Contents

Nephrology

Medical Masterclass third edition

Editor-in-Chief

Dr John D Firth DM FRCP
Consultant Physician and Nephrologist
Addenbrooke's Hospital
Cambridge
UK

Nephrology

Editor

Dr Andy C Fry PhD FRCP
Consultant in Nephrology and Acute Medicine
Addenbrooke's Hospital
Cambridge
UK

Third edition

Disclaimer

Although every effort has been made to ensure that drug doses and other information are presented accurately in this publication, the ultimate responsibility rests with the prescribing physician. Neither the publishers nor the authors can be held responsible for any consequences arising from the use of information contained herein. Any product mentioned in this publication should be used in accordance with the prescribing information prepared by the manufacturers.

The information presented in this publication reflects the opinions of its contributors and should not be taken to represent the policy and views of the Royal College of Physicians of London, unless this is specifically stated.

Every effort has been made by the contributors to contact holders of copyright to obtain permission to reproduce copyrighted material. However, if any have been inadvertently overlooked, the publisher will be pleased to make the necessary arrangements at the first opportunity.

List of contributors

Dr Anil Chalisey MB BChir MRCP(UK)
Centre for Cellular and Molecular
Physiology
Nuffield Department of Medicine
University of Oxford
Oxford
UK

Dr Andy C Fry PhD FRCP
Consultant in Nephrology and Acute
Medicine
Addenbrooke's Hospital
Cambridge
UK

Dr Elizabeth Wallin MA MB BChir
DPhil MRCP(UK)
Nephrology Specialist Registrar
Lister Hospital
Stevenage
UK

Dr Vivian Yiu
Consultant Nephrologist
West Suffolk NHS Foundation Trust
Bury St Edmunds
Suffolk
UK

Acknowledgements

The third edition of Medical Masterclass has been produced by a team. The names of those who have written and edited are clearly indicated, and along with all these contributors I gratefully acknowledge the contributions of those who wrote and edited the first and second editions. This third edition is based on their foundations, and some of their material has been retained. But my acknowledgements must not stop there, because the Medical Masterclass would not have been published without the efforts of many other people. Naming names is risky, but I must name Claire Daley, who has worked as editor of the third edition with a wonderful combination of quietness and efficiency, and with an attention to detail that has made me feel triumphant if I have ever spotted a misplaced comma in a proof.

Dr John Firth DM FRCP
Medical Masterclass Editor-in-Chief

The authors are very grateful to Dr RM Hilton, Dr JE Scoble, Dr JA Amess and Dr EC Morris for their help in sourcing some of the medical images appearing in this book. The editor would also like to thank Dr D Davies.

Cover image courtesy of: GJPL / CNRI / Science Photo Library

Published by:
Royal College of Physicians of London
11 St Andrews Place
Regent's Park
London NW1 4LE
United Kingdom

Typeset by Manila Typesetting Company, Makati City, Philippines

Printed by The Lavenham Press Limited, Suffolk

First edition published 2001
Reprinted 2004
Second edition published 2008
Updated and reprinted 2010
Third edition published 2018

ISBN: 978-1-86016-666-2 (this book)
eISBN: 978-1-86016-667-9 (this book)
ISBN: 978-1-86016-670-9 (set)
eISBN: 978-1-86016-671-6 (set)

Royal College of Physicians of London
11 St Andrews Place
Regent's Park
London NW1 4LE
United Kingdom
Tel: +44 (0)20 3075 1379
Email: medical.masterclass@rcplondon.ac.uk
Web: www.rcplondon.ac.uk/medicalmasterclass

Preface

This third edition of Medical Masterclass is produced and published by the Royal College of Physicians of London. It comprises 12 books and an online question bank. Its aim is to interest and help doctors in their first few years of training, to enable them to improve their medical knowledge and skills, and to pass postgraduate medical examinations, most particularly the MRCP(UK): Part 1, Part 2 and PACES (the practical assessment of clinical examination skills that is the final part of the exam).

The 12 textbooks are divided as follows: two cover the scientific background to medicine; one is devoted to general clinical skills, including medicine for older people, palliative care and specific guidance on exam technique for PACES; one deals with acute medicine; and the other eight cover the range of medical specialties.

The medical specialties are dealt with in eight sections:

> Case histories – you are presented with letters of referral that are commonly received in each specialty and led through the ways in which the patients' histories should be explored, and what investigations and/or treatments should follow, as in Station 2 of PACES.

> Physical examination scenarios – these emphasise solid and reliable clinical method, logical analysis of physical signs and sensible clinical reasoning ('having found this, what would you want to do next?'), as in Stations 1 and 3 of PACES.

> Communication and ethical scenarios – you are presented with difficult issues that can arise in each specialty. What should you actually say in response to the 'frequently asked (but nonetheless tricky) questions', as required in Station 4 of PACES?

> Brief clinical consultations – how should you take a focused history and perform a focused examination of a patient who has a medical problem when there isn't much time? This section explains how to do this while working as a medical registrar on take, or in Station 5 of PACES.

> Acute presentations – what are your priorities if you are the doctor seeing a patient in the emergency department or the medical admissions unit? The material in this section is relevant to all parts of the MRCP(UK) exam.

> Diseases and treatments – concise structured notes that are of particular relevance to the Part 1 and Part 2 exams.

> Investigations and practical procedures – short and concise notes.

> Self-assessment questions – in the form used in the Part 1 and Part 2 exams.

The online question bank, which is continually updated, enables you to take mock Part 1 and Part 2 exams, or to be selective in the questions that you tackle (if you want to do 10 questions on cardiology, or any other specialty, then you can do so). You can see how your scores compare with those of others who have attempted the same questions, which helps you to know where to focus your learning.

I hope that you enjoy using the Medical Masterclass to learn more about medicine. I know that medicine is tough at the moment, with hospital services under unprecedented pressure and the medical registrar bearing more than their fair share of the burden. But careers are a long game, and being a physician is a wonderful occupation. It is sometimes intellectually and/or emotionally very challenging, but with these challenges come great rewards, and few things give more substantial satisfaction than being a doctor who provides good care for a patient. The Medical Masterclass should help you do to that, as well as to pass the MRCP(UK) exam along the way.

Dr John Firth DM FRCP
Medical Masterclass Editor-in-Chief

Key features

We have created a range of icon boxes that sit among the text of the various Medical Masterclass books. They are there to help you identify key information and to make learning easier and more enjoyable. Here is a brief explanation:

This icon is used to highlight points of particular importance.

Key point

A patient with a normal physical examination, a normal ECG and a normal echocardiogram is at very low risk of significant arrhythmia.

This icon is used to indicate common or important drug interactions, pitfalls of practical procedures, or when to take symptoms or signs particularly seriously.

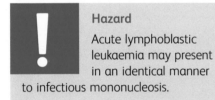

Hazard

Acute lymphoblastic leukaemia may present in an identical manner to infectious mononucleosis.

Case examples / case histories are used to demonstrate why and how an understanding of the scientific background to medicine helps in the practice of clinical medicine.

Case history

A man with a renal transplant is immunosuppressed with ciclosporin, azathioprine and prednisolone. He develops recurrent gout and is started on allopurinol.

Nephrology

Authors
Dr A Chalisey, Dr AC Fry, Dr E Wallin and Dr V Yiu

Editor
Dr AC Fry

Editor-in-Chief
Dr JD Firth

The nephrology section of the second edition of Medical Masterclass was written by Dr AC Fry, Dr JD Gillmore, Dr CA O'Callaghan, Dr SA Summers and Professor PH Maxwell (editor). This third edition of Medical Masterclass contains entirely new material, but many sections from the second edition have been retained and updated, and we gratefully acknowledge the contribution of these authors.

Nephrology: Section 1

1 PACES stations and acute scenarios

1.1 History taking

1.1.1 Dipstick haematuria

Dear Doctor,

Re: Mr Charles Oatway, aged 43 years

This airline pilot was found to have a positive urine dipstick test for blood at an insurance medical. Repeat testing confirms this and also shows a trace of protein. He has no symptoms. His blood pressure (BP) is 142/94 mmHg and there are no other abnormalities on examination. I would be grateful for your advice regarding diagnosis and management.

Yours sincerely,

Introduction

The definition of non-visible haematuria is more than three red blood cells per high power field. This is most commonly detected by urine dipstick testing, rather than direct microscopy. However, urine dipstick tests are very sensitive and are capable of detecting concentrations of red blood cells at the upper limit of the normal range for red cell excretion. Positive urine dipstick tests for blood occur in 2.5–13.0% of men, and in most cases this is not associated with significant disease. Recognised causes of haematuria are shown in Table 1.

Key point

Isolated non-visible haematuria is very common.

The clinical approach depends on the age of the patient (Fig 1).

> In a young person, haematuria is usually glomerular in origin – most frequently as a result of immunoglobulin (Ig) A nephropathy – and tumours are rare.

> In an older patient, tumours within the kidney or urinary tract are an important cause.

> Stones can cause haematuria at any age.

Key point

In older patients (≥40 years) with haematuria the first priority is to identify or exclude malignancy in the urinary tract.

In younger patients malignancy is very infrequent and a glomerular cause (eg IgA nephropathy or thin membrane disease) is more likely.

History of the presenting problem

Although the patient is said to be asymptomatic, the following symptoms are worth asking carefully about.

Have you ever seen blood in your urine, and if so, when?

Blood present at the start of micturition usually comes from the urethra or prostate; that at the end of the stream from the bladder. Blood clots are unusual with glomerular bleeding. Episodes of visible haematuria, especially occurring at the same time as – or just after – a mild upper respiratory tract infection (often termed 'synpharyngitic haematuria'), suggest IgA nephropathy, as does visible haematuria followed by persistent non-visible haematuria. However,

Table 1	Differential diagnosis of haematuria[1]		
Type of pathology	**Source of bleeding**	**Common**	**Other causes**
Benign	Kidney Urinary tract / bladder	Glomerulonephritis – especially IgA nephropathy Thin membrane disease / benign familial haematuria UTI Prostatic disease – benign Urinary stone disease	Interstitial nephritis Adult polycystic kidney disease Alport syndrome Loin pain haematuria syndrome Papillary necrosis Medullary sponge kidney
Malignant	Anywhere in urinary tract	Bladder cancer	Renal cell carcinoma

1 Also consider: trauma and gynaecological bleeding.
Ig, immunoglobulin; UTI, urinary tract infection.

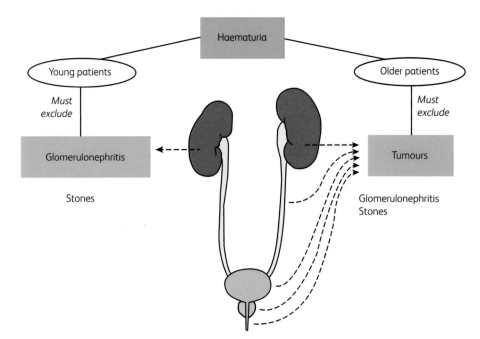

Fig 1 The approach to the investigation of haematuria depends on the age of the patient.

remember that visible haematuria also occurs with stones and tumours.

Have you had any pain in the loins, abdomen, groins or genitalia?
Ask about previous pain in the loins, the abdomen, the groins and the external genitalia. Pain is consistent with stones or tumours, polycystic kidney disease, loin pain haematuria syndrome, renal infection or infarction. Painless haematuria is consistent with tumours, glomerulonephritis, interstitial nephritis or a bleeding disorder.

Other relevant history
General history
Ask about the following: recent trauma or heavy exercise, which can cause haematuria on dipstick testing; joint pains or skin rashes that would suggest a multisystem disorder (eg systemic vasculitis); and a sore throat or other recent infection, raising the possibility of a post-infective glomerulonephritis (when haematuria typically occurs 2 weeks after the sore throat, rather than at the same time). Also ask about other medical conditions including diabetes mellitus and sickle cell disease, both of which predispose to renal papillary necrosis.

Urinary symptoms
Has there been any dysuria or increased urinary frequency which would suggest infection? Is there a poor urinary stream or hesitancy, or a poor flow and dribbling, either of which suggest prostatic or bladder pathology? Has the patient ever passed stones, grit or gravel in the urine?

Family history
Has anyone in the family had kidney problems? (eg polycystic kidney disease or Alport syndrome). Other important inherited causes of haematuria include sickle cell disease and sickle trait. Many patients with haemophilia or von Willebrand disease experience non-visible or visible haematuria.

Travel history
Has the patient travelled to areas where *Schistosoma haematobium* is prevalent? Infection can cause urinary tract granulomas and tumours.

Drug history
Ask specifically about analgesics, which can cause papillary necrosis and therefore haematuria. However, note that this does not happen with occasional use of painkillers and has become very uncommon since phenacetin was withdrawn from compound analgesic preparations. The typical story – now rarely encountered – would be of chronic headache or back pain, with the patient consuming 10–20 or more analgesic tablets per day for many years.

Plan for investigation and management
After explaining to the patient that under normal circumstances you would examine him carefully to confirm that there are no physical abnormalities apart from the raised BP, you would then plan further investigations as follows.

Dipstick urinalysis and microscopy
Proteinuria combined with haematuria suggests intrinsic renal disease, especially glomerulonephritis. Interstitial nephritis is less likely. If there is dipstick proteinuria, as in this case, then quantify this by measuring the urinary albumin:creatinine ratio (ACR) or protein:creatinine ratio (PCR) in a spot urine sample (or with a 24-hour collection).

Dysmorphic red cells on microscopy suggest glomerular bleeding, but morphological changes can occur as artefacts after collection of the sample; the distinction of dysmorphic cells (from the kidney) from non-dysmorphic cells (from the urinary drainage system) requires special expertise and is not a routine or reliable test in most centres. If seen, red blood cell casts indicate active glomerular inflammation.

Key point
Red cell casts indicate active glomerular inflammation.

Blood tests

Check plasma urea and creatinine. Note or calculate the estimated glomerular filtration rate (eGFR) (routinely reported by most laboratories) based on sex and age (see Section 3.2). Remember that there can be a substantial fall in GFR before serum creatinine rises out of the normal range. If renal function is normal, BP is normal and there is no significant proteinuria, significant medical renal pathology is very unlikely.

Imaging

Image the renal tract to exclude stones and assess renal size and anatomy. The best way of doing this is to perform both of the following:

> plain radiograph (kidneys, ureter and bladder) – looking for stones

> ultrasonography of the urinary tract – to measure renal size (preferably length of each kidney in centimetres: not 'normal' or 'small'), look for renal masses and carefully examine the bladder wall.

Other imaging approaches can be useful in some cases: intravenous urogram (IVU) to determine whether small calcific lesions are urinary stones and whether stones are causing obstruction; and computerised tomography (CT) with contrast (CT urogram) can be useful to look at the entire urinary tract for causes of haematuria.

Urine cytology and cystoscopy

In an older person (≥40 years), arrange cystoscopy to look for a tumour in the lower urinary tract. Urine cytology may be useful in increasing the suspicion of malignancy, but cannot be used instead of cystoscopy since it is not sufficiently sensitive to rule out a tumour.

Renal biopsy

If there is hypertension, proteinuria and impaired renal function, glomerular disease is likely and renal biopsy may be performed to make a precise diagnosis. But note that in cases of isolated haematuria with normal renal function and no proteinuria, a renal biopsy is not recommended since it will not lead to a change in management.

Key point
Renal biopsy is usually indicated if there is significant proteinuria, renal impairment or unexplained systemic symptoms.

Review

See the patient in clinic with the results of the investigation and recheck their renal function.

Further discussion

In many cases of non-visible haematuria, no specific diagnosis will be made unless a renal biopsy is undertaken, and even then no diagnosis will be established in 50% of cases. However, the commonest recognised cause in a young, otherwise-well patient is IgA nephropathy, for which there is no specific treatment.

Any patient with persistent non-visible haematuria should have annual urinalysis, monitoring of their BP and measurement of their serum creatinine to enable calculation of their eGFR. If this monitoring shows development of proteinuria or significant decline in renal function then further investigation, eg renal biopsy, may be appropriate.

It is important to consider that giving a patient a 'renal diagnosis' may adversely affect their ability to obtain life insurance and may have implications for their employment. Clearly this patient has hypertension (if the value of 142/94 mmHg is confirmed on other readings) and the fact that he has haematuria increases the argument for treating this, because strict control of BP slows the progression of renal damage in patients with renal disease. In addition, renal disease increases the risk of vascular disease and therefore the likely benefit of antihypertensive therapy.

1.1.2 Pregnancy with renal disease

Letter of referral to the nephrology outpatient clinic

Dear Doctor,

Re: Mrs Patricia Redwood, aged 30 years

Please would you see this woman who has just discovered that she is pregnant for a second time. She had what was thought to be pre-eclampsia at 34 weeks in her first pregnancy 3 years ago and was induced at about 35 weeks – I am pleased to say that her baby boy is quite well.

About 2 months ago we saw her for contraceptive advice because she was considering going back onto the oral contraceptive pill. Her blood pressure was 142/86 mmHg (confirmed on repeated measurement), she had positive urinalysis for protein, and her creatinine was slightly elevated at 122 μmol/L (normal range 60–110). Following discussion, she decided to continue to use barrier contraception and is now pregnant.

I think she almost certainly has mild chronic kidney disease (CKD) and would be grateful for your advice.

Yours sincerely,

Key point
A creatinine outside the normal range is often dismissed as mildly elevated – remember it equates to loss of about 50% of normal GFR for age and weight.

Introduction

Pre-eclampsia is the most common medical complication of pregnancy, affecting 5–7% of previously healthy women. Pre-existing renal disease (eGFR <60 mL/min, hypertension, or proteinuria) increases the risk of pre-eclampsia, and in women with pre-eclampsia it is easy to overlook evidence of pre-existing renal disease.

The reported incidence of renal disease during pregnancy is relatively low. This is predominantly because significant renal insufficiency or renal failure is associated with reduced fertility and because both are more prevalent in women beyond childbearing age. Another important reason is that women with a mildly elevated creatinine are often not reported as having renal disease, despite a significant drop in eGFR.

Pregnancy in women with kidney disease may result in a worsening of renal function and is associated with increased fetal morbidity and mortality. When counselling women with renal impairment one has to consider both the risk to the mother and the risk to the fetus/baby.

Risk of maternal renal disease to the fetus

Women with an elevated baseline serum creatinine have a higher risk of pre-term labour, which increases with the degree of renal insufficiency (11–20% if creatinine <125 µmol/L, 39–64% if creatinine 125–250 µmol/L, and above 80% if creatinine >250 µmol/L), and infants are usually small for their gestational age. However, advances in neonatal intensive care have improved fetal outcomes so that the survival of babies is now routine, even when born as early as 27 weeks gestation. Chances of a successful pregnancy are 89% if the pre-existing creatinine is <250 µmol/L but drop to 46% if >250 µmol/L.

Risks of pregnancy to the mother with renal disease

As a woman's degree of renal insufficiency increases, the risk that renal function will worsen during pregnancy rises sharply – a tendency that is exaggerated by the presence of

hypertension. The risk of decline in renal function during pregnancy in women with creatinine <125 µmol/L is small. In women with a pre-existing serum creatinine between 125 and 250 µmol/L, 43% may have a decline in renal function either during pregnancy or between 6 weeks and 6 months postpartum. In women with a pre-existing serum creatinine >250 µmol/L the risk of decline in renal function is considerably higher, with as many as one in three women requiring dialysis during or shortly after pregnancy. Among women with moderate or severe renal disease the deterioration in renal function is usually irreversible.

History of the presenting problem

Was there any evidence of renal disease in the past, especially early in the course of her first pregnancy? Blood pressure and urinalysis will have been checked at the time of booking in the first pregnancy: significant proteinuria early in the pregnancy would prove that she had renal disease before she had pre-eclampsia. It is also important to ask directly whether she has ever had her urine or blood tested at any other times. If there were urinary abnormalities in the past this would constitute strong evidence of underlying chronic renal disease. By contrast, if the urine had been tested and showed no blood or protein, this would be consistent with a more acute renal problem.

Renal impairment of the degree described in this case is very unlikely to cause symptoms, but there may be clues that renal function is not normal, and an appropriate history may reveal clues as to what has caused renal damage. Ask the following questions.

> Do you have to get up at night to go to the toilet? This suggests lack of urinary concentrating ability and commonly occurs in people with renal impairment, although it is, of course, also quite common in people with normal kidney function.

> Did you have infections in your urine as a child? Did you have trouble with wetting the bed? Either could suggest reflux nephropathy.

> Have you ever passed blood in your urine? Episodes of visible haematuria would suggest IgA nephropathy.

> Does anyone in your family have a kidney problem or high BP? This could suggest autosomal dominant polycystic kidney disease.

> Do you ever take medicines, herbal remedies or painkillers? Interstitial nephritis or (much less likely, see Section 1.1.1) analgesic nephropathy are possibilities.

> Have you had any skin rashes, trouble with your joints or eye problems? These might suggest systemic lupus erythematosus (SLE), vasculitis or an interstitial nephritis.

> Have you had any other pregnancies? Spontaneous abortions might suggest an anticardiolipin antibody syndrome.

Other relevant history

The patient's feelings about her pregnancy should be gently explored. This should not be a main focus in Station 2 of PACES, although counselling a woman with significant renal disease about the risks of pregnancy could certainly feature in Station 4. However, if the conversation is led in this direction by the patient – or by the examiner – then it will be important to explain that at this level of kidney function, although the risks to the patient and the baby are slightly increased, and more intensive monitoring than usual will be recommended, the likelihood of a successful outcome for the baby is very high and the pregnancy is unlikely to result in an acceleration in the course of kidney disease. If the woman knows she wants more children in the future, then she needs to understand that kidney disease often progresses over time, and that if her kidney function became worse the risks would be higher.

Plan for investigation and management

Investigation
Investigation of the patient (not including standard renal and obstetric investigations that have already taken place) should include:

> urine dipstick for haematuria, proteinuria and glycosuria

> urine microscopy and culture for infection (asymptomatic bacteriuria occurs in up to 7% of pregnancies)

> spot urinary ACR or PCR for quantification of proteinuria

> serum creatinine to estimate GFR (remember GFR normally increases and creatinine falls in pregnancy) (Fig 2)

> baseline liver function tests, serum urate and lactate dehydrogenase (LDH) – this patient is at increased risk of pre-eclampsia and haemolysis, elevated liver enzymes and low platelets (HELLP syndrome)

> full blood count (FBC) and blood film – looking for platelet count and evidence of haemolysis

> renal ultrasound – this might show scars, which would establish a diagnosis of reflux nephropathy or cysts.

The history may suggest other investigations (eg immunological tests if there is any suggestion of SLE or a systemic vasculitis). Note that renal biopsy can be performed safely in pregnancy if necessary.

Investigation of the fetus (not including standard obstetric tests) should include close monitoring for intrauterine growth retardation with serial ultrasonography.

Management
Management of known renal disease in pregnancy involves:

> meticulous BP control, using drugs that are known to be safe in pregnancy (this will often require alteration of medication)

> avoidance of salt

> low-dose aspirin

> heparin, if there is a high risk of thrombosis (eg nephrotic syndrome)

> antibiotic prophylaxis in those with recurrent urinary tract infections (UTI).

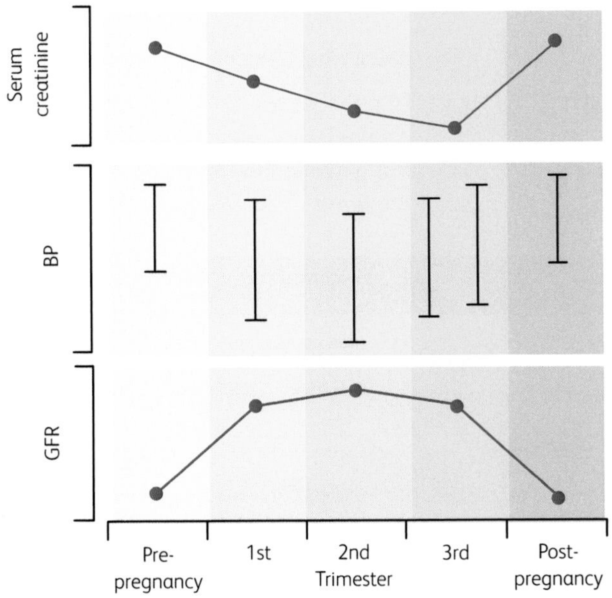

Further discussion

Pre-eclampsia
Pre-eclampsia is more common in first pregnancy, when with a new partner and in multiple pregnancies. It is also more common in those with renal impairment. The risk is 10–20%, 60% and up to 100% in women with pre-existing serum creatinine of <125 μmol/L, 125–250 μmol/L and >250 μmol/L, respectively. The definitive management of pre-eclampsia is delivery of the baby, and the balance to strike is between risk to the baby (prematurity and intrauterine death) and risk to the mother (convulsions and irreversible renal impairment).

Reflux nephropathy
The incidence of vesicoureteral reflux (VUR) is as high as 1:4 in the children of patients with reflux nephropathy. It is therefore recommended that children of a patient with reflux nephropathy should be screened for VUR soon after birth, usually with a micturating cystogram.

Pregnancy in patients on renal replacement therapy
Pregnancy is extremely uncommon among dialysis-dependent patients due to reduced fertility. The likelihood of successful pregnancy is substantially higher if the patient becomes pregnant before needing dialysis than if she conceives while on maintenance dialysis. The management of the pregnant dialysis patient is to increase both dialysis dose and frequency, minimise cardiovascular instability and fluid shifts, and monitor anticoagulation carefully. Careful monitoring of intrauterine growth is required.

Renal transplantation restores fertility. A period of 1 year after transplantation is recommended before contemplating pregnancy. Immunosuppressive drug therapy must be altered – mycophenolate mofetil (MMF) and sirolimus should be avoided and the dose of calcineurin inhibitors often needs increasing with close monitoring

Fig 2 Schematic diagram illustrating the changes in blood pressure, serum creatinine and glomerular filtration rate during pregnancy.

of levels. Regardless of renal function, transplant recipients have an increased risk of pre-eclampsia.

1.1.3 A swollen young woman

Dear Doctor,

Re: Miss Gemma Blyth, aged 21 years

Thank you for seeing this young woman who is usually fit and well. She presented to the practice last week complaining of breathlessness and increasingly swollen legs over the past fortnight. On examination she had bilaterally oedematous legs. Urine dipstick testing showed 3+ of proteinuria but no haematuria. I would be grateful for your further assessment.

Yours sincerely,

Introduction

There are many causes of breathlessness and ankle swelling in a young woman, including cardiopulmonary conditions such as cardiomyopathy and primary pulmonary hypertension. However, in this scenario urinalysis by the general practitioner (GP) – a very simple test – indicates that the patient is likely to be nephrotic.

Key point

The nephrotic syndrome consists of:

> proteinuria of >3 g in a 24-hour urine collection – in the absence of the other features this is referred to as nephrotic-range proteinuria

> hypoalbuminaemia – serum albumin <35 g/L

> peripheral oedema.

Complications of the nephrotic state include the following.

> Oedema, pleural effusions and ascites.

> Hypercoagulability due to loss of clotting factors in the urine; there is increased risk of venous and arterial thromboembolism, including renal vein thrombosis.

> Increased susceptibility to bacterial infection, due to urinary loss of immunoglobulins (especially IgG) and complement, which increases susceptibility to infection with encapsulated organisms. In addition, bacteria thrive in areas of oedematous tissue where skin fragility allows easy entry.

> Hyperlipidaemia – in particular, marked elevation of low-density lipoprotein (LDL) cholesterol and triglycerides.

> Increased risk of acute renal failure, often because these patients have intravascular volume depletion.

The nephrotic syndrome results from glomerular disease and has many potential causes, as shown in Table 2.

History of the presenting problem

From the brief information in the referral letter, which describes a young woman with no past medical history, a primary glomerular disease would appear to be the most likely cause of the nephrotic syndrome. However, the patient should clearly be asked about previous personal or family history of renal disease before pursuing the history of the nephrotic state.

> Oedema – detectable oedema implies at least a 2 L increase in extracellular fluid. In the nephrotic syndrome there is often a 10 L increase in extracellular fluid volume. How long has the patient noticed this? Did it come on suddenly? Rapid onset of severe oedema is more common in minimal change nephrotic syndrome. Has her weight changed – and by how much?

> Urine – has the patient noticed a change? Heavy proteinuria causes frothy urine and this can help to date the onset of problems.

Table 2	Causes of the nephrotic syndrome in adults	
Condition	**Common**	**Less common**
Primary glomerular disease	Minimal change disease FSGS Membranous nephropathy	Other glomerulonephritides[1]
Secondary glomerular disease	Diabetes mellitus SLE Amyloidosis Drugs, eg gold, penicillamine, NSAIDs and captopril	Malignancy related Other autoimmune rheumatic disorders Infection related[2]

1 Other common glomerulonephritides only rarely present with nephrotic syndrome (eg IgA nephropathy).
2 Infections are not common causes of nephrotic syndrome in the developed world, but in other parts of the world they are, eg malaria.
FSGS, focal segmental glomerulosclerosis; NSAIDs, non-steroidal anti-inflammatory drugs; SLE, systemic lupus erythematosus.

Other relevant history

Are there any clues to the cause of the nephrotic syndrome, especially the secondary glomerular diseases listed in Table 2?

> SLE – an important consideration in a young woman. Is there anything in the history to suggest this?

> Minimal change disease – this often relapses and remits: has she ever had this problem before? It may also follow an upper respiratory tract infection.

> Drugs – a range of over-the-counter and prescribed medication can cause the nephrotic syndrome (eg non-steroidal anti-inflammatory drugs (NSAIDs)), as can intravenous drug abuse.

> Possibility of amyloidosis – primary amyloid light-chain (AL) amyloidosis would be a very unlikely cause of nephrotic syndrome in a patient of this age, but any chronic inflammatory condition can be associated with secondary amyloid, eg rheumatoid arthritis or bronchiectasis.

> Possibility of malignancy – this would be a most unlikely cause of the nephrotic syndrome in a young patient, but could be in someone older: is there any history suggestive of underlying malignancy? Carcinoma can cause membranous nephropathy; lymphoma is associated with minimal change disease; and, multiple myeloma with amyloidosis.

> Infection – a number of infections may cause the nephrotic syndrome; hepatitis B is associated with membranous nephropathy, hepatitis C with both cryoglobulinaemia and membranous nephropathy, and HIV with a form of focal segmental glomerulosclerosis (FSGS) termed collapsing FSGS. Does the patient have any risk factors for these infections?

> Family history – Alport syndrome (see Section 2.8.2) can be associated with nephrotic-range proteinuria, and familial forms of other glomerulonephritides are recognised (eg FSGS).

Is there evidence of any complications of the nephrotic state, in particular of venous thromboembolism? Ask the patient if one leg has been more swollen than the other or if she has experienced breathlessness, chest pain or haemoptysis.

Plan for investigation and management

Investigations
Bedside tests

Repeat dipstick urinalysis – check proteinuria and see if non-visible haematuria is present. The latter can occur in minimal change disease, but if heavy (more than 1+) it suggests another diagnosis. The urine should be sent for microscopy of the spun deposit – red cell casts point to active glomerular inflammation.

Key point
Oedema and (low-grade) dipstick proteinuria occur in other settings besides nephrotic syndrome – eg in congestive cardiac failure (CCF).

Blood biochemistry

Check renal and liver function and serum cholesterol.

> Serum creatinine – may be high in some types of the nephrotic syndrome, eg membranous glomerulonephritis, and in older patients with minimal change glomerulonephritis or with renal vein thrombosis.

> Serum albumin – this is low (by definition) in those with nephrotic syndrome, and especially so in less well-nourished patients (eg older patients), those with systemic disease (hepatic albumin synthesis reduced) and in those with gross proteinuria (eg >10 g/24 h).

> Cholesterol – this will be elevated and may be very high (>10 mmol/L) when proteinuria is gross.

Key point
Nephrotic syndrome results in hypercholesterolaemia.

Quantitation of proteinuria

This is traditionally performed by measurement of the protein content of a 24-hour urinary collection, but this has now been superseded in routine clinical practice by estimation from a spot urine sample, either by measuring the albumin:creatinine ratio (ACR) or protein: creatinine ratio (PCR). The normal ACR in adults is <2.5 mg/mmol (men) or 3.5 mg/mmol (women): those with nephrotic range proteinuria will have an ACR >200 mg/mmol (or PCR >300 mg/mmol).

Other blood tests

Check the following:

> inflammatory markers – C-reactive protein (CRP) and erythrocyte sedimentation rate (ESR)

> evidence of SLE – anti-nuclear antibody (ANA), double-stranded DNA (dsDNA) and further specific tests if indicated

> serum complement levels – C3 and/or C4 may be depressed in SLE or some forms of primary glomerulonephritis (eg membranoproliferative disease)

> immunoglobulins/paraprotein measurement or serum/urine protein electrophoresis – although myeloma and primary amyloidosis are extremely unlikely at this age

> anti-neutrophil cytoplasmic antibodies (ANCA) – patients with ANCA-positive vasculitides can occasionally present with the nephrotic syndrome, but this would be very unusual

> FBC and clotting screen – a renal biopsy will be needed to establish a precise diagnosis

> blood glucose

> HIV and hepatitis screening – if indicated from the history.

Radiological tests

Perform:

> Chest radiograph – this may show pleural effusions and may also reveal an underlying malignancy in older patients that is associated with membranous nephropathy.

> Renal ultrasonography – in most cases renal size will be normal or increased, the latter caused by oedema or infiltration (eg amyloid).

Renal biopsy

Renal biopsy is almost always recommended to determine the cause of nephrotic syndrome in adults. The situation is different in children, where minimal change disease accounts for over 90% of cases and biopsy is reserved for those with renal impairment, failure to respond to corticosteroids, frequent relapses or an atypical clinical course.

Key point
Renal biopsy in the nephrotic syndrome

In children, 90% of nephrotic syndrome is due to minimal change disease – renal biopsy is reserved for those who do not respond to steroids, and those with renal impairment or an atypical course.

In adults the range of causes is much wider and renal biopsy is almost always recommended.

Management

Management is based on general treatment measures for any patient with the nephrotic syndrome, which can be started before a precise diagnosis is established, and specific treatment for the underlying renal condition, once this is known.

General treatment measures

These include the following.

> Salt-restricted diet – often fluid restriction is also necessary.

> Loop diuretics – usually oral furosemide (frusemide) or bumetanide; the latter may be better absorbed from the oedematous gut mucosa. Dose escalation is often needed and resistant cases may require the addition of oral metolazone or admission for intravenous diuretics, very occasionally combined with infusion of intravenous 20% human albumin.

> Daily measurement of the patient's weight is the best means of assessing fluid balance – the usual aim being to titrate diuretic dosage to achieve a loss of 0.5–1 kg per day.

> If the nephrotic patient is immobile, prophylactic subcutaneous low-molecular-weight heparin is indicated.

> Angiotensin-converting enzyme (ACE) inhibitors have been shown to reduce proteinuria and the risk of progressive loss of renal function in patients with nephrotic syndrome. Most patients should be started on an ACE inhibitor, but this needs balancing against blood pressure and monitoring of renal function.

Specific treatment measures

Specific therapy for the underlying kidney problem may be instituted once the result of the renal biopsy is known. In this particular clinical scenario, minimal change disease is at the top of a list of likely diagnoses, but biopsy confirmation is necessary before therapy is commenced. See Section 2.3 on 'Glomerular diseases' for details of individual conditions and their treatment.

Further discussion

Would you anticoagulate this patient?
Anticoagulation and antiplatelet agents are often used to reduce the risk of thromboembolic complications, but these should not be commenced before renal biopsy has been performed. As a general rule of thumb, low-dose aspirin (75 mg daily) is appropriate if the serum albumin is >20 g/L, and anticoagulation with warfarin (international normalised ratio (INR) 2.0–3.0) would be advocated by many nephrologists if it is <20 g/L. However, note that it is not necessary to commence warfarin therapy if a rapid response to treatment is predicted – as would be the case in minimal change disease.

Should the patient be treated for hypercholesterolaemia?
Statin therapy is often used to treat the hypercholesterolaemia of patients with the nephrotic syndrome, but – as with warfarin – there is little point in doing this if the underlying condition is expected to respond rapidly once treatment is initiated. However, if the nephrotic state is expected to persist for months or years (eg FSGS), and particularly if the patient has other cardiovascular risk factors, then statin therapy is appropriate. Statins may also have an additional antiproteinuric effect.

How can the patient monitor their condition?
Usefully, many patients can be taught how to weigh themselves daily and make appropriate adjustments to diuretic dosage. They can also be supplied with urinalysis reagent strips to enable them to monitor their proteinuria. This is particularly useful for patients with minimal change disease as it enables them to reduce their steroid dose once they are in remission (absence of protein on urine dip) and also to monitor for relapse.

The patient is hypertensive – how should this be treated?

The management of fluid overload by dietary salt restriction and diuretics may be adequate to treat hypertension. If the nephrotic state persists and hypertension is still present then as discussed above the agents of choice are ACE inhibitors, due to their additional effect in reducing proteinuria. Angiotensin-receptor blockers (ARBs) have a similar effect and can be used if ACE inhibitors are not tolerated.

1.1.4 Rheumatoid arthritis with swollen legs

Letter of referral to the nephrology outpatient clinic

Dear Doctor,

Re: Mrs Edna Smith, aged 60 years

Thank you for seeing this woman with a long-standing history of rheumatoid arthritis, for which she has had various treatments. Over the last 2 or 3 months she has noticed increasing swelling of her ankles. On dipstick urinalysis she has 3+ proteinuria (on two occasions). I have checked her biochemistry – her creatinine is elevated (170 µmol/L; normal range 60–110) and her albumin is low (17 g/L; normal range 37–49 g/L). Both were normal 1 year ago. I would be grateful for your advice as to the cause of this and regarding her management.

Yours sincerely,

Introduction

This woman almost certainly has the nephrotic syndrome, which could be confirmed by estimating the PCR or ACR in a spot sample. Many different pathological processes in the glomerulus

can cause this clinical syndrome (see Table 2), and in adults a renal biopsy will almost certainly be indicated to establish which of these is present in order to guide prognosis and to determine whether specific treatment (eg corticosteroids for minimal change nephrotic syndrome) is possible. The history provides clues as to the underlying glomerular process and is crucial in determining what therapeutic interventions and investigations will be indicated before the biopsy.

An immediate issue in this case is that the patient clearly has impaired renal function: is this stable or is it deteriorating? It may be that previous monitoring indicates that the problem is long standing and stable, but a diagnosis needs to be made rapidly if it is not. If you are not sure about this then you should either arrange for the serum creatinine to be measured again – to ensure there is no acute deterioration – or see the patient promptly to arrange investigation.

Key point

Renal failure is best avoided

Remember that a single measurement of creatinine does not tell you whether renal function is stable or deteriorating rapidly. If there is any doubt, get the creatinine rechecked a few days later: if it turns out to be rising then the tempo of the investigation should be very rapid.

History of the presenting problem

Most of the issues discussed in Section 1.1.3 are equally applicable here, but there should be particular emphasis on the following.

> Is there anything to suggest chronic renal disease? As mentioned above, a previous serum creatinine measurement would be invaluable, but have there been any previous abnormalities on urinalysis? A history

of hypertension might also suggest a long-standing renal problem.

> Drugs: what medication is the patient taking now and what have they taken in the past? Ask specifically about over-the-counter drugs – patients do not always count them as medicines. In a patient with rheumatoid arthritis, remember particularly that NSAIDs can cause minimal change nephrotic syndrome (and also acute and chronic interstitial nephritis – but these are not causes of the nephrotic syndrome) and that penicillamine and gold can both cause membranous nephropathy. Anti-tumour necrosis factor (TNF) therapies used in rheumatoid arthritis (eg etanercept, infliximab) have also been linked with membranous nephropathy.

> Activity of arthritis: how bad and for how long? As a generalisation, the longer and the more active the arthritis, the greater the chance of secondary amyloidosis.

> Features that might suggest malignancy: the nephrotic syndrome, in particular when caused by membranous glomerulonephritis, can be a complication of malignancy in the older patient. Is there any evidence of this? Has there been any weight loss? Has their bowel habit changed?

> The presence of worsened constitutional symptoms with joint pains, rashes or night sweats might indicate the development of a vasculitis as a complication of rheumatoid arthritis.

Plan for investigation and management

The investigations described in Section 1.1.3 will be relevant in this case, with particular note of the following.

> Is their creatinine rising? If it is, then renal biopsy is needed without delay.

> Serum immunoglobulins plus serum and urine electrophoresis

(for paraprotein): myeloma and other plasma cell dyscrasias are common in this age group.

> Renal ultrasonography: are there two normal-size, unobstructed kidneys? If both kidneys are small (<9 cm in length), this indicates chronic disease and biopsy is much less likely to reveal a treatable diagnosis.

> Chest radiograph: any suggestion of malignancy?

> Does the patient have a low threshold for investigation of gastrointestinal (GI) symptoms? This might indicate malignancy.

> Check iron status and faecal occult bloods, pursuing GI investigation if there is evidence of iron deficiency and/or GI blood loss.

> Renal biopsy: will certainly be required to establish a diagnosis in this case.

 Key point
Although a renal biopsy will almost certainly be required in a patient with nephrotic syndrome, a proper history and examination are still essential.

General management of the nephrotic syndrome will be as described in Section 1.1.3; specific management will be determined by the precise diagnosis.

Further discussion

Diuretics
Massive oedema cannot be ignored and needs relief, but note the dangers of overdiuresis, particularly in older patients who can easily feel totally exhausted, develop postural hypotension with risk of falls and suffer acute deterioration in renal function. Hence:

> Aim for 0.5–1.0 kg weight loss per day (Fig 3).

> Cut back on the diuretics if this degree of weight loss is being exceeded.

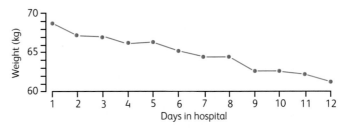

Fig 3 Weight chart of a patient with nephrotic syndrome treated with intravenous diuretics (furosemide (frusemide) 160 mg once daily). Their weight decreases at a satisfactory rate (8 kg over 12 days in hospital).

> Tell patients to check their weight daily at home and omit/stop diuretics if they lose >1 kg/day.

 Key point
Furosemide may be poorly absorbed due to gut oedema and is also sequestered by albumin in the renal tubule, so high doses are often required in the nephrotic syndrome. Bumetanide may be better absorbed.

Angiotensin-converting enzyme inhibitors
Any patient with proteinuric renal disease and renal impairment will benefit from an ACE inhibitor (or ARB) to reduce proteinuria and the rate of progression of renal failure (see Section 2.1.2).

Statins
Lipids are invariably deranged in the nephrotic syndrome, but the relationship to cardiovascular risk is not yet clear. There are animal experiments to suggest that lipid-lowering drugs may alter the course of progressive renal failure, but there are no reliable human data concerning this. Statins reduce cholesterol effectively and should be considered if the nephrotic state persists.

Anti-inflammatories and analgesics
Remember that NSAIDs cause a predictable fall in GFR. This does not generally cause clinical problems in those with normal renal function, but can do so when kidney function is impaired. If at all possible, this woman should avoid using them and take regular simple analgesics, eg paracetamol, for her musculoskeletal pains. Also note that opiates can accumulate in those with renal impairment, and regular doses of co-proxamol and similar agents could lead to nausea and drowsiness in this case.

Thrombotic tendency
There should be a high index of clinical suspicion when symptoms that could represent a thrombotic complication occur. Of particular note is renal vein thrombosis, which can present with the following:

> flank/back pain

> increasing proteinuria

> haematuria: increased non-visible and sometimes visible

> rising creatinine.

If suspected, the diagnosis can be made by Doppler ultrasonography (requires considerable technical skill), CT or renal arteriography (looking at the venous phase). If any thrombosis does occur, then anticoagulation should continue for as long as the patient remains nephrotic.

1.1.5 A blood test shows chronic kidney disease

Dear Doctor,

Re: Mr Peter Ward, aged 38 years

This garage mechanic came to see me with a vague history of fatigue a week ago. He was hypertensive (160/104 mmHg). His blood tests showed Na⁺ 134 mmol/L (normal range 137–144), K⁺ 4.8 mmol/L (normal range 3.5–4.9), urea 21 mmol/L (normal range 2.5–7.0), creatinine 370 μmol/L (normal range 60–110), eGFR 17 mL/min/1.73 m², haemoglobin 101 g/L (normal range 130–180), mean corpuscular volume (MCV) 89 fL (normal range 80–96), white blood cell count (WCC) 4.2 × 10⁹/L (normal range 4.0–11.0) and platelets 254 × 10⁹/L (normal range 150–400).

Please consider investigation of his chronic kidney disease (CKD) and advise concerning further management.

Yours sincerely,

Introduction

The emphasis in the history-taking station of PACES is clearly on conditions that present to medical outpatient clinics, but how do you know that this is CKD? The answer is that you cannot be sure from the information provided: this could be acute kidney injury (AKI) that is potentially reversible and you must recognise this in your approach to and discussion of the case.

The definition of CKD requires that renal dysfunction has persisted for more than 3 months. Renal function is usually described in terms of GFR; most clinical laboratories routinely report an eGFR along with creatinine values, and this is used to classify patients as being in CKD stage I through to stage V (see Section 2.1).

How will you establish whether the renal failure is acute or chronic?

> Further values of creatinine and eGFR are required – any previous blood tests would be useful, and it is urgent to obtain current values to check that renal function is not deteriorating rapidly.

> A renal ultrasound is very important – reduced renal size would prove that there is CKD, but even if this is the case there may still be an element of acute-on-chronic renal failure.

Key point

Take an exhaustive approach before concluding that renal failure is chronic.

History of the presenting problem

How long has the patient had renal failure?

Renal failure does not produce dramatic symptoms. Ask specifically about the following.

> Energy: many patients with advanced renal failure simply notice that they are exhausted all the time; this is due mainly to uraemia and renal dysfunction, but anaemia also plays an important role.

> Concentration: uraemia causes mental dulling.

> Breathing: anaemia may cause breathlessness on exertion and fluid retention can cause pulmonary oedema.

> Appetite, nausea or vomiting: uraemia causes anorexia and, when advanced, nausea and vomiting.

> Nocturia: the normal kidneys elaborate concentrated urine at night; they cannot do this when they fail and this leads to nocturia, a significant symptom in a young man

or woman (prostatism being a much more common cause in older men).

> Itching: a symptom of uraemia.

How long has the patient had a renal problem?

Are there any clues from the past? Take a detailed history of any contact with medical services. Approach this from several angles – ask the patient the following questions.

> Have you ever had kidney disease or swelled up in the past?

> Has anyone ever taken your BP before now and told you it was high?

> Have you ever had your urine tested?

> Have you ever had a medical for work or insurance purposes?

> Have you ever had a blood test or had blood taken? Knowing that the eGFR was normal or abnormal 3 months ago would be a crucial piece of information – CKD is defined as an abnormal eGFR persisting for at least 3 months.

> In women, ask about previous pregnancies – did they have high blood pressure / proteinuria / pre-eclampsia? Has their blood pressure been measured when prescribing hormonal contraception?

What is the cause of renal failure?

Explore all avenues that might suggest a diagnosis or aetiological factor, in particular, determine the following.

> Recent illnesses such as diarrhoea or upper respiratory tract infection, which in retrospect may have heralded the start of the illness, would favour an acute aetiology.

> Multisystem disease? Any previous rashes, painful or swollen joints, eye pain, haemoptysis, numbness, weakness or tingling – these may point to a systemic inflammatory illness such as vasculitis (see Section 2.7).

> Urinary tract symptoms: childhood recurrent infections or enuresis suggest reflux nephropathy (see Section 2.4). Recurrent haematuria associated with upper respiratory tract infections could point to IgA nephropathy (see Section 2.3). Has the patient had urinary stones?

> Drug history: this should include over-the-counter medications, illicit drugs, and traditional and herbal remedies, because all of these have been known to cause renal failure.

> Family history of kidney disease or of deafness (see Section 2.8).

> Is there a history of diabetes mellitus?

Plan for investigation and management

Investigations
The key issue is to determine whether the renal failure is acute or chronic, which can only reliably be done on the basis of previous measurements of renal function or ultrasonographic demonstration of small kidneys (Fig 4).

Certain chronic renal failure
If renal failure is chronic then the investigations shown in Table 3 are required. Further pursuit of a specific diagnosis is likely to have a poor yield, make little difference in terms of subsequent management and potentially risk complications. In particular, a renal biopsy would not be useful.

Key point
A renal biopsy is relatively contraindicated in patients with small kidneys – it is technically difficult, has a high complication rate, and the pathological findings are very likely to be non-specific.

Uncertain diagnosis
In some cases it is not certain whether renal failure is acute or chronic. It is then necessary to carry out tests to rule out potentially reversible diagnoses (Table 4), and in some cases a renal biopsy may be indicated even if the kidneys are reduced in size.

If there is any doubt about the findings on ultrasonography or if they seem at odds with the clinical setting, ask an experienced radiologist to repeat the study or consider CT, which is less operator dependent (Fig 5).

Management
There is no specific treatment for chronic renal failure, but particularly note the following.

> ACE inhibitors and angiotensin receptor antagonists slow the progression of chronic renal disease, but remember to check the serum

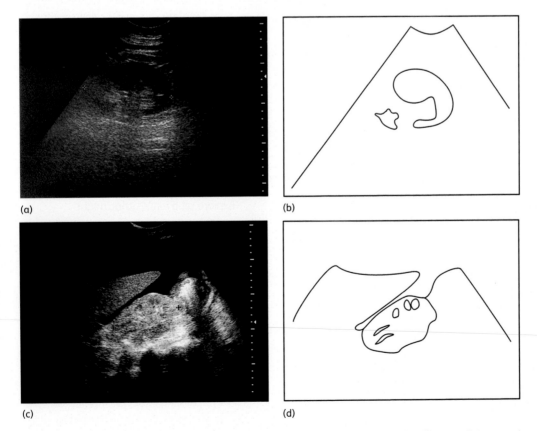

(a)

(b)

(c)

(d)

Fig 4 Urinary tract ultrasonography showing **(a, b)** a normal kidney and **(c, d)** a small, hyperechoic kidney without clear corticomedullary differentiation that is consistent with chronic renal failure.

Table 3 Investigations in the evaluation of chronic renal failure

Investigation	Purpose
FBC and haematinics	Evaluation of contributory factors to anaemia
Calcium, phosphate and PTH	Assessing degree of secondary or tertiary hyperparathyroidism
Lipid profile	Cardiovascular disease is accelerated by chronic renal failure and is the main cause of death
Hepatitis B and C serology, and HIV testing (after counselling)	Positive patients will need specific haemodialysis arrangements. All patients who are HBsAg negative should be vaccinated against hepatitis B
ECG and chest X-ray	Evidence of LVH and/or IHD

ECG, electrocardiogram; FBC, full blood count; HBsAg, hepatitis-B surface antigen; IHD, ischaemic heart disease; LVH, left ventricular hypertrophy; PTH, parathyroid hormone.

Table 4 Investigations to help exclude a possible acute aetiology

Investigation	A normal result is likely to exclude the following diagnoses
Blood count and film	HUS
CRP	Any inflammatory disease
Serum and urine electrophoresis / paraprotein measurement	Myeloma
Anti-GBM	Anti-GBM disease
ANCA plus ELISA for anti-MPO or PR3	ANCA-associated vasculitides
C3, C4 and autoantibody screen	Connective tissue diseases, SLE, MCGN, cryoglobulinaemia and infection-related glomerulonephritis

ANCA, anti-neutrophil cytoplasmic antibodies; CRP, C-reactive protein; ELISA, enzyme-linked immunosorbent assay; GBM, glomerular basement membrane; HUS, haemolytic uraemic syndrome; MCGN, mesangiocapillary glomerulonephritis; MPO, myeloperoxidase; PR3, proteinase 3; SLE, systemic lupus erythematosus.

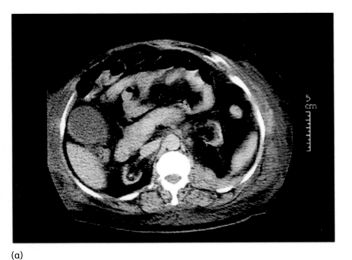

(a)

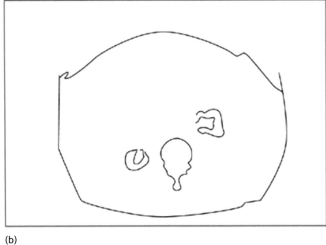

(b)

Fig 5 Abdominal CT scan demonstrating small kidneys with little renal cortex, which is consistent with chronic renal failure.

creatinine 7–10 days after initiating or adjusting treatment to ensure there is no acute deterioration (a rise in creatinine of up to 30% or fall in eGFR of <25% can be tolerated, but a more substantial change suggests the possibility of renal arterial disease and should lead to the drug being stopped and consideration given to imaging the renal vessels). Also remember that these drugs may exacerbate the common tendency to hyperkalaemia in those with advanced CKD.

> Cardiovascular morbidity and mortality are extremely high in patients with renal impairment: all require a full cardiovascular risk assessment, followed by attempts aiming to deal with reversible factors such as smoking, hypertension and lipids.

> Treatment of anaemia – invariably, most patients with CKD will eventually require treatment with erythropoiesis-stimulating agents (ESAs). However, prior to this, it is necessary to look for and correct iron deficiency, which is a very common finding in those with CKD (see Section 2.1).

> Treatment of hyperparathyroidism (see Section 2.1).

> Dietary advice: may be appropriate and is most commonly to restrict potassium intake.

Further discussion

This patient has an eGFR of 17 mL/min/1.73 m^2, and so has CKD stage IV (see Section 2.1), but is on the cusp of CKD stage V. His renal disease is likely to progress and he will require long-term renal replacement therapy (RRT). Telling a patient this can be devastating. The reaction is often similar to that seen in bereavement, with progression through shock, grief and denial before reaching acceptance. Accurate information and continued support are essential and best provided by a team which includes doctors, dietitians and specialist nurses. Breaking of bad news such as this may

feature in PACES Station 4, but it will be important to also demonstrate an appropriately sympathetic way of talking to the patient in a Station 2 scenario such as this (as is certainly the case in routine clinical practice).

1.1.6 Diabetes with chronic kidney disease

Letter of referral to the nephrology outpatient clinic

Dear Doctor,
Re: Mr David Marshall, aged 55 years

Please would you see this man who has had diabetes for the past 10 years, treated with metformin and gliclazide. He is not a frequent attender at the surgery, but he came in last week to consult me about erectile dysfunction. I did some blood tests which showed that his creatinine was elevated at 160 μmol/L (normal range 60–110). I would be grateful for your advice about his management.

Yours sincerely,

Introduction

Diabetic nephropathy is the commonest cause of end-stage renal failure (ESRF) in the Western world and its incidence is increasing; in 2013 in the UK, diabetes was the primary renal diagnosis in 25% of new RRT patients. In the USA, >35% of people with ESRF have diabetes, and up to 20% of type 1 diabetics eventually develop end-stage renal disease. Only about 10% of patients with type 2 diabetes develop end-stage renal disease, but due to the higher prevalence of type 2 diabetes (five- to ten-fold) they are the commonest diabetics treated for renal failure. Genetic factors appear to play an important role in the development of diabetic nephropathy and some ethnic groups, particularly

African Americans, persons of Hispanic origin, Native Americans and Indo-Asians, are predisposed to renal disease as a complication of diabetes. Interestingly, the likelihood of developing new diabetic nephropathy declines 20 years after the onset of type 1 diabetes, suggesting that some individuals are relatively protected.

The initial aim in dealing with this case must be to determine whether the overall history is consistent with diabetic nephropathy or if there are any features to suggest an alternative diagnosis. Between 10% and 30% of patients with diabetes who have renal disease are discovered to have a non-diabetic cause of nephropathy.

The duration of diabetes is important. In general, the risk of diabetic nephropathy is higher when the duration of diabetes is up to 20 years, although type 2 diabetics may have had the condition for several years before becoming aware of it. Renal impairment is preceded by hyperfiltration, microalbuminuria and macroalbuminuria. Hypertension is usually present early in the course of the disease. Diabetic nephropathy is more common if diabetic control has been poor, and the condition is unusual in the absence of any diabetic retinopathy.

Key point

Diabetic nephropathy is very common, but diabetics with renal impairment may have another diagnosis – for example obstructive uropathy, a plasma cell dyscrasia or renovascular disease.

History of the presenting problem

Related to renal disease

Although the referral letter suggests that the patient has no systemic symptoms other than erectile dysfunction and the strong suspicion is that he has diabetic nephropathy, it is important to probe the history thoroughly as he may have renal failure due to a cause other than diabetes. Crucially, this might be acute and potentially reversible. The questions relating to past medical history and potential causes of renal failure listed in Section 1.1.5 would all be appropriate in this case.

Related to diabetes

It is important to ask about the following.

> Monitoring of diabetes – how is the patient assessing his diabetic control? Occasional patients are still using urine testing, which is certainly inappropriate in the presence of renal disease. How often is he checking his blood sugar, at what times of day and what values have been obtained? Part of the management of diabetic nephropathy is to optimise diabetic control.

> Hypertension – has his BP been checked regularly and does he know what readings have been obtained? Obtaining good control of BP will be crucial in this case, whatever the cause of renal impairment.

> Retinopathy – has the patient ever been told there is a problem with his eyes? Are his eyes checked regularly for signs of diabetic damage? Has he ever had laser treatment?

> Neuropathy – does he get any numbness, pins and needles or funny feelings in his toes and/or fingers, which would indicate peripheral neuropathy?

> Macrovascular disease – has he suffered angina / myocardial infarction, transient ischaemic attacks / amaurosis fugax / stroke, or intermittent claudication? If these are prominent features, then renovascular disease requires consideration.

> Feet – has he had ulcers, which could be caused by neuropathy, ischaemia, or both?

Key point

Diabetic nephropathy with renal impairment is almost always associated with some diabetic retinopathy – if this is not present, you need to seek another renal diagnosis.

Other relevant history

It will be important to obtain a proper smoking history: the combination of diabetes, renal impairment and smoking is devastating to health.

Plan for investigation and management

Investigation

Investigations aim to determine whether diabetic nephropathy is the most likely cause of the renal impairment and should include the following.

Urine tests

Stick testing would typically reveal significant proteinuria (2+ or more) without haematuria in a patient with renal impairment due to diabetic nephropathy. Quantitate proteinuria by estimation of urinary ACR – an ACR >3 mg/mmol (termed microalbuminuria) is clinically significant. Overt proteinuria is when the ACR is >30 mg/mmol. Non-visible haematuria and the absence of proteinuria are both unusual in diabetic nephropathy, and either of these findings should raise the possibility of another diagnosis. If non-visible haematuria is observed, then urine microscopy should be performed: the presence of red cell casts would strongly suggest that diabetic nephropathy was not the diagnosis.

Blood tests

Serum creatinine to determine the current level of renal function and rate of decline (if previous values are available). Cholesterol and triglycerides to help quantitate cardiovascular risk. HbA$_{1C}$ to determine medium-term

glycaemic control. FBC – erythropoietin deficiency and thus renal anaemia often occur relatively early in the course of diabetic renal disease.

To rule out other causes of renal impairment, consider serum (and urine) protein electrophoresis – plasma cell dyscrasias are a common cause of renal impairment in this age group – and also immunological tests including ANCA, ANA and complement to exclude immunologically mediated renal disease (but note that hypocomplementaemia may be a feature of cholesterol embolisation syndrome).

Urinary tract ultrasonography

By contrast with most other causes of chronic renal failure, renal size is often normal in patients with diabetic nephropathy. Disparity in renal size (>1.5 cm difference in kidney length) may suggest renovascular disease or reflux nephropathy, and irregular renal outlines may indicate congenital dysplasia / reflux nephropathy / chronic pyelonephritis. Check that the patient's bladder empties properly: neglected obstruction is a common cause of renal impairment in older men.

Other tests

Perform an electrocardiogram (ECG) to look for evidence of previous myocardial infarction or left ventricular hypertrophy.

Conduct magnetic resonance angiography if the history, examination findings or ultrasonography suggest renovascular disease, but only if you would proceed to angiography and renal artery angioplasty/stenting if renal artery stenosis is demonstrated.

Consider renal biopsy if there are any features to suggest a non-diabetic cause of the renal impairment other than renovascular disease, eg an absence of previous proteinuria or retinopathy, a sudden onset of nephrotic syndrome or the presence of red cell casts on urine microscopy.

Key point

It is usually not appropriate to perform a renal biopsy if the history and clinical findings are consistent with diabetic nephropathy – the chances of doing harm are greater than the chances of revealing anything that would help management.

Management

Aside from issues common to all diabetics, eg regular eye and foot checks, issues of particular importance in this case are:

> Review of current drug therapy – metformin can cause lactic acidosis in advanced renal impairment and the National Institute for Health and Care Excellence (NICE) advises that it should be discontinued if the serum creatinine exceeds 150 µmol/L or eGFR is <30 mL/min/1.73 m^2.

> BP control – the most important determinant of the rate of progression of diabetic renal impairment is BP, which should be maintained as low as tolerated (<130/80 mmHg if achievable without unacceptable side effects), with first-line therapy being an ACE inhibitor. Other antihypertensive agents may need to be added. The combination of ACE inhibitor and ARB together is no longer recommended due to the increased risk of adverse events. Modest restriction of salt intake can help to achieve BP targets.

> Management of cardiovascular risk – encourage the patient to stop smoking (if necessary) and take exercise; reduce cholesterol using a statin.

> Glycaemic control – improvement may slow the progression of early diabetic nephropathy but is less important than BP control.

Key point

Management of diabetic nephropathy is with ACE inhibitors and additional antihypertensive agents as necessary, aiming for BP <130/80 mmHg.

Key point

Management of cardiovascular risk and macrovascular arterial disease is essential in patients with diabetic nephropathy.

Further discussion

Renovascular disease

Renovascular disease may coexist with diabetic nephropathy and should be considered in all diabetic patients with renal impairment, hence – as stated in Section 1.1.5 – it is always important to check renal function 7–10 days after starting an ACE inhibitor or ARB to ensure there is no acute deterioration. Whether to undertake angioplasty and stenting of stenotic lesions in renovascular disease needs careful consideration and is discussed in Section 1.1.7.

Prognosis of diabetic nephropathy

Diabetic nephropathy is usually inexorably progressive and patients with diabetes have a reduced survival rate compared to other causes of renal failure. Once RRT is instituted, 5-year survival among patients with diabetic nephropathy is significantly reduced compared to those with another cause of their renal failure, particularly in patients under the age of 65.

1.1.7 Atherosclerosis and renal failure

Letter of referral to the nephrology outpatient clinic

Dear Doctor,
Re: Mr Harry Scott, aged 65 years

I would be grateful if you would see this man and advise on his renal failure, which seems to have developed since he left hospital. He is a heavy smoker and has been hypertensive for 10 years. One month ago he was admitted with chest pain and a suspected acute coronary syndrome (ACS). His troponin (Tn) was not elevated, he was started on an ACE inhibitor, and he was put on the waiting list for a coronary angiogram (not yet done). I was asked to check his renal function, and this shows that his creatinine – which was normal when he was discharged from hospital – is now markedly elevated at 260 µmol/L (normal range 60–110). What should be done about this?

Yours sincerely,

Introduction

Renovascular disease is an important cause of renal dysfunction and resistant hypertension. In patients with atherosclerotic renovascular disease there is usually evidence of cardiovascular, cerebrovascular and peripheral vascular disease.

History of the presenting problem

Renovascular disease

It is very likely that this man has this condition, which produces no specific symptoms, but it is worth asking the following questions.

> Has he felt dizzy and been hypotensive since starting the ACE inhibitor? Hypertension related to renovascular disease often responds dramatically to ACE inhibitors.

> Has he had episodes of sudden onset severe shortness of breath suggesting 'flash pulmonary oedema'? Renovascular disease can cause such problems, which may have been better since starting on the ACE inhibitor, but this is uncommon and episodes of breathlessness are generally much more likely to have a cardiac explanation.

Other vascular disease

There is a strong association between renovascular disease and peripheral vascular disease, hence probe carefully for symptoms suggesting intermittent claudication, amaurosis fugax or transient ischaemic attacks.

Key point

The best predictor of renovascular disease is evidence of peripheral vascular disease.

Other causes of acute renal impairment

It is very important to consider other possible causes by pursuing the following aspects of the history.

> Pre-renal failure – since discharge from hospital, has the patient had any illness that would predispose him to this, eg diarrhoea/vomiting, or any symptoms to suggest volume depletion, eg postural dizziness?

> Urinary obstruction – has he had any difficulty passing urine, any back pain, any haematuria or passed any stones?

> Renal inflammatory condition – has he felt unwell in any way? Systemic features (fever, etc) are not expected with renovascular disease and could support a diagnosis of pre-renal failure or of a renal inflammatory condition. Has he had any symptoms that might suggest a multisystem disorder, eg joint pains or nasal/sinus problems?

> Has he noticed any skin rash, particularly on the feet, which may suggest cholesterol emboli, or if it is more widespread may be due to drug hypersensitivity associated with an acute interstitial nephritis? And relating to the latter, has he taken any other new drugs (including over-the-counter medicines – especially NSAIDs)? Has he had aching muscles? He will almost certainly be on a statin and could have developed rhabdomyolysis.

Other relevant history

Patients at risk of renal atherosclerosis have the same risk factors as patients with atherosclerosis elsewhere: he smokes, but is he diabetic?

Plan for investigation and management

Given the high index of clinical suspicion that this patient has renovascular disease with acute deterioration in renal function caused by the ACE inhibitor, your immediate action should be to stop this drug, which may lead to improvement in renal function.

Investigation

Blood pressure (including postural readings)

Urinalysis

Significant proteinuria (more than 1+) and/or haematuria (more than trace) would not be expected in renovascular disease: if present then consider cholesterol embolism or other renal inflammatory condition.

Blood tests

Check renal function: is this getting worse, has it stabilised or is it improving? Check FBC and clotting screen (this man may require an interventional procedure), and also inflammatory markers and myeloma/autoimmune/vasculitis screens depending on clinical suspicion.

Urinary tract ultrasonography

This is the first-line imaging test in any instance of unexplained acute deterioration in renal function. The finding of a unilateral atrophic kidney or a discrepancy in renal length of >1.5 cm may predict underlying renovascular disease. Ultrasound will also exclude obstruction with a high degree of reliability (but not total reliability).

Key point

Urinary tract ultrasonography should be performed urgently in any patient with unexplained acute deterioration in renal function.

Imaging for renal artery stenosis

The standard screening tests are magnetic resonance angiography or CT angiography, proceeding to formal angiography, which remains the gold standard for diagnosis and also enables therapeutic angioplasty/stenting.

Management

The following are essential:

> Stop smoking – aside from general vascular considerations, smoking is an independent risk factor for the progression of renal disease.

> Aspirin and cholesterol-lowering therapy (eg statin) to reduce cardiovascular risk, although it is not proven that they influence the progression of renovascular disease.

> Blood pressure control.

If renovascular disease is proven, then consider angioplasty and/or stenting.

Further discussion

Which patients should have occlusive renal artery lesions angioplastied (dilated) and stented?

This remains controversial. Recent trials have shown that patients with atheromatous renal artery stenosis and hypertension / renal impairment should not be offered radiological intervention routinely, even if this would be technically straightforward. However, most nephrologists would recommend angioplasty/stenting for:

> bilateral stenoses with acute deterioration in renal function, especially in the context of initiation of ACE inhibitor or ARB

> small kidney on one side and tight stenosis affecting the opposite kidney

> episodes of flash pulmonary oedema not explained by left ventricular dysfunction.

1.1.8 Recurrent loin pain

Dear Doctor,

Re: Mr Lawrence Perkins, aged 46 years

This man, with no past medical history of note, has had several episodes over the past few years of severe right-sided flank pain, following which he has sometimes noticed gravel in his urine. He recently had a particularly severe attack when away on holiday that took him to the emergency department of the local hospital, where he required diclofenac and pethidine to ease the pain. Stimulated by this, he came to see me. I would be grateful for your advice as to what we should do about his kidney stones.

Yours sincerely,

Introduction

Urinary tract stones are a common problem. Patients typically present when stones enter the ureter, causing colic and/or obstruction. If present in the renal pelvis, they make UTI much harder to eradicate. Aside from confirming the history of loin pain and passage of gravel/stones in this case, the history must focus on the well-recognised predisposing factors for stone formation. In deciding on the correct treatment, it will be very important to determine the chemical composition of the patient's stones (if possible) because different types of stone require different treatments.

History of the presenting problem

To confirm that the patient has had pain from urinary stones

Renal colic is usually of sudden onset and very painful; it is typically in the loin, radiating to the suprapubic area, and is often spasmodic in nature, occurring in waves lasting from 30 minutes to 1 hour. Nausea and vomiting are common symptoms. The patient may notice haematuria, and dysuria is common when stones are in the bladder or passing through the urethra. Strong analgesia may be required. As in this case, an episode of pain followed by passing a stone or grit in the urine establishes the diagnosis.

Previous episodes

There will often be a previous history of urinary stone disease, as seems to be the case here. Ask the patient directly whether they have had any tests done for these in the past: 'Have you ever had X-rays or scans done to look at the kidneys or bladder? Have you ever seen an urologist or a kidney doctor?' In routine clinical practice it would not be at all uncommon for a patient not to have mentioned these to their GP, and in PACES the instruction to the patient could well say 'do not mention this unless asked directly'.

Other relevant history

Ask about the following risk factors for urinary stones.

> Fluid intake – 'What do you drink over 24 hours on a typical day?' Go through this carefully: 'When you get up, what do you drink at breakfast; and then during the morning; and at lunch?' and so on. Low fluid intake is a major risk factor for formation of all types of stones.

> Diet – high oxalate intake (spinach, tea, nuts and chocolate) and high protein intake predispose to calcium stones (the commonest sort).

> Time in hot climates – increased perspiration leads to decreased urine output (UO), hence stones are much commoner in hot climates. This might be relevant in this case if the man has spent 10 years working in the tropics: once stones form they are very slow indeed to resolve, even if the precipitating factor is removed.

> Hypertension.

> UTIs – these predispose to stones and are also more likely in those with stones.

> Gout – suggesting increased uric acid production and excretion, and is a risk factor for uric acid stones.

> Drugs promoting crystalluria can rarely cause stones, eg triamterene and indinavir.

> Family history of stone disease – if many family members are affected then obviously consider genetic causes, including medullary sponge kidney.

Also consider the following.

> Are there other symptoms suggesting hypercalcaemia and/or hyperparathyroidism (such as thirst, polyuria, abdominal pain, depression or aching bones)?

> Increased oxalate absorption from short bowel syndrome – has this patient had any intestinal surgery?

Plan for investigation and management

Investigation

Examination of the urine

Spot urine sample – check standard urinalysis, urinary pH (with a pH meter), specific gravity and microscopy for crystals, and then send for culture – a pH of >7 with phosphate crystals is suggestive of magnesium ammonium phosphate / calcium phosphate 'infection stones'; hexagonal cystine crystals are diagnostic of cystine stones.

24-hour urine collections – two are required; one in a container with acid as a preservative for the checking of volume and excretion of creatinine, calcium, magnesium, sodium, potassium, phosphate, oxalate and citrate; the other in a plain container to be analysed for volume, creatinine, pH, urate and a qualitative test for cystine.

Chemical examination of the stone (if available)

Ask the patient if they have saved a stone: sometimes people do but may not volunteer this information, only revealing it if asked directly. Expect to find one of the following:

> calcium oxalate/phosphate – common and not specific

> uric acid – uricosuria

> cystine – cystinuria

> magnesium ammonium phosphate, usually with calcium phosphate – suggests stones caused by chronic infection with urea-splitting bacteria.

Key point

Always ask the patient if they have saved any stone/gravel that they have passed – analysis is crucial to direct specific treatment.

Blood tests

Check renal function plus serum sodium, potassium, calcium, magnesium, phosphate, bicarbonate, urate, albumin and alkaline phosphatase. Consider measuring parathyroid hormone.

Imaging

The test to perform at the first outpatient attendance would be an abdominal X-ray of the kidneys, ureter and bladder, which would show any radio-opaque stones. The single most useful test to look for stones within the urinary tract would be an unenhanced CT of the kidneys, ureters and bladder. Ultrasonography of the kidneys would be the appropriate test if obstruction were suspected, but there is nothing in the letter of referral to suggest that this is likely in this case.

Management

The management of patients with urinary stones includes general measures and specific measures based on the type of the stone, where this is known.

General measures to decrease stone formation

Ensure the patient:

> drinks enough water to increase their urinary output to over 2,000 mL daily

> decreases their animal protein intake

> reduce their dietary oxalate: spinach, tea, nuts and chocolate.

Key point

Whatever the cause of urinary stones, get the patient to drink more.

Specific measures for specific stones

These are:

> calcium oxalate/phosphate stones – potassium citrate and thiazide diuretics

> urate stones – potassium citrate and allopurinol

> 'infection stones' – these require eradication of urinary sepsis: prolonged antibiotic therapy (3–6 months) is often required – note that these stones are associated with alkaline urine and are not helped by giving alkali such as potassium citrate

> cystine stones – D-penicillamine, captopril or alpha-mercaptopropionylglycine.

Underlying medical causes of stones – such as hyperparathyroidism – need to be treated, and CKD, if present, would require management along conventional lines (see Section 2.1).

Further discussion

What happens if a symptomatic stone doesn't pass?

Urinary obstruction must be relieved, usually by percutaneous antegrade nephrostomy. Stone removal can be effected by percutaneous endoscopic or ureteroscopic procedures, or by external shock wave lithotripsy, depending on the site, size and type of stone, and on the availability of technical expertise. Open surgery to remove urinary stones is rarely required, but remains the best option in some cases.

1.2 Clinical examination

1.2.1 Polycystic kidneys

Instruction

This patient has noticed abdominal swelling – please examine their abdomen.

General features

Is there any evidence of renal failure or renal replacement therapy (RRT)?

> Look for arteriovenous fistulae (AVF) in the arms to indicate treatment with haemodialysis, or scars over the forearms and in the elbows that might be due to attempts to create such fistulae.

> Look in the root of the neck and below the clavicles for tunnelled dialysis catheters, or scars indicating that these may have been inserted in the past: they typically enter the internal jugular vein low down in the neck and exit the skin 3–8 cm below the clavicle in the mid-clavicular line.

> Is there a peritoneal dialysis (Tenckhoff) catheter *in situ*, indicating peritoneal dialysis treatment?

Has the patient had neck surgery, perhaps a parathyroidectomy?

Abdominal examination

The instructions state that the abdomen will be swollen: is this symmetrical or not? Does it look like fluid, suggesting ascites and (most probably) a hepatological case?

Look carefully for scars – these might be from previous Tenckhoff catheters, which are inserted in the midline about 5 cm below the umbilicus and tunnelled to exit laterally, or related to renal transplant operations, which leave a 'hockey-stick' incision in either the right or left iliac fossa.

The most likely finding is bilateral abdominal masses, in which case it is essential to have a logical technique for distinguishing between bilateral polycystic kidneys and hepatosplenomegaly. Remember the five clinical features that can be used to do this.

> Can you get above the masses? This indicates that they are renal: you cannot get above a liver or spleen.

> How do the masses move on respiration? A kidney moves 'up and down'; a spleen moves 'down and across' (towards the right iliac fossa).

> Are the masses ballotable? Push firmly up in the renal angle with one hand

while pressing down into the abdomen with the other – a kidney will move forwards and be palpable by the 'upper' hand (and movement with respiration may be better appreciated). The liver or spleen will not be ballotable.

> Percussion note – kidneys are resonant (usually – overlying gas-filled small bowel), but the liver and spleen are dull (always).

> Can you feel a notch? This is a feature of some spleens.

Remember that polycystic enlargement of the liver is a common finding in polycystic kidney disease and do not be thrown if you can feel what you think is a kidney on the left side and what you think is a liver on the right: you are probably correct. If you can't feel both kidneys, also look for the scars of a nephrectomy – polycystic kidneys may be removed due to symptoms or to create space for future transplantation. Also examine the patient for inguinal hernias (or evidence of previous repair) since these are associated with polycystic kidney disease.

If asked whether you would like to extend your examination of the patient, say that you would want to check their BP and perform fundoscopy looking for signs of end-organ hypertensive damage.

Key point

Polycystic kidneys range in size from barely larger than normal kidneys to being so large that they distend the abdomen – in the latter case they can be confused with ascitic distension and may be hard to feel as distinct masses.

Key point

Remember that patients with polycystic kidneys, particularly women, can have a very large polycystic liver.

Further discussion

For further discussion see Section 2.8.

1.2.2 Transplant kidney

Instruction

Examine this patient's abdomen (with hockey-stick scar visible in iliac fossa).

General features

Look for evidence of:

> an underlying condition causing renal failure: treatment or complications of diabetes, hearing impairment (Alport), facial rash (systemic lupus erythematosus (SLE)) or collapsed nasal bridge (ANCA-associated vasculitis)

> previous RRT: AVF (haemodialysis), scars on neck or upper chest from central lines, or an abdominal scar (continuous ambulatory peritoneal dialysis (CAPD) catheter)

> complications of long-standing renal impairment: parathyroidectomy scar and carpal tunnel release (dialysis-related amyloid).

Numerous features are commonly found in the general examination of transplant recipients, many of which are the direct consequence of immunosuppressive drugs:

> steroids – 'moon face', 'buffalo hump', central obesity, acne, bruising, thin skin and striae

> ciclosporin – gingival hyperplasia and hirsutism

> sirolimus (rapamycin) – mouth ulcers, acneiform rash, ankle oedema

> long-standing immunosuppression – 'field change' in skin of sun-exposed areas, typically face and backs of hands; warts; actinic keratoses; and scars from removal of squamous/basal cell carcinomas.

Abdominal examination

The typical sign is a scar in the right or left iliac fossa beneath which there is a palpable smooth mass, which may feel very superficial or may be quite deep – this is the transplanted kidney. Listen over the transplant for a bruit, which may indicate transplant renal artery stenosis. Look carefully at the other iliac fossa for another transplant, which may be small and shrunken (a previous failed graft).

Palpate carefully for polycystic kidneys (see Section 1.2.1).

Further discussion

What are the common causes of renal failure?
These include:

> diabetes mellitus is the commonest cause of end-stage renal failure (ESRF) in the UK – 20–30% and increasing

> biopsy-proven glomerulonephritis – 15%, with IgA disease the single commonest form

> congenital dysplasia/reflux nephropathy/chronic pyelonephritis – 10–15%

> autosomal dominant polycystic kidney disease – 5%

> obstruction – 5%

> renovascular – 5%

> multisystem autoimmune/vasculitis – 5%

> cause unknown – 20–30%.

1.3 Communication skills and ethics

1.3.1 Renal disease in pregnancy

Scenario

Role: you are a junior doctor in a nephrology outpatient clinic.

Scenario: Mrs Lucy Booth is a 27-year-old woman who is known to have reflux nephropathy with moderate renal impairment. She is hypertensive and taking lisinopril 10 mg daily. She attends the nephrology clinic every 6 months for review.

Her routine pre-clinic investigations demonstrate proteinuria (1.2 g/24 hour) and creatinine 196 μmol/L (normal range 60–110) (eGFR 28 mL/min). Her BP is 156/90 mmHg.

She tells you that she is planning to start a family. This is something that she has said before and a previous letter in the notes from the renal consultant to the patient's GP has documented that there would be considerable risks: at least a 50% chance of significant rapid deterioration in the patient's renal function, at least 50% chance of pregnancy-related complications (such as pre-eclampsia), and at least a 50% chance of fetal loss.

Your task: to explain the implications of pregnancy with regard to the patient's renal condition.

Key issues to explore

What is her understanding of the risks of pregnancy to her own health, and what does she think the chances are of her having a healthy baby? What does she understand about the risks to pregnancy caused by her medication?

Key points to establish

> Pregnancy poses very significant risk to her own health.

> There is a high chance that pregnancy will not be successful.

> ACE inhibitors (lisinopril) are contraindicated in pregnancy.

> That you will try to give her the best care, whatever she decides about pregnancy.

Appropriate responses to likely questions

Patient: I feel perfectly well, so I must be fit enough to have a child.

Doctor: it's obviously good that you feel well, but I am afraid that this does not mean that there aren't any problems. Kidney disease does not make people feel ill until it is very bad indeed; but the fact that your blood pressure is high, that you have protein in the urine and the blood test showing that kidney function is about 30% of normal all mean that the risks of pregnancy would be very high.

Patient: what do you mean by very high?

Doctor: I mean that there's at least a 50% chance that the stress of pregnancy would make your kidneys get significantly worse; and at least a 50% chance that the pregnancy would not go well, so you would not end up with a healthy baby. This includes a significant risk of miscarriage, the baby being born early or underweight and also pre-eclampsia. This can be life-threatening for both you and the baby.

Patient: you and all the other doctors are just trying to frighten me, aren't you?

Doctor: no, we're trying to give you the proper facts. I'd like to be able to tell you that there aren't any problems, but that wouldn't be true. The risks of pregnancy for you are much higher than they are for a woman who doesn't have kidney problems, and it's important that you understand this.

Patient: if I do get pregnant, then what would you do?

Doctor: we'd try and look after you as well as we can. We would want to see you in clinic as soon as you knew you were pregnant, and we would monitor your blood pressure and kidney function very carefully. And if things were going wrong, we would talk to you about it. You would need to have follow up with both the kidney and the obstetric teams. We would also need to monitor you closely for urine infections.

Patient: if I am going to get pregnant, should I do anything before?

Doctor: we should try and get better control of your blood pressure and we should change the blood pressure tablet, because lisinopril – the one you're taking at the moment – can cause problems in pregnancy. You would have a better chance of a good pregnancy outcome if you conceived when your blood pressure is well controlled. This may take a few months on a new tablet regime.

Patient: if I have a child, will they develop the same kidney problems as me?

Doctor: it's not inevitable, but it is possible that they might. If this was a concern, then the baby could have scans done to see.

1.3.2 A new diagnosis of myeloma

> ### Scenario
> **Role:** you are a junior doctor working on a renal ward.

Scenario: Mr Albert Foster is a 76-year-old man who was admitted with new renal impairment (creatinine 350 µmol/L (normal range 60–110)), anaemia (haemoglobin 85 g/L (normal range 130–180)), and back pain for which he was taking ibuprofen. Investigations revealed a raised erythrocyte sedimentation rate (ESR) (105 mm/1 h (normal threshold <20)), an 8 g paraprotein band on protein electrophoresis, and urine test was positive for Bence Jones protein. His initial corrected calcium was elevated at 2.9 mmol/L (normal range 2.20–2.60). A kidney biopsy showed cast nephropathy. A skeletal survey showed lytic lesions in the spine and pelvis. He underwent a bone marrow biopsy that showed a 15% plasma cell infiltrate suggestive of multiple myeloma.

His case was discussed with the renal and haematology consultants. It was felt that he would require supportive management initially to treat his hypercalcaemia and hopefully improve his renal function. He would then require disease-specific chemotherapy, potentially bortezomib with dexamethasone. However, there is a possibility that his renal function may continue to deteriorate, he would be at risk of infections, and he would have a reduced life expectancy (around 3–4 years after first presentation).

Your task: to explain the diagnosis of myeloma and renal failure to the patient and discuss what this means for his future.

Key issues to explore
What is his understanding of the situation?

Key points to establish

> The link between myeloma and renal impairment.

> Initial supportive therapy can reverse acute kidney injury (AKI).

> Chronic kidney disease (CKD) may progress to end stage despite chemotherapy.

Appropriate responses to likely questions
Patient: what is myeloma?

Doctor: myeloma is a type of cancer of the blood. It affects the white blood cells that produce antibodies … things that normally fight infections. These are produced from your bone marrow, but unfortunately some of them have become cancerous. These abnormal cells can weaken bones, leading to the bony pain that you have experienced. The abnormal antibodies can also block the filters in your kidneys, leading to worsening kidney function.

Patient: is that why my kidneys are not working properly?

Doctor: yes, although there are also other factors. Your blood calcium level was very high and this can cause dehydration as well as direct kidney damage. The ibuprofen that you were taking for your back pain can also cause kidney problems … it can reduce blood flow to the kidneys, and sometimes it can cause inflammation in the kidneys as well. We hope that giving you fluids through a drip, lowering the calcium with medication, and stopping the ibuprofen will improve your kidney function … but we don't know if it will return to normal, and I'm afraid that there's quite a high chance that it might not.

Patient: what happens if my kidney function doesn't get better?

Doctor: around half of patients with myeloma have impaired kidney function when they first get diagnosed. Many recover some kidney function with treatment, usually within the first 6 weeks, but it is rare that kidney function completely recovers. In around 20% of cases kidney function continues to deteriorate despite treatment, and we would then offer dialysis treatment … artificial kidney treatment. Do you know anything about this? Have you known anyone who's been on a kidney machine?

Patient: how will I get rid of the myeloma?

Doctor: you have already been referred to the haematology team who are specialists in looking after myeloma and other blood disorders. They will discuss further treatment with you, which is likely to involve steroids and a drug to reduce the production of the abnormal antibodies.

Patient: but can the myeloma be cured?

Doctor: I'd like to say something different, but I'm afraid that's not likely … the treatment that we have is unlikely to get rid of the myeloma altogether, but it can certainly help to control the disease.

Patient: will I die from this?

Doctor: I'm not hiding anything when I say that I don't know … as I've said, I'm afraid it's unlikely that the myeloma can be completely cured, but the outlook depends on how well it responds to treatment. If the initial response is good, then you may well be OK for several years.

1.3.3 Is dialysis appropriate?

Scenario

Role: you are a junior doctor working on a renal ward.

Scenario: a 78-year-old retired lecturer was found to have metastatic carcinoma 3 months previously. No primary site has been identified and previously he declined further investigation and treatment. He has been more short of breath for the last week and confused for about 2 days.

He has chronic renal failure, cause unknown – previous imaging has shown that both of his kidneys are of reduced size and his serum creatinine was 300 µmol/L (normal range 60–110) 2 months ago (eGFR 20 mL/min/1.73 m^2).

He is brought to the emergency department by his son who was visiting him. His BP is 70/50 mmHg. Blood tests show creatinine 670 µmol/L, urea 38 mmol/L (normal range 2.5–7.0) and potassium 7.2 mmol/L (normal range 3.5–4.9). You are called to give advice on the management of his renal failure. You discuss this with the renal consultant who is on call and they say that dialysis would not be appropriate and that he should be managed conservatively.

Your task: to explain the management plan to the patient's son, who is upset.

Key issues to explore

What is the son's understanding of his father's condition? Does he know about the diagnosis of malignancy, and does he know that his father declined further investigation and treatment?

Key points to establish

> The background of malignancy.

> The patient's wishes are more important than anyone else's – he is confused now, but when competent to make decisions he declined intervention.

> The patient is dying and heroic medical interventions would not change that, as well as being contrary to his wishes.

> That you will ensure that the patient is not distressed, and will look after him until he dies.

> That decisions about treatment are medical decisions – the son is not to be asked to make them, and must not be given the impression that he is being asked to do so.

Appropriate responses to likely questions

Son: why is my father so ill?

Doctor: it's difficult to be sure what has caused the recent deterioration, but there's at least two things going on. First, he has got cancer that has spread through his body. Secondly, his kidney function … which was previously running at about 20% of normal … has got worse. The kidneys control the levels of salts in the blood and also remove toxins, and the level of toxins and salts in your father's blood are now very abnormal. They are at a level that might be responsible for his confusion, and also the fact that the heart is not pumping properly.

Son: I thought kidney failure could be treated with dialysis.

Doctor: you are right, it can be. We can do the job of the kidneys with a dialysis machine, and this is something we do for lots of people every day ... but dialysis treatment tends to lower the blood pressure, and his blood pressure is already very low ... he would not be strong enough for the treatment, and if we tried to give it I think he might die more quickly. I think we ought to concentrate on making him as comfortable as possible.

Son: but there must be something you can do – some tests.

Doctor: I don't think that any more tests will help your father at the moment. We know that your father has got widespread cancer, which we cannot cure ... and when he was able to tell us his wishes he was quite clear that he didn't want more tests and treatments, and it's important that we respect his view. We cannot make him better, and it would be wrong to put him through lots of tests that won't alter anything when he's dying. We must make sure that he is as comfortable as possible.

Son: but don't you think that's wrong? I can't understand why he didn't want to be treated.

Doctor: I understand why you find that difficult, but people are different, and he has a cancer which he knew we couldn't cure. Perhaps that's why he was

so clear that he did not want more tests and treatments. Even people who are well in other ways often find some of the tests and treatments we do very draining.

Son: what is going to happen if you don't give my father treatment for his kidney failure?

Doctor: I think whatever we do he is going to pass away quite soon, and it's likely to be within the next few hours.

Son: is he suffering?

Doctor: no, I don't think so. The toxins in the blood affect the brain, which is why he is confused. As they build up he is likely to become sleepy, but if he seems to be distressed in any way, we will give him some medicine to make him more comfortable. When his heart stops, we won't be trying to resuscitate him – we will let him die peacefully.

Son: what should I do now?

Doctor: is there anyone else in the family who would want to know the situation? If there is, it would be very helpful if you could explain things to them, and let them know how ill he is. If they'd like to speak to me, then please let me know. Apart from that, I would suggest that you simply sit with him and talk to him at the moment ... it's difficult to know how much he understands at the moment, but he may find that comforting.

1.3.4 Stopping dialysis

Scenario

Role: you are a junior doctor working on a renal ward.

Scenario: Mr Jones is an 84-year-old man who has been on haemodialysis for the past 3 years with ESRF due to renovascular disease. He no longer has any significant urine output (UO). He has recently been admitted with cough, shortness of breath and weight loss. He has been diagnosed with lung cancer with liver and bony metastases. The oncologists have indicated that no active treatment options are available. He has recently struggled with hypotension on dialysis, and has had to stop several sessions early. He has reducing mobility and is now unable to look after himself at home.

He has been talking with his dialysis nurse about stopping dialysis. The view of the renal multidisciplinary team (MDT) is that this would be a reasonable course of action.

Your task: to discuss withdrawal from dialysis with the patient and explore his concerns.

Key issues to explore

> What are the main reasons why he would like to withdraw from dialysis?

> What is his understanding regarding his subsequent treatment and prognosis? (Does he have capacity to make this decision?)

> What are his wishes for end-of-life care?

Key points to establish

> Dialysis is becoming increasingly difficult for the patient.
> The background malignancy means that prognosis is very poor.
> The patient's wishes for the dialysis withdrawal process and advanced care planning.

Appropriate responses to likely questions

Patient: why has dialysis become so difficult?

Doctor: I am sorry that you have been finding dialysis a struggle. Your blood pressure has been dropping low each time, and this makes you feel lightheaded and washed out. It's happening because dialysis is a strain on the body and the heart, and I'm afraid that you're not as strong as you were … like all of us, you're getting older, and the cancer is sapping your strength.

Patient: what about the cancer? Does this mean that I will die soon anyway?

Doctor: I'm not hiding anything when I say that I can't give a precise answer … as you know, the cancer has spread to the liver and bones, and I'm sorry to say that there isn't any treatment we can give to get rid of it. We will certainly treat any symptoms that you develop from the cancer, but we can't make it better. I can't be precise about timing … weeks … possibly months.

Patient: I've been thinking about it for a while … I want to stop dialysis … I've had enough … can I do that?

Doctor: yes you can … as long you fully understand the implications, then yes you can.

Patient: if I stop dialysis, what will happen? How long will I live?

Doctor: when patients stop dialysis they often don't notice any difference for the first week or so – it's just like

they've missed a few sessions. But after that the waste products slowly build up in the blood … you feel more drowsy and your appetite goes … and eventually the poisons build up to a level where they stop your heart and you die in your sleep. Patients like yourself who don't pass any urine will usually live for between 1 and 3 weeks after stopping dialysis.

Patient: are there any unpleasant symptoms?

Doctor: sometimes patients feel sick, and we can give injections to help that … and sometimes the breathing can become difficult, and if that happens we can give something – morphine – to help.

Patient: will I suffer or be in pain?

Doctor: no, the toxins usually removed by dialysis will build up and you will become more sleepy as time passes. Dying from kidney failure is normally a peaceful process … but if you do have any symptoms such as pain or shortness of breath, we will treat these with medications to keep you as comfortable as possible.

Patient: I haven't talked to my family about this … I think it will upset them … what do you think?

Doctor: I understand what you say, and I think you're right … I'd expect them to be upset … but they do need to know about this, and after the shock of being told I suspect that they'll understand. Perhaps it would be a good idea if we arranged to speak to them together? Do you think that would be helpful?

Patient: if I do stop dialysis, then what happens – do I stay here?

Doctor: we need you to think about where you would like to be after stopping dialysis. Some patients are very keen to be at home – with any extra help that is needed – while others want to be in a hospice or to

stay in hospital. We would need to plan this with you and your family … but we will try to do whatever we can to support your wishes.

1.3.5 The patient who is not fit for a renal transplant

Scenario

Role: you are a junior doctor on the renal ward.

Scenario: Mr John Bennett is a 68-year-old man with ESRF secondary to type 2 diabetes who has recently started on dialysis. He also has a history of hypertension, peripheral vascular disease and is a smoker of 20 cigarettes per day. He has been admitted with a delayed presentation of an ST elevation myocardial infarction, which has been treated with aspirin, clopidogrel and atorvastatin. He had an echocardiogram that showed severe left ventricular impairment and a subsequent angiogram demonstrating severe triple vessel disease that is to be treated with medical management only. His blood pressure is 90/50 mmHg.

He had previously been due to attend the transplant assessment clinic as he was keen to proceed with a live-related transplant from his brother. He wishes to discuss his transplant options with you. The view of the nephrology consultant is that it is not appropriate for Mr Bennett to be offered a kidney transplant given his recent myocardial infarction, poor left ventricular function and unreconstructable coronary disease.

Your task: to explain the decision regarding transplant listing and the implications for the patient's future care.

Key issues to explore

> What is his understanding of the current situation and diagnosis?

> What does he understand about the risks of transplantation?

Key points to address

> He has had a significant cardiac event that has significantly impacted his cardiac function.

> His peri- and postoperative risks of a cardiac event are too high for renal transplantation to be considered.

> You will continue to look after him on dialysis and help optimise his medical conditions.

> He does not have the right to demand a transplant, but he can request a second opinion.

Appropriate responses to likely questions

Patient: I had been due to attend the transplant assessment clinic before I got admitted. Can I still be listed for a kidney transplant?

Doctor: I'm afraid that you have had a significant heart attack that has affected the main pumping chamber in the heart. This is now not functioning very well and we know that there are significant blockages in the arteries around the heart. A kidney transplant is a big operation and you would be at very high risk of having another heart attack during, or just after, the operation … we think that the risks would be too high.

Patient: but I feel fine now. I didn't even have any chest pain. Once this heart problem gets treated, can I go ahead with the transplant?

Doctor: I'm glad that you now feel well, but sometimes patients with diabetes like yourself do not feel pain when they have a heart attack … I'm afraid that you had quite a big heart attack, and this has led to significant damage to the heart's main

pumping chamber and is why your blood pressure is now low. I'd like to say something different, but this means that the risks of trying to give you a transplant would be too high.

Patient: so are you saying that I won't be able to have a kidney transplant?

Doctor: yes, I'm sorry, but we just think that it would be too dangerous to try to perform the operation, and we don't think that you will be able to have a kidney transplant.

Patient: is there anything I can do to help?

Doctor: it would be good for you to stop smoking as this can worsen the artery blockages, and for you to have good blood sugar control … both of these things will probably cut down the chances of you having another heart attack, but I'm afraid that they aren't going to undo all the damage to your heart that's already happened.

Patient: do I just have to take your word for all this, or can I have a second opinion?

Doctor: no, you don't just have to take my word for this … I could arrange for you to speak to the consultant about things if that would be helpful … but if you wanted another opinion from someone else entirely, either we could recommend someone to you, or you could discuss with your GP and ask them to make a referral.

Patient: so what will happen now? Will I just carry on with dialysis?

Doctor: yes, we will continue to look after you on dialysis. We know that you will be needing dialysis for the rest of your life, so we need to make arrangements to do this as well as possible. We will continue to work with your heart doctors and your GP to monitor and treat your other medical conditions.

1.4 Brief clinical consultations

1.4.1 The breathless dialysis patient

Scenario

Role: you are a junior doctor on duty for the renal dialysis unit.

Scenario: the dialysis nurses have noticed that Mr Smith, a 65-year-old dialysis patient, seems to be more breathless than usual. They have given him his normal dialysis session, which has now been completed, and they have asked you to review him on the dialysis unit before he is allowed to go home. What is the most likely diagnosis? Would you allow him to go home?

Introduction

Breathlessness is a very common problem among dialysis patients. There are many potential causes that can arise before, during and after dialysis (Table 5), but the commonest cause by far is volume overload leading to pulmonary oedema. A focused history should narrow the differential diagnosis in most cases by concentrating on timing of onset and presence or absence of associated symptoms such as chest pain, fever or light-headedness. Catastrophic causes such as air embolus are fortunately rare but require immediate treatment and resuscitation.

Beginning the encounter

Doctor: hello, my name is Dr A. I understand that the problem is that you were breathless when you were on dialysis earlier, is that correct?

Patient: yes.

Doctor: before we go into the details of that, can you tell me if you have any other major medical problems? Any problems with the heart or the lungs?

Table 5 Causes of dyspnoea in dialysis patients	
Common	Volume overload
	Arrhythmia
	ACS
	Sepsis / chest infection
	Anaemia
	Hypotension
Less common	PE
	Dialyser reaction
	Reaction to medication
	Air embolus
	Haemolysis

ACS, acute coronary syndrome; PE, pulmonary embolism.

Patient: [gives list (with doctor politely but firmly discouraging lengthy detail.)]

Doctor: *and are you on any medications or tablets?*

Patient: [gives list (and will probably have been asked to produce a written list.)]

These introductory questions will provide useful clinical context and may immediately give a clue to the likely diagnosis, eg are there any drugs that predispose to arrhythmia? Is there a significant history of coronary artery disease?

Focused history

Doctor: *tell me about when the shortness of breath started* [Table 6]. *Were you short of breath before you started your dialysis? Have you been short of breath leading up to dialysis* [were they dyspnoeic walking in to the unit]? *Did you sleep normally last night* [or was there orthopnoea or paroxysmal nocturnal dyspnoea (PND)]? *It is vital to be specific with regards to the timing – if it started after dialysis, how long into the session? Did it start immediately*

after your line was connected to the machine, minutes after starting dialysis, towards the end of the session?

Doctor: *was it associated with any other symptoms? Did you have any chest pain, fevers, sweats, rigors? Do you feel lightheaded or have leg cramps?*

Doctor: *has this ever happened to you before on dialysis?*

The following specific questions might also be helpful in this case.

> Do you often feel short of breath before your dialysis session? – suggests fluid overload and a need to reduce the patients target (dry) weight.

> Do you know how your weight today and your target (dry) weight on dialysis?

> Have you lost weight recently? – if a patient is losing flesh weight and their target weight on dialysis has not been adjusted, then they will inevitably become fluid overloaded.

> Have you had a history of heart disease or narrowed heart valves? – would suggest the possibility of cardiac pulmonary oedema.

In routine clinical practice you would also take a history from the patient's dialysis nurse. In PACES this will not be possible, but the examiner may ask: 'If you could speak to the patient's dialysis nurse, what would you ask them?'

Table 6 Timing of dyspnoea – clues to diagnosis	
Timing	**Cause**
Before dialysis	Volume overload
	Sepsis/chest sepsis
	Anaemia
Soon after start of dialysis (minutes)	PE
	Dialyser reaction
	Haemolysis
End of dialysis	Hypotension
Any time during dialysis	ACS
	Arrhythmia
	Reaction to medication
	Air embolus

ACS, acute coronary syndrome; PE, pulmonary embolism.

- Was this patient significantly heavier than their target weight when they arrived for dialysis today? Is this a recurrent problem?

- Do they have problems with their access – is it infected or have they recently had intervention?

- Have they missed any dialysis sessions or doses of their erythropoiesis-stimulating agent (ESA)?

- Have they recently changed to a different preparation of intravenous iron or heparin?

Focused examination

Concentrate specifically on the cardiovascular and respiratory systems. Check the following:

- well/ill/very ill – a judgement from the foot of the bed is very important

- pulse rate and rhythm

- respiratory rate – and explain to the examiner that you would check oxygen saturations

- pulse character (check at carotid): is it slow rising?

- BP: ask the examiner for this, which may prompt them to show you an observation chart

- jugular venous pressure (JVP) – very important to look for this properly, with the patient's neck supported and relaxed: it's one part of the examination where the examiner can see the physical sign as well (and perhaps better) than you can

- heart sounds and murmurs (quick auscultation and apex, aortic area and neck, not a full examination)

- percussion of lung bases

- chest auscultation – fine inspiratory crackles? Unilateral or bilateral? Bronchial breathing? Wheeze? – the most likely finding will be bilateral basal crackles due to pulmonary oedema

- peripheral oedema.

Other relevant examination:

- presence of sepsis: fever, warm peripheries, bounding pulse (not likely in PACES)

- signs of anaphylactoid reaction: flushing, rash, angioedema (vanishingly unlikely in PACES)

- pallor of mucosal membranes

- dialysis access – arteriovenous fistula (AVF) or tunnelled line (exit site and tunnel not inflamed).

Questions from the patient

[Assuming that the diagnosis is fluid overload, and he feels a bit better after dialysis:]

Patient: *why did I feel short of breath?*

Doctor: I think that the most likely reason is that you had fluid overload – there was excess fluid which built up on your lungs. This could have been caused by you drinking too much fluid, or the fact that we haven't got your target (dry) weight right. Another possibility is some problem with the heart, but that seems much less likely.

Patient: *is there something I can do to prevent this from happening again?*

Doctor: keeping to the fluid restriction recommended is an important way to reduce the build-up of fluid before dialysis sessions. Keeping

to a low-salt diet is also vital (to help you drink less), and we may need to bring down your target (dry) weight … and to do this we may need to increase your dialysis treatment time to ensure that we can remove the correct amount of fluid.

Patient: *I'm feeling better, can I go home now?*

Doctor: I'm pleased that you're feeling better, and I suspect that the problem is that you've got a bit too much fluid on board … but I'd like to get an electrical recording of your heart – an ECG – done to check that it looks OK. If it does, and you're still feeling better, then I think it will probably be OK for you to go home, but I'll phone the renal registrar to check that they're happy with this.

Questions from the examiner

Examiner: *if the patient had become hypotensive during the dialysis session, what may have caused this?*

Doctor: this happens in 5–30% of all dialysis treatments and is usually due to rapid ultrafiltration (taking too much fluid off too quickly) or an incorrectly prescribed target weight (where the dialysis prescription aimed to remove too much fluid) or it could be due to autonomic dysfunction. Patients at increased risk include those who have diabetes, biventricular failure, lower blood pressure or have been on dialysis for a longer time.

Examiner: *what can be done to reduce the frequency of hypotension occurring?*

Doctor: it is important to accurately assess the patient's target weight and counsel the patient to reduce interdialytic weight gain ... if they drink too much between dialysis sessions and many litres of fluid therefore have to be removed during dialysis to get them back to their target weight, then they're more likely to have hypotension on dialysis. It may be necessary to increase the dialysis treatment time to allow for adequate ultrafiltration or cool the dialysate. Patients should also be advised to not take their antihypertensives prior to dialysis and to avoid eating during the treatment.

Further discussion

ECG – features to look for include signs of acute (or old) ischaemia, sinus rhythm, PR interval, heart block, left ventricular hypertrophy, right heart strain or S1Q3T3 (suggestive of pulmonary embolism (PE), which is unlikely in this clinical context).

In other circumstances the following investigations would be of relevance:

> Chest X-ray – look for cardiac size, prominent pulmonary vasculature, pulmonary oedema, consolidation, pleural effusion(s).

> Bloods – electrolytes, creatinine, FBC, liver function tests, inflammatory markers, haematinics, blood cultures (if appropriate), cardiac enzymes.

> Cardiac monitoring during dialysis – if there is a strong suspicion of arrhythmia triggering breathlessness during dialysis and the resting ECG is unremarkable.

1.4.2 A renal transplant patient with a fever

Scenario

Role: you are a junior doctor on a medical take shift.

Scenario: Mr John Bushell, a 60-year-old man who had a renal transplant 8 months previously, contacted the transplant ward as he was feeling unwell and feverish. The senior nurse on the ward advised him to attend his local emergency department, where he was found to have a temperature of 38.7°C. What is the likely diagnosis, and what is your management plan?

Introduction

In the first year following a transplant of any kind, the immunosuppressive burden is higher than in subsequent years, hence the risk of infection is highest in the first year. The differential diagnosis is wide (Table 7). In the context of immunosuppression, patients are at increased risk of any normal infection, such as a urinary tract infection (UTI) or gastroenteritis, and they are also at risk of opportunistic infections. You should ask about specific symptoms and look for signs of opportunistic infection.

Although fever is due to infection until proved otherwise, non-infective causes must be considered. Acute rejection can lead to an inflammatory response and patients can present with fever, but this is rarely a prominent feature. Rarer but more serious causes of fever, such as PTLD and other malignancies, also come into the reckoning. Although most malignancies would be uncommon this soon after transplant, PTLD, an Epstein–Barr virus (EBV)-driven lymphoproliferative disorder, most commonly presents in the first year post transplant.

Table 7 Causes of fever in a transplant patient

Time post transplant	General cause	Transplant-specific cause
Early (days to weeks)	Infection – urinary tract, respiratory tract, gastroenteritis, viral, eg influenza Healthcare-associated infection, eg MRSA, VRE, *Clostridium difficile* Post-surgical complications, eg wound infection, transfusion reactions Allergic reactions to new medications	Opportunistic infections, eg candidiasis Infection transmitted from donor Transplant-specific surgical complications, eg urine leak Acute rejection episode (ACR or ABMR)
Within first year	Infection (usually community acquired) Rarer infections, eg subacute bacterial endocarditis Solid organ or haematological malignancy (rare <1 year)	Opportunistic infections, eg CMV, PJP, toxoplasmosis Reactivation of TB Acute rejection episode (ACR or ABMR) PTLD (peak period, 50% within first year)
Late (months to years)	Infection (usually community acquired) Solid organ or haematological malignancy (more common than general population)	Acute rejection episodes (less common) Opportunistic infections (less common) PTLD

ABMR, antibody-mediated rejection; ACR, acute cellular rejection; CMV, cytomegalovirus, MRSA, methicillin-resistant *Staphylococcus aureus*; PJP, *Pneumocystis jirovecii* pneumonia; PTLD, post-transplant lymphoproliferative disorder; TB, tuberculosis; VRE, vancomycin-resistant *Enterococcus*.

Beginning the encounter

Doctor: *hello, my name is Dr A, I understand that the problem is that you are feeling unwell and feverish, and the sister on the transplant ward suggested you come to the hospital: is that right?*

Patient: yes.

Doctor: *before we get onto the details of that, can you tell me what was the cause of your original kidney disease? Do you have any other medical problems?*

Patient: [gives list (with doctor politely but firmly discouraging lengthy detail).]

Doctor: *and do you have a list of your medications? Have there been any changes lately?*

Patient: [gives details (and will probably have been asked to produce a written list).]

These introductory questions will provide useful clinical context and may immediately give a clue to the likely diagnosis, eg if the azathioprine or mycophenolate mofetil have been stopped or reduced, this may indicate that the patient had leukopenia and is at enhanced risk of bacterial sepsis; if a prophylactic antimicrobial, eg valganciclovir, has recently been stopped, this may have allowed the relevant infection (cytomegalovirus (CMV)) to develop.

Focused history

Doctor: *now please tell me how you have been feeling over the past few days. When did you start to feel unwell and what symptoms did you have?* [Press for specific symptoms such as cough, dysuria. Ask if anyone else has been unwell. Ask about pain over the transplant, which may indicate pyelonephritis or rejection.]

Doctor: *have you had any other problems with infections since your transplant (eg recurrent urinary tract infections)?*

Doctor: *with regards to your transplant, was the operation straightforward or did you have any complications?* [Ask about any infections, repeat operations, any plastic left *in situ*, eg urinary stent, mesh from hernia repair.]

Doctor: *and I asked you before about medications, but can I just double check, have any of these been missed or stopped recently?*

The following specific questions might also be helpful in this case.

> Time course – this may give you an idea of the potential diagnosis. How long have you felt unwell? A few hours or days would tend to suggest a standard infection, eg urinary or community-acquired chest infection, a few weeks should make you consider opportunistic infections or PTLD.

> Has anyone else been unwell? – it is important to remember that patients on immunosuppression are not only more prone to infection, but their symptoms may be worse, a gastroenteritis that lasted 2 days in a relative may last much longer in a transplant patient.

> Site of infection – if not previously covered, specific questions that might suggest a site of infection include the following. Do you have a cough or are you bringing anything up? Have you had any abdominal pain, diarrhoea or vomiting? Do you have burning or stinging passing your urine?

> Possibility of renal transplant rejection – this is an unlikely diagnosis in this scenario, but relevant questions would be: Do you have any pain or swelling over the graft? Have you noticed any reduction in the amount of urine you are producing? Have you missed any doses of your immunosuppression recently or have any doses been reduced?

Transplant patients are generally very well informed about their medications, and what each one is used for. They will also usually be able to tell you quite a lot of detail about their operation and any complications, as well as what kind of donor their kidney came from. Live donor kidneys often function better and are less prone to rejection, but may be less well matched (if from unrelated donors), and therefore require higher immunosuppression. Kidneys from deceased donors are more prone to delayed graft function and this is a risk factor for rejection. Infection can also be transmitted from the donor to the recipient, but this is rare.

Focused examination

This scenario should prompt a focused assessment of the three major potential causes of fever and malaise:

> infection – examine any system where the patient has indicated symptoms, eg chest

> rejection – examine the graft for tenderness and swelling

> PTLD – examine for lymphadenopathy in the cervical and inguinal regions.

If there are no good clues as to the source of the problem from the history, proceed as follows:

> well/ill/very ill – a judgement from the foot of the bed is very important; bacterial infection is most likely if the patient appears to be very ill, but this is not likely in PACES

> vital signs – temperature, BP: ask the examiner (they may show you an observation chart)

> hands – warm or cold; check for splinters

> eyes and conjunctivae – inspection only

> mouth, tongue and fauces

> lymphadenopathy – cervical, axillary

> chest – 'give a cough', rapid auscultation of heart and lungs

> abdomen – look for swelling or redness, particularly over scars; palpate the graft, noting if it is tender; check for hepatomegaly, splenomegaly,

palpable kidneys (polycystic) and inguinal lymphadenopathy

> ask to dipstick the urine, the examiner may provide you with the result.

Questions from the patient

[Assuming that the patient does not look very unwell, but the cause of fever is not apparent:]

Patient: why do you think I have a fever?

Doctor: I'm not sure, but it is common in transplant patients in the first year after their operation. It could be an infection, but you don't seem to have any symptoms that would suggest where that might be … but the medications you are taking can reduce symptoms and signs of infection (steroids in particular can mask the inflammatory response), so we should do a few more tests to check if there is any infection in your blood or urine, and do an X-ray of your chest.

Patient: I remember a doctor in the transplant clinic talking about a virus … C-M-something: could it be that?

Doctor: I know what you're thinking of … the virus is called cytomegalovirus – CMV for short – and it is a common cause of fever in transplant patients. That's one of the things we'll be looking for.

Patient: I am worried that this might be rejection instead of infection, is that likely?

Doctor: I agree that it's possible for rejection to cause a fever, but it's not the most likely thing at all … but we are going to check your kidney blood tests … if you had rejection bad enough to cause a high fever, then we'd certainly expect that to show up when we measure kidney function.

Patient: do I need to be admitted? All my care up to now has been in the transplant centre.

Doctor: we need to see the results of the tests we've talked about before we decide. If your kidney function and blood count are OK, and if a test of your urine and a chest X-ray are OK, then you'll be able to go home, and I'll call the transplant service to get them to see you in their clinic or on their ward tomorrow … but if these tests do show something that needs treatment in hospital right away, then we'll need to get on and do what's needed.

Questions from the examiner

Examiner: what kind of infections would you expect in a patient 8 months out from transplant?

Doctor: at this time point, community-acquired infections would be most likely, for example urinary tract infections caused by *Escherichia coli*, or respiratory tract infections caused by *Streptococcus pneumoniae*. I would also be concerned about viral infections such as influenza, and would check a vaccination history. But at this point prophylaxis for some of the opportunistic infections may have been stopped, and so I would be concerned about infections such as CMV, and want to consider fungal infections such as *Pneumocystis jirovecii*.

Examiner: if the patient looked pretty well, but had this high fever of 38.7°C, which of the things you've listed would be most likely?

Doctor: I don't know the patient's CMV status, or that of their recipient, but I think that CMV infection would be most likely, and I'd like to do a blood polymerase chain reaction (PCR) test for CMV.

Examiner: and if it wasn't CMV, and had been grumbling on for some weeks, what would you consider next?

Doctor: in that case I'd be concerned about a couple of infections that can present in this way … infective endocarditis and tuberculosis (TB) … and I would also be concerned about the possibility of PTLD … and the investigation to pursue that possibility would be a CT of chest, abdomen and pelvis.

Examiner: what do you know about cytomegalovirus?

Doctor: it is a common pathogen, transmitted by close contact with an infected individual, as it is transmitted in bodily fluids. Primary infection usually occurs in childhood or as a young adult and is often asymptomatic, but can give an infectious-mononucleosis-type syndrome. The virus remains latent following primary infection, and seropositivity rises with age. It rarely reactivates unless patients are immunosuppressed, but is an important infection in transplant patients. Typically symptoms are non-specific, with fever, malaise and weight loss, but it can cause gastrointestinal (GI) symptoms, bone marrow suppression, pneumonitis and chorioretinitis in severe cases.

Further discussion

It is important to remember that by far the commonest organisms causing infections in transplant patients are the same organisms that affect the rest of the population. This is in part because transplant patients are given antimicrobial prophylaxis against the most common or serious opportunistic infections.

In the early postoperative period, infections are likely to be identical to those usually experienced by surgical patients – UTIs with the usual pathogens, wound infections from skin flora, and chest infections from either community-acquired or hospital-acquired pathogens. It is also important to consider infections that may be transmitted from the donor. This information will be available to the recipient team at the time of offer, and often patients are given prophylactic antibiotics, eg a week of co-amoxiclav if the donor had a sensitive UTI at the time of donation.

Prophylaxis against infection

For a kidney transplant patient, the following are standard in the UK.

> Co-trimoxazole (sulfamethoxazole 400 mg plus trimethoprim 80 mg) to prevent *P jirovecii* pneumonia, usually continued for 6-months post transplant (consider nebulised pentamidine if patients are sensitive to co-trimoxazole, but seek advice).

> Valganciclovir to prevent CMV reactivation / primary infection. Prior to transplant, the seropositivity of both donor and recipient will be known:

>> if both are positive, or the donor is negative but recipient positive, then prophylaxis is typically continued for 3 months

>> if the recipient is negative but donor positive then prophylaxis typically continues for 6 months, as the risk of primary infection is high

>> if both are negative (ie have never contracted CMV) then no prophylaxis is required, although some centres use aciclovir to prevent other herpes viral or EBV infection/reactivation, particularly in patients receiving very heavy immunosuppressive load (eg T-cell depleting monoclonal antibodies).

> Fluconazole or nystatin to prevent candida infection, particularly oral/oesophageal infection.

> Prophylaxis against specific infections depending on risk factors, eg antivirals for patients who are hepatitis B surface antibody positive, antituberculous medication for those from high-risk backgrounds.

Post-transplant lymphoproliferative disorder

PTLD is the second commonest malignancy in transplant patients after skin malignancy. It occurs in up to 2% of kidney transplant recipients, although rates are higher in all other solid-organ transplants. Half of cases occur in the first year after transplant, although it can occur at any time. It is a viral-driven, predominantly B-cell lymphoproliferative disorder, from reactivation of latent EBV. Risk factors include mismatch between donor and recipient in terms of EBV status (a seropositive donor organ in a seronegative recipient) and higher immunosuppressive burden. Patients who have had T-cell depleting antibodies such as alemtuzumab (Campath) or anti-thymocyte globulin for induction therapy or treatment of rejection are at particularly high risk, as T cells are the key immune cells involved in identification and deletion of malignant cells.

There is a wide differential for the symptoms of PTLD, which are often non-specific, eg fever, weight loss, malaise, night sweats. Symptoms can resemble infection with lymphadenopathy and graft dysfunction, but can also involve other organs, eg small intestine, liver. A biopsy is required to make the formal diagnosis of PTLD prior to commencing treatment.

Early disease may be treatable just with reduction in immunosuppression, but patients may require specific treatment. Rituximab is widely used in PTLD, as it targets CD20, a marker expressed on the surface of B cells, and hence will lyse the malignant cells. Success rates are high, and it can induce remission in around half of the patients. Those who do not respond will often require systemic chemotherapy. Prognosis is variable; younger patients who are EBV positive, are diagnosed early and have good response to reduction in immunosuppression tend to do well with

low rates of relapse, but around 10% lose their grafts to rejection. Older patients or those whose disease responds poorly to treatment, or who require systemic chemotherapy, tend to have much poorer survival, and death is either due to progressive disease or treatment toxicity.

Key point

The causes of fever in transplant patients are varied. However, common pathogens are common and immunosuppression may mask specific symptoms; therefore do a comprehensive infection screen and consider empirical antibiotics after cultures have been taken if the patient is very unwell. Involve the transplant team early and check graft function as a priority.

1.4.3 Fever in a dialysis patient

Scenario

Role: you are a junior doctor on duty for the renal dialysis unit.

Scenario: Mr Kofi Waring, a 63-year-old haemodialysis patient who dialyses through a tunnelled dialysis line, was noted to have a temperature of 38.3°C when he attended for his regular dialysis session. The nurse looking after him has asked you to review him. What is the likely diagnosis, and how should he be managed?

Introduction

Fever is a common presentation in dialysis patients. It may be detected as an incidental finding when checking the patient's temperature prior to dialysis, or may be accompanied by associated symptoms depending on the underlying cause.

Bacterial infections are the commonest cause of fever in dialysis patients, and the 'big three' are respiratory tract infections, UTIs and dialysis access site infections, which account for 70% of all causes of fever (Table 8). Your approach to this case must be to exclude these before considering less likely possibilities. Many dialysis patients are immunocompromised due to diabetes or ongoing immunosuppression (eg for underlying vasculitis or the presence of a failing/failed transplant) and hence are at risk for opportunistic infections. In patients on peritoneal dialysis (PD), PD peritonitis must be considered.

Non-infective causes of fever are much less common than infective, but include malignancy, connective tissue or autoimmune diseases (either primary or a relapse of the patient's underlying condition), drug-induced, dialysis-associated (allergic reactions to components of dialysis circuit), and late rejection (if transplant still *in situ*). Many patients receive blood

transfusions while on dialysis – if this is the case, then transfusion reactions should also be considered.

Beginning the encounter

Doctor: hello, my name is Dr A, the dialysis nurses tell me that you have got a fever, is that right? … were you aware of this?

Patient: yes.

Doctor: before we get onto the details of that, can you tell me what was the cause of your original kidney disease and whether you have any other medical problems?

Patient: [gives list (with doctor politely but firmly discouraging lengthy detail).]

Doctor: and do you have a list of your medications? Have there been any changes lately?

Patient: [gives details (and will probably have been asked to produce a written list).]

These introductory questions will provide useful clinical context and may immediately give a clue to the likely diagnosis.

Focused history

Doctor: tell me about how you've been feeling over the last few days. [Press for specific symptoms related to potential sites of infection (eg cough, sputum production, breathlessness, dysuria, pain or redness around dialysis access sites, abdominal pain). Ask if anyone else has been unwell.]

Ask specifically about any problems with dialysis recently.

> Have there been any problems with dialysis access that may suggest infection?

> Have they had any recent dialysis access interventions (eg a new dialysis catheter insertion or change)?

> For patients on PD, has the PD fluid been cloudy, have they had any abdominal pain or diarrhoea?

Table 8 Causes of fever in dialysis patients	
Infectious diseases	Bacteria: respiratory tract[1] urinary tract,[1] dialysis access site[1] (haemodialysis catheter, peritoneal dialysis catheter, AV fistulae or graft) peritoneal infections[1] (eg PD peritonitis), intra-abdominal infections infective endocarditis metastatic abscess (most typically from dialysis catheter related primary source).
	Opportunistic: viruses (CMV, EBV) fungi (*Candida, Aspergillus*).
Malignancies	
Connective tissue or autoimmune diseases	Relapse of underlying condition (eg MPA, GPA, SLE) or *de novo* condition (eg GCA/PMR or any other).
Dialysis-related	Reaction to membranes or circuit components, puncture needles, endotoxin contamination.
Other	Drug reaction, transfusion reaction, other causes seen in general population, eg upper respiratory tract viral infection.[1]

1 Commonest causes.
AV, arteriovenous; CMV, cytomegalovirus; EBV, Epstein–Barr virus; GCA, giant cell arteritis; GPA, granulomatosis with polyangiitis; MPA, microscopic polyangiitis; PD, peritoneal dialysis; PMR, polymyalgia rheumatica; SLE, systemic lupus erythematosus.

Ask about other potential causes of fever.

> Have there been constitutional symptoms (eg myalgia, arthralgia) that may suggest viral infection – particularly if others have been affected – or (less likely) an underlying vasculitis or malignancy?

> Does a transplant remain *in situ* and is there any pain or tenderness around it?

Check timing of symptoms.

> A few days is suggestive of a 'standard' viral or bacterial infection, whereas a few weeks to months may suggest opportunistic infections, vasculitis / connective tissue disease or malignancy.

> If the patient only develops symptoms while on dialysis, this may be the first sign of an access infection (especially tunnelled line infection), or may be an allergic reaction to components of the dialysis circuit or drugs administered during dialysis.

Focused examination

The obvious requirement is to look for evidence of infection:

> Well/ill/very ill – a judgement from the foot of the bed is very important; bacterial infection is most likely if the patient appears to be very ill, but this is not likely in PACES.

Dialysis access – examine this carefully:

> Haemodialysis catheter – is there redness or tenderness at the exit site over the tunnel? It is sometimes possible to express pus from the tunnel (most unlikely in PACES).

> Arteriovenous fistula (AVF) – is this red or inflamed? Is this patent (can you feel a thrill and/or hear a bruit)? Thrombosis of a fistula is often associated with a notable inflammatory reaction.

> PD catheter – is there redness or tenderness at the exit site over the

tunnel? It is sometimes possible to express pus from the tunnel (most unlikely in PACES).

Respiratory and chest:

> respiratory rate and saturations

> percussion – dullness suggestive of effusions (empyema?)

> auscultation of chest – bronchial breathing?

Cardiovascular:

> signs of sepsis – tachycardia, bounding pulse, warm peripheries

> peripheral signs of infective endocarditis – splinter haemorrhages, Osler's nodes

> auscultation – heart sounds and murmurs.

Abdominal:

> tenderness – localised (eg over a renal transplant graft, suprapubic, renal angle, or over a polycystic kidney) or generalised (eg with PD peritonitis – unlikely in PACES)

> ask to dipstick urine (if the patient produces any).

Other relevant examinations:

> lymphadenopathy – malignancy, infection

> percuss the patient's spine – any tenderness (discitis)?

> joint swelling/redness – septic arthritis, gout and pseudogout are all common in renal patients.

Questions from the patient

[Assuming that the history and examination do not suggest an obvious cause:]

Patient: *why do you think I have a fever?*

Doctor: the likeliest cause is an infection, but I'm not sure what the source of this might be. We need to do a few tests to work out the reason … we will start off with blood and urine samples, and also do an X-ray of your chest.

Patient: *will you need to change my dialysis catheter?*

Doctor: there's no obvious indication to do that at present. If we discover that your fever is related to a catheter infection, we can hopefully manage this with antibiotics … we will decide exactly what to do when we have the test results back, but sometimes – if a temperature is due to an infection of a dialysis catheter – then it is necessary to change this.

Questions from the examiner

Examiner: *what would your initial management strategy for this patient be?*

Doctor: as part of my standard investigations, I would take a full set of baseline bloods including inflammatory markers, and if the patient produces urine, also perform a urine dipstick. As with any patient with a fever, I would take blood, urine and sputum cultures. I would take the blood cultures both peripherally and ask trained staff to take cultures from the dialysis catheter if I suspected a catheter-related infection. I would also request a chest X-ray, and if the patient had a new murmur I would also consider an echocardiogram. If there was a clear source of infection or if there were signs of sepsis, then I would also start antibiotics as per local policy.

Examiner: *what organisms might be responsible for infection in this patient?*

Doctor: the most commonly isolated organisms in this context are staphylococci, Gram-negative bacilli and streptococci.

Further discussion

Management of dialysis catheter-related bloodstream infection can be difficult. To treat the infection, the most obvious solution is often to remove the catheter and administer appropriate antibiotics, but in patients with difficult access this may not always be the best approach as it may not be easy to replace the removed access, which would mean the patient would be unable to dialyse. These two needs have to be balanced.

For uncomplicated coagulase-negative staphylococcal or enterococcal infections, it is often possible to leave the catheter in and treat with systemic antibiotics and antibiotic lock therapy for 10–14 days. For infection with Gram-negative bacilli the line should usually be removed and the patient treated with systemic antibiotics. However, if it is necessary to try and salvage the line because the patient has very difficult access, a trial of intensive systemic antibiotic therapy and antibiotic locks may be considered first. For patients with a tunnel infection, line removal is usually required. If there is infection with *Staphylococcus aureus*, or fungi, then the line should be removed promptly as the risk of severe sepsis and complications such as endocarditis, osteomyelitis or septic thrombi is high.

Antibiotic treatment for catheter-related infections usually involves vancomycin and an aminoglycoside with therapeutic drug monitoring. Both can be given intravenously on haemodialysis, with monitoring (blood levels) and dosing on subsequent dialysis sessions.

Peritoneal-dialysis (PD) associated peritonitis:

> Samples of fluid from a drain bag (and usually the whole bag) are sent for microscopy and culture.

> The finding of >100 white blood cells per mm³ in the drainage fluid indicates peritonitis.

> Once samples have been sent, treatment should be initiated with intraperitoneal and oral antibiotics depending on the local protocol (a common protocol is for intraperitoneal vancomycin and oral ciprofloxacin, given until culture results are known).

> Speak to your local renal service / nephrologists early to guide treatment and further management.

1.4.4 Chest pain in a patient on dialysis

Scenario

Role: you are a junior doctor on duty for the renal dialysis unit.

Scenario: Mr Tareq Dean, a 65-year-old man, attended for his regular haemodialysis session today. Three hours into dialysis he developed chest pain and the nursing staff stopped his treatment. You have been called to come and assess him. What is the most likely diagnosis, and how should he be managed?

Introduction

Chest pain is common in dialysis patients, and occurs (in at least a mild form) in 2–5% of dialysis sessions. Patients with end-stage renal failure (ESRF) are at significantly increased risk of cardiovascular complications and chest pain should be taken seriously. Chest pain may be caused by typical pathology (eg angina), or by dialysis-specific problems (Table 9). Angina is common, induced by fluid shifts and (relative) hypotension.

Cardiovascular disease accounts for about a third of deaths in patients on dialysis. This is broadly similar to the proportion in the general population, but patients on dialysis have a far higher relative risk of death for their age. The relative risk of death of a dialysis patient aged 35–39 years is increased 16-fold, and it is still three- to four-fold elevated in those aged over 80 years (data from the UK Renal Registry report 2014).

Beginning the encounter

Doctor: hello, my name is Dr A, I understand that the problem is that you have been having some chest pain on dialysis today: is that right?

Patient: yes.

Doctor: before we get onto the details, can you tell me if you have any other major medical problems? Any problems with the heart in the past?

Patient: [gives list (with doctor politely but firmly discouraging lengthy detail).]

Doctor: and are you on any tablets or medications?

Patient: [gives details (and will probably have been asked to produce a written list).]

These introductory questions will provide useful clinical context and may immediately give a clue to the likely diagnosis, eg if the patient volunteers a history of angina or heart attack.

Table 9 Chest pain in patients on dialysis	
Dialysis-specific problems	Dialysis disequilibrium Dialyser reactions Intradialytic hypotension Air embolism
Unrelated to dialysis process (but may be induced by physiological stress of dialysis)	Angina[1] ACS[1] Arrhythmia Mesenteric ischaemia Gastritis PE

1 Common causes that require exclusion.
ACS, acute coronary syndrome; PE, pulmonary embolism.

Focused history

Doctor: so how were you feeling when you came into dialysis today? Were you feeling well – did you feel your normal self? Any chest pain beforehand? [Symptoms preceding treatment obviously eliminate any diagnoses where dialysis is the cause, but dialysis may have made symptoms worse, eg through (relative) hypotension if ischaemic.]

Doctor: have you had problems with chest pain when you've been on dialysis before? [Recurrent symptoms on dialysis may reflect vascular disease and recurrent relative hypotension (angina, mesenteric ischaemia) or repeated exposure to an inducing agent (dialyser reactions).]

Doctor: can you tell me a bit more about the pain – where did you feel it, radiation, nature of pain, etc? [Standard questions about the pain may help focus further history taking, eg if a 'good' cardiac description is provided.]

Doctor: did you get any other symptoms with it – palpitations, shortness of breath, wheeziness, nausea? [Palpitations may increase the likelihood of there being an underlying arrhythmia; diaphoretic symptoms may be consistent with a cardiac cause; wheeze can be found in dialyser reactions.]

Focused examination

General features:

> Well/ill/very ill – a judgement from the foot of the bed is very important; a patient with chest pain who looks very ill is likely to have a serious cause, eg myocardial infarction.

> Vital signs – ask the examiner if they have a record of the patient's temperature, pulse and blood pressure: this may prompt them to show you an observation chart.

Concentrate on the cardiovascular status of the patient – check the following:

> peripheral perfusion

> heart rate and rhythm

> blood pressure

> volume status – JVP and peripheral oedema

> oxygen saturation.

Perform a brief examination:

> heart sounds and murmurs

> chest – is there normal air entry, or wheeze, or bibasal crackles?

> epigastric tenderness

> dialysis access – assess any tunnelled line (exit site and tunnel – no erythema or discharge) and/or AVF (thrill, erythema).

State that you would want to know:

> The patient's usual target (or 'dry') weight and their weight before dialysis today – ie did they attend dialysis with 4 kg of fluid overload, and is removing this excess fluid inducing hypotension?

> Their blood pressures throughout dialysis (especially when they were in pain) – if low, was this before or after the pain started?

Questions from the patient

[On the assumption that history and examination have revealed no clear cause:]

Patient: why have I had chest pain, doctor?

Doctor: I'm not sure, but we need to perform a few simple tests to find out. I haven't found anything untoward examining you, but I want to see your heart tracing, and check a blood test to make sure there isn't any sign of heart damage.

Patient: I feel fine now, can't I just go home?

Doctor: I'm pleased that you're feeling OK now, but I do need to see the results of these tests before I let you

go home ... I need to make sure that the pain wasn't caused by a serious problem with your heart.

Patient: but the transport is waiting for me, I have to go now.

Doctor: I know it's inconvenient, but I really do think we need to check things out before we let you go ... I will speak with the dialysis nurses and we'll get the tests carried out as quickly as possible, and we'll sort out transport later if you are able to go home.

Questions from the examiner

Examiner: what tests do you want to do, and why?

Doctor: the most important tests I'd like to check are an ECG and a cardiac troponin to look for evidence of an acute coronary event. I'd also want to check a biochemical screen and an FBC – if the patient has had ischaemic cardiac pain, then anaemia is a common exacerbating factor in dialysis patients.

Examiner: how useful are troponin measurements in patients on dialysis?

Doctor: cardiac troponin (Tn) levels (both Tn-I and Tn-T) may be stably elevated in dialysis patients, but they can still be used as part of the diagnosis of acute coronary syndrome (ACS) – serial measurements are important to assess for a dynamic change over time (eg 3–6 hours after symptoms).

Further discussion

ECG changes in ACS – Dialysis patients are more likely to have an abnormal resting/baseline ECG, and they are less likely to have an ST elevation myocardial infarction than non-dialysis patients.

Tn measurements in dialysis patients – Stable elevations of Tn-I and Tn-T may be present in many dialysis patients – if elevated, they predict poorer long-term cardiovascular outcomes. Elevation post-myocardial infarction also has prognostic significance – as in the general population. There is no significant difference in clinical practice between Tn-I and Tn-T measurements in dialysis patients.

Dialyser reactions – Allergic reactions to the dialysis membrane are uncommon with modern synthetic membranes. Symptoms can include chest and back pain, nausea, vomiting and hypotension. Anaphylactic reactions with wheeze, urticaria, flushing, coughing and diarrhoea are extremely rare.

1.5 Acute scenarios

1.5.1 A worrying electrocardiogram

Case history

A previously fit 74-year-old man presented to his GP after feeling unwell for 4 weeks with anorexia, and more recently nausea, vomiting and breathlessness. He was found to have crackles at both lung bases and a grossly enlarged bladder. He was referred to the surgical admissions unit where blood tests identified renal impairment: Na$^+$ 134 mmol/L (normal range 137–144), K$^+$ 8.9 mmol/L (normal range 3.5–4.9), urea 72 mmol/L (normal range 2.5–7.0) and creatinine 1,208 µmol/L (normal range 60–110). A urinary catheter was inserted.

Introduction

What should you check immediately?

Key point

This patient has severe hyperkalaemia, a life-threatening complication of renal impairment that requires urgent treatment – an ECG should be performed and treatment instituted immediately, before extensive history taking or full examination.

Assessment of severity of hyperkalaemia

The main risk of hyperkalaemia to the patient is cardiac arrest, and the ECG is the best guide of the severity of hyperkalaemic toxicity. There are progressive ECG changes as the serum potassium rises, starting with tenting of the T waves (affecting all leads!); followed by diminished P waves with lengthening of the PR interval and broadened QRS complexes; and finally a sine wave pattern before the onset of either asystole or ventricular fibrillation. This patient's ECG showed a sine-wave pattern (Fig 6a) requiring immediate treatment.

Treatment of hyperkalaemia

Treatments for hyperkalaemia are shown in Table 10.

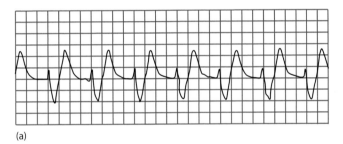
(a)

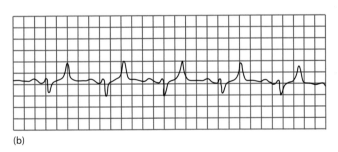
(b)

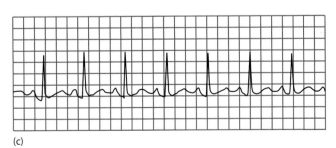
(c)

Fig 6 ECG findings in a patient with hyperkalaemia. **(a)** Initial ECG with [K$^+$] 8.9 mmol/L showing a sine-wave pattern: peaked T waves, broad QRS complex and absent P waves. **(b)** ECG after 40 mL 10% calcium gluconate: the P waves have returned and the complexes are starting to narrow – the T waves are still peaked. **(c)** Normal ECG after serum potassium had been restored to normal levels by dialysis.

Treatment should be instituted if there are any ECG changes of hyperkalaemia

Calcium counteracts the cardiotoxicity of hyperkalaemia by stabilising the myocardium. It acts as soon as it gets to the heart, and its effect lasts for about 1 hour. It should be given intravenously in 10 mL aliquots and repeated as necessary, until the ECG improves significantly (Fig 6b). Calcium does not reduce the serum potassium concentration.

Give calcium as a slow infusion (10 mL 10% calcium gluconate over 30 min) if the patient is taking digoxin – high calcium concentrations potentiate the cardiotoxicity of digoxin.

After calcium, then give insulin and dextrose, which should lower the serum

Table 10 Treatment of hyperkalaemia

Treatment	Dosage	Effect
Intravenous calcium	Calcium gluconate 10% in 10 mL aliquots IV by 'slow push' (2 minutes)	Stabilises myocardial cells and counteracts the cardiac toxicity of hyperkalaemia
Intravenous insulin and dextrose	10 units soluble insulin in 50 mL 50% dextrose infused over 20 minutes	Insulin induces cellular uptake of K^+ by activating Na/K-ATP-ase. Dextrose prevents hypoglycaemia
Nebulised β-adrenergic agents	Salbutamol 10–20 mg neb	Induces cellular uptake of K^+ by activating Na/K-ATPase
Oral or rectal ion exchange resins	Calcium resonium 15 g oral tds	Removes K^+ from the body by binding in the GI tract; 1 g of resonium binds 1 mmol of K^+ (NB takes several days to have an effect)
Haemodialysis	For 2 hours using dialysis fluid with low K^+	Removes K^+ from the body by diffusion across semipermeable membrane

ATP, adenosine triphosphate; GI, gastrointestinal; IV, intravenous; neb, nebulised.

potassium by about 1 mmol/L within 1–2 hours. Nebulised beta agonists may be used as additive therapy (and have been shown to augment the effect of insulin/dextrose) but up to 40% of patients do not respond, particularly those with dialysis-dependent renal failure or on systemic beta-agonist therapy, so do not use them alone unless intravenous access is difficult or insulin/dextrose is not immediately available. The patient should have regular monitoring of their blood sugars for 6 hours after insulin/dextrose infusion – hypoglycaemia is common.

The effects of insulin and dextrose will last for 3 or 4 hours: unless the patient has a form of renal impairment that is likely to recover quickly (as might be possible in this case with the relief of obstruction), use this time to arrange transfer to renal / intensive care unit (ICU) services for dialysis/haemofiltration.

Key point

If the ECG shows severe changes of hyperkalaemia – tented T waves with diminished P waves or broadened QRS complexes – give intravenous calcium immediately.

Note that none of the treatments mentioned above actually remove potassium from the body. This can be accomplished by renal excretion (if kidney function can be restored), dialysis or (to a limited degree) by ion-exchange resins. In obstructive nephropathy, relief of the obstruction will often lead to an immediate diuresis with potassium removal, but even in these cases, when hyperkalaemia is severe, dialysis will often be necessary.

What else should you check?
The man is breathless, most likely due to pulmonary oedema. Before embarking on details of history and examination, make sure that he does not require urgent attention for this. After checking his airway, breathing and circulation decide which of four categories the patient is in: well, ill, very ill or peri-arrest? If peri-arrest, call for ICU help immediately – don't wait for cardiac arrest. Note the following:

> Can he talk – if so, how many words at a time?

> Is he using his accessory muscles to breathe?

> Is he exhausted?

> Is there cyanosis?

> Check vital signs: pulse rate; respiratory rate (beware of the patient with a normal respiratory rate who is exhausted, death may be imminent!); and BP.

> Peripheries – is he cold and shut down?

> Cardiac examination – JVP (likely to be grossly elevated) and gallop rhythm.

> Chest examination – crackles or wheeze.

If the patient is very ill or worse:

> sit them upright, assuming that pulmonary oedema and not hypotension is the main problem

> give them high-flow oxygen via reservoir bag

> attach pulse oximeter – monitor oxygen saturation

> attach cardiac monitor

> establish large-bore intravenous access.

What are the likely diagnoses in this patient?
The combination of acute kidney injury (AKI) with clinical evidence of urinary retention is usually the result of

long-standing bladder outflow obstruction. This is most often caused by benign prostatic hypertrophy, although other possibilities should be considered (see Table 11).

Bladder outflow obstruction with renal impairment is a common clinical scenario, accounting for up to 30% of cases of AKI in community-based studies. In such cases there is often a long history of urinary outflow symptoms and presentation is notoriously late.

History of the presenting problem

When immediate treatment for hyperkalaemia and pulmonary oedema has been given then take a full history, concentrating on the following.

Symptoms relating to renal impairment
There is often a non-specific prodrome with malaise, fatigue and sometimes nausea. As renal impairment advances, these rapidly progress with the development of vomiting, confusion and eventually coma.

Symptoms related to urinary outflow obstruction
Chronic retention is usually painless, in contrast to the restless agony of acute retention. Ask about lower urinary tract symptoms (LUTS), eg frequency (most common and earliest symptom), urgency and difficulty with micturition (poor stream).

Symptoms related to specific pathology
If obstruction is caused by pathology other than benign prostatic hypertrophy, then specific symptoms may be elicited. Prostate or other pelvic malignancy may be indicated by loss of weight, haematuria or bone pain. Although almost certainly not the explanation in this man, kidney/bladder stones should be considered as a potential cause.

Symptoms related to infection
UTI is present in at least 50% of patients presenting with AKI caused by bladder outflow obstruction.

Examination: general features

Before you started to take a history, you rightly made a general assessment of this patient and initiated any necessary emergency treatment.

Examination: abdominal system

When the patient's condition permits, look for evidence of causal pathologies (see Table 11), especially:

> lymphadenopathy and hepatomegaly – suggesting malignancy

> rectal examination – benign prostatic hyperplasia or malignancy

> neurological signs in the legs – this is unlikely to be bladder outflow obstruction resulting from spinal cord pathology, but the diagnosis should not be missed!

Record the residual urine volume immediately post-catheterisation, as well as colour and signs of infection, and the rate of urine output (UO).

Investigation

Key point

If they are available, past biochemistry results indicate the chronicity of renal damage and the level of recovery to expect – check the notes; check the pathology laboratory records; and ask the GP.

Blood tests
Repeat electrolytes and renal function; FBC; clotting screen; liver and bone function tests; prostate-specific antigen; and blood cultures (if suspicion of sepsis).

Chest radiograph
To assess for pulmonary oedema, and also (although much less likely) for secondaries in lungs or bones.

Ultrasonography of urinary tract
This is required urgently in any patient with an unexplained acute deterioration in renal function. A large residual bladder volume in combination with bilateral hydronephrosis (Fig 7) is diagnostic of obstructive nephropathy caused by a bladder outflow obstruction.

Management

Pulmonary oedema
The spectrum ranges from mild breathlessness on exertion to respiratory

Frequency	Diagnosis
	Table 11 Differential diagnosis of renal impairment with a large bladder
Common	Obstructive nephropathy caused by benign prostatic hypertrophy
Less common	Obstructive nephropathy caused by prostatic carcinoma Obstructive nephropathy cause by other pelvic malignancy, eg cervical or uterine Incidental acute urinary retention with another cause for renal impairment
Uncommon	Obstructive nephropathy caused by a neurogenic bladder, eg spinal cord compression Obstructive nephropathy caused by other bladder outflow pathology, eg urethral stricture

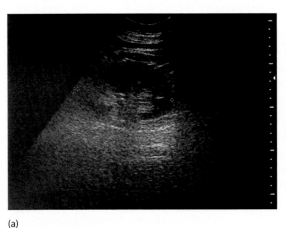
(a)

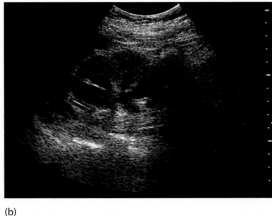
(b)

Fig 7 Renal ultrasonography: **(a)** normal kidney and **(b)** hydronephrotic kidney with marked pelvicalyceal dilatation.

failure leading to respiratory arrest. All patients should receive high-flow oxygen and be sat upright. Those who are severely compromised with an increasing respiratory rate, fatigue and hypoxia require transfer to the ICU with the option for ventilation if necessary. In others, intravenous nitrates may be sufficient until fluid can be removed by either diuresis – perhaps after the relief of obstruction in this case – or dialysis with fluid removal by ultrafiltration.

Hyperkalaemia and fluid overload causing pulmonary oedema are the most common indications for urgent dialysis; others are given in Table 12.

Volume depletion and fluid replacement

Although this man's initial problem is pulmonary oedema from fluid overload, relief of obstructive nephropathy is often followed by excessive diuresis, associated with sodium, potassium, bicarbonate, calcium and magnesium wasting. This happens when the tubules have 'forgotten' how to concentrate the urine, and means there is a risk of volume depletion, which could compromise recovering renal function. Note the following.

> Fluid status (postural blood pressure, JVP and weight) and biochemistry should be checked frequently.

> Care needs to be taken with the sodium content of intravenous fluid; alternating physiological (0.9%) saline and 5% dextrose is usually an appropriate choice.

> Large quantities of potassium may need to be given (20–40 mmol/L); this requires close monitoring.

If the patient is polyuric (passing >3 L urine/day), give a total daily fluid input equal to the measured output of the day before. This will achieve a gentle negative balance; but you will need to monitor volume status carefully.

Table 12	Indications for urgent dialysis
Condition	**Indication**
Hyperkalaemia	Different patients respond differently to hyperkalaemia: if there are severe ECG changes that do not respond to medical treatment then intervention is required
Pulmonary oedema	This is the commonest life-threatening manifestation of salt and water overload in AKI. All patients should receive high-flow oxygen and be sat upright. Other holding measures while preparations for dialysis are made include intravenous nitrates, low-dose morphine and (in very extreme circumstances) venesection
Uraemia	Severe uraemia (urea >50 mmol/L, normal range 2.5–7.0) is a relative indication. When associated with encephalopathy or pericarditis then urgent dialysis is required
Severe acidosis	This is usually a reflection of the severity of metabolic derangement and it is difficult to suggest a particular value for blood pH that demands intervention. A pH <7.2 or base excess of <–10 should certainly prompt early intervention and consideration of dialysis

AKI, acute kidney injury; ECG, electrocardiogram.

Key point

Don't chase your own tail! Avoid driving a post-obstructive diuresis with huge volumes of replacement fluid.

If urine output does not continue after catheterisation

The urethral catheter will drain the bladder, but there may be coincident ureteric obstruction. This is particularly common in prostate carcinoma, which can spread to encase the ureters. Repeat the ultrasonography to determine whether catheterisation has relieved the hydronephrosis. Consider CT to assess the retroperitoneum and involve the urology team.

Other possibilities are that the kidneys may have been chronically damaged by obstruction, or there may be acute tubular necrosis (ATN) (see Section 1.5.2) – resulting in this patient from the combination of hypoxia, sepsis and poor perfusion. Also consider other causes of renal impairment – how convincing was the evidence of obstruction and what was the residual urine volume?

1.5.2 Postoperative acute kidney injury

Case history

A 73-year-old man presented with a Duke's B carcinoma of the descending colon for which he had a hemicolectomy. Preoperatively his serum creatinine was normal (103 μmol/L, normal range 60–110), but his urine output (UO) fell after he left the operating theatre recovery suite. Initially the surgical team managed this with intravenous fluids and boluses of furosemide, but 24-hours postoperatively his UO was 10 mL/hour and his creatinine had risen to 180 μmol/L.

Table 13 Causes of ATN[1]	
Haemodynamically-mediated ATN	**Toxic ATN**

Reduced circulating volume:
    Blood loss
    Excessive GI fluid loss, eg diarrhoea
    Burns
	Drugs which are toxic to renal epithelial cells:
	    Gentamicin
	    Amphotericin

Low cardiac output	Rhabdomyolysis
Systemic sepsis	Radiocontrast nephropathy

Drugs inducing renal hypoperfusion:
    NSAIDs
    ACE inhibitors
    ARBs	

1 Note that many patients suffer more than one of these insults.
ACE, angiotensin-converting enzyme; ARBs, angiotensin-II receptor blockers; ATN, acute tubular necrosis; GI, gastrointestinal.

Introduction

The most common cause of postoperative acute kidney injury (AKI) is acute tubular necrosis (ATN). ATN may be the end result of a variety of insults to the kidneys, many of which cause hypoperfusion and initially cause pre-renal AKI (Table 13). By definition, pre-renal AKI will be corrected immediately when normal perfusion is restored.

Management of AKI depends on identification and correction of the cause, treating life-threatening complications (eg hyperkalaemia and pulmonary oedema) and providing supportive treatment, including renal replacement therapy (RRT), when required.

History of the presenting problem

When confronted with a patient with impaired renal function, it is always important to establish whether this is acute or chronic. In this case the preoperative creatinine clearly indicates an acute deterioration. In dealing with this patient consider the following.

Causes of hypoperfusion (pre-renal)
The following may lead to ATN:

> intraoperative haemodynamic details (usually from anaesthetic

charts) including blood loss, fluid replacement, BP, urinary output (if measured) and time on cardiac bypass (if relevant)

> postoperative haemodynamic details, including blood loss, fluid replacement, urinary and other fluid outputs (GI losses and drains etc), and BP

> evidence of hypoxia (eg low oxygen saturation or dyspnoea)

> details of all medications, particularly non-steroidal anti-inflammatory drugs (NSAIDs), ACE inhibitors/ARBs causing hypoperfusion but also nephrotoxic drugs such as some antibiotics

> evidence of sepsis, eg fever, hypotension, acute-phase response and wound discharge

> evidence of cardiac dysfunction, eg postoperative chest pain may go unnoticed but can be an indication of myocardial infarction.

Causes of post-renal renal impairment

> Bladder outflow obstruction, particularly in older men due to prostatic enlargement – is the catheter properly positioned and draining freely?

> Bilateral ureteric obstruction is very uncommon but may occur

postoperatively due to retroperitoneal haemorrhage or inadvertent ligation of the ureters (eg during hysterectomy).

Intrinsic causes of renal impairment
The following would be very unlikely in this case:

> acute tubulointerstitial nephritis, usually due to drugs
> disease of the small blood vessels, eg thrombotic microangiopathy (TMA) associated with drugs.

Examination
As always the first priority is to make an overall assessment of the patient: are they well, ill, very ill or peri-arrest? See Section 1.5.1 for discussion. Check in particular for features to support the diagnoses of renal hypoperfusion or post-renal problems.

Evidence of likely renal hypoperfusion

> hypotension and postural hypotension (lying and sitting/standing for 3 minutes)
> low JVP
> presence of sepsis – warm peripheries, bounding pulse, hypotension and wound infection
> evidence of low cardiac output – cold peripheries, thready pulse and hypotension
> murmur and/or chest crepitations may suggest low cardiac output / hypoxaemia
> blood or fluid loss, eg wound haematoma, full drains.

Evidence of post-renal renal impairment

> enlarged bladder due to outflow obstruction.

In any patient that is acutely unwell or who has renal impairment, it is crucial to establish current volume status.

Evidence of fluid overload

> raised JVP
> gallop rhythm
> basal crackles in the chest suggesting pulmonary oedema
> peripheral oedema shows that there is an increase in overall body salt and water: even a trace of ankle oedema usually corresponds to at least 3 L of expansion.

Evidence of intravascular fluid depletion
All of these suggest renal hypoperfusion is likely:

> hypotension / postural hypotension
> low JVP.

Evidence to support specific renal pathologies

> loin pain – can occur with hydronephrosis, rarely with acute renovascular occlusion or embolisation, and more commonly with retroperitoneal haematoma
> 'trash feet' as part of cholesterol embolisation syndrome, particularly after vascular operations

> drug rash associated with tubulointerstitial nephritis
> enlarged bladder indicating urinary obstruction.

Investigation
The diagnosis of the cause of this man's acute deterioration in renal function is likely to be made on the basis of his history and physical examination. However, appropriate investigations will assist in making a diagnosis in some cases and be necessary to assess the severity of metabolic disturbance and progress in all.

Assessment of severity and progress
Several staging systems have been developed to assess AKI and the risk of progression. Different systems use different criteria, but all rely on assessment of serum creatinine and UO. The Kidney Disease: Improving Global Outcomes (KDIGO) guidelines are most commonly recommended to diagnose and stage AKI, with diagnosis requiring one of the following:

> a rise in creatinine of >26 μmol/L in 48 hours
> a rise in creatinine to >1.5 times the baseline (the best figure in the last 3 months)
> UO of <0.5 mL/kg/hour for >6 consecutive hours.

The KDIGO stages of AKI are based on the Acute Kidney Injury Network (AKIN) guidelines and are broadly classified as shown in Table 14.

Table 14	KDIGO stages of AKI	
Stage	**Serum creatinine**	**Urine output**
1	Increase ≥26.5 μmol/L in 48 hours or to ≥1.5–1.9 × baseline	<0.5 mL/kg/hour for >6 consecutive hours
2	Increase to ≥2–2.9 × baseline	<0.5 mL/kg/hour for >12 hours
3	Increase to ≥3 × baseline or creatinine > 354 μmol/L or need for RRT	<0.3 mL/kg/hour for >24 hours or anuria for 12 hours (anuria <400 mL/day)

KDIGO, Kidney Disease: Improving Global Outcomes; RRT, renal replacement therapy.

When assessing the patient, identifying the stage of AKI allows assessment of prognosis, including the likelihood of recovery of renal function and of mortality.

Additionally, you should consider investigations to assess potential causes and complications.

> blood tests – electrolytes (watch for hyperkalaemia), creatinine, liver/bone function tests, C-reactive protein (CRP), FBC (consider postoperative bleeding) and clotting screen; also arterial blood gases (if the patient is very ill or worse) for acid–base status

> chest radiograph – to look for features of pulmonary oedema and/or postoperative pneumonia.

Diagnosis of the cause of AKI

> Urine dipstick for blood and protein – if the cause is pre-renal or ATN one would not expect more than protein + and blood +: more haematuria or proteinuria in a non-catheter specimen should prompt consideration of a renal inflammatory cause of AKI – but this would be extremely unlikely in this context.

> Screen for sepsis – cultures of wound swab, blood, urine and sputum (if any).

> Ultrasonography of urinary tract (if a clinical diagnosis of hypovolaemia is not clear-cut) – looking for features of obstruction.

Note that measurement of urinary sodium concentration, urinary creatinine or urea concentration, and urine osmolality are of no value in this context: whether the patient has pre-renal AKI or ATN will be determined by their response to resuscitation.

Other tests

> ECG – deterioration could have been caused by a perioperative myocardial infarct.

Management

Treat life-threatening complications (eg hyperkalaemia and pulmonary oedema), decide if urgent haemodialysis (or a renal opinion!) is required and assess whether the patient should be transferred to the intensive care unit (ICU) – all as described in Section 1.5.1.

Optimise circulating volume, oxygenation and (hopefully) renal perfusion: the aim is to correct possible renal hypoperfusion while avoiding dangerous fluid overload and pulmonary oedema. If renal function improves immediately with fluid infusion, the diagnosis is pre-renal AKI.

Monitor fluid input and output carefully – a urinary catheter is required.

Key point

Fluid management of the patient with postoperative AKI associated with hypovolaemia

> Resuscitate – give intravenous 0.9% saline rapidly until the JVP is seen easily and the postural hypotension is abolished.

> Maintain optimal intravascular volume – give fluid input equal to measured outputs plus 500–1,000 mL/day; examine the patient twice daily for features of volume depletion (low JVP or a postural fall in BP) or overload (tachypnoea or basal crackles) and then adjust fluid input appropriately.

Key point

In the patient with AKI, always look at the drug chart and stop drugs that have adverse renal haemodynamic effects when the circulation is disturbed (NSAIDs, ACE inhibitors and ARBs) or are nephrotoxic (eg aminoglycosides).

Regularly repeat measurements of serum electrolytes and creatinine. Particular attention should be paid to the trend as well as the absolute values of abnormalities: if these are getting worse day by day, do not wait until they are extreme before seeking advice from renal services. Once the need for RRT becomes clear, usually in the context of oliguria and worsening renal function, there is no point in delaying its commencement until there is an emergency indication.

Always consider sepsis and have a low threshold for commencing broad-spectrum (non-nephrotoxic) antibiotics.

Hazard

There is no good evidence that prognosis of AKI is beneficially altered by measures such as loop diuretics and dopamine – they should not be used.

Nutritional support should be commenced early in AKI.

Key point

The management of AKI can be summarised as follows:

> treat life-threatening complications (may require urgent haemodialysis)

> restore and maintain renal perfusion

> investigate and correct the cause, while continuing supportive management.

Further comments

Haemodialysis or haemofiltration?
Intermittent haemodialysis is the renal replacement modality used on renal units for most patients with renal impairment but without failure of other organs (isolated AKI). Patients who are haemodynamically unstable or who have failure of more than one organ require management in intensive care, where continuous renal replacement therapies such as haemofiltration or haemodiafiltration are the norm. These techniques have the advantage of cardiovascular stability, optimal circulatory volume manipulation and the ability to create space for enhanced nutritional replacement. However, in randomised trials in a variety of settings there is no evidence that one treatment modality is better than the other.

Outcome of AKI
Although most patients with ATN have potentially recoverable renal function, the mortality of patients with this condition is high: 40–45% of those who require acute RRT will die. This reflects the poor outcome of those who have ATN as a component of multi-organ failure: if a patient has failure of three or four organs, mortality is 80–90%. By contrast, mortality is <10% in patients with isolated AKI.

The renal outcome of those patients who survive is roughly that 60% will recover normal renal function, 30% are left with chronic kidney disease (CKD) and 10% remain dialysis dependent.

1.5.3 Renal impairment and a multisystem disease

Case history

A 26-year-old woman presented to the emergency department with several weeks of intermittent pleuritic chest pain and joint pain. She was found to have dipstick proteinuria, a creatinine of 225 µmol/L (normal range 60–110) and anaemia with fragments on the blood film.

Introduction

What is the first priority in a young woman with pleuritic chest pain?
The first priority is to establish that the patient does not have pulmonary embolism (PE).

Features suggesting a multisystem disorder
Arthralgia, anaemia and impaired renal function all clearly suggest a multisystem disorder. History and examination are crucial in narrowing down the differential diagnosis. Considered analysis of the findings of simple tests such as urinalysis, plasma biochemistry and haematology will often give a clear lead to the underlying pathology, and is essential in determining the urgency of the situation. Joint and chest pains in a young woman with renal impairment raise a strong clinical suspicion of systemic lupus erythematosus (SLE) (see Section 2.7.5).

History of the presenting problem

Pleuritic chest pain
The differential diagnosis of intermittent pleuritic chest pain going on for some weeks includes PE, musculoskeletal pain, pericarditis and rarer causes of pleurisy, such as autoimmune disease. It is clearly very important to pursue the possibility of PE, so ask about previous thromboembolism, leg/calf pain or swelling, breathlessness and haemoptysis. If the patient has musculoskeletal pain, this may be positional – do any particular movements bring it on? Does moving into any particular position improve it? Pericarditis would be supported by any 'cardiac radiation' of the pain, and also if it were eased on sitting forward.

Joints
What is the pattern of joint involvement? Which joints are affected? Is the distribution symmetrical and does this change over time? Is there a diurnal pattern? Is there swelling, stiffness or discoloration? Is the pain eased or worsened by movement? These features are important in the differential diagnosis of arthritis.

Renal disease
Until renal impairment is far advanced, it is asymptomatic, although patients with the nephrotic syndrome may notice frothy urine and will (by definition) have oedema.

Other relevant history
Are there other features that would support the diagnosis of SLE (Fig 8)? Ask about the following:

> skin rashes, especially ones that are photosensitive

> Raynaud's phenomenon

> myalgia

> neurological abnormalities – seizures or psychiatric disturbances

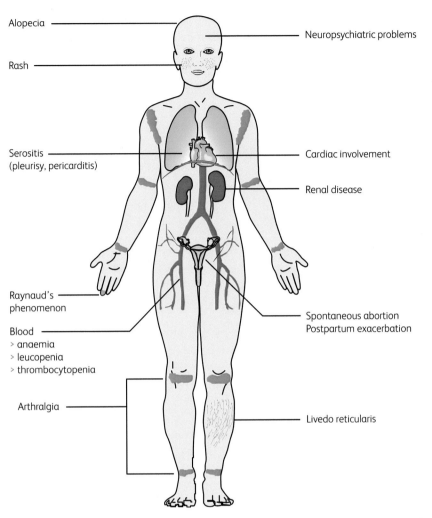

Alopecia

Rash

Serositis
(pleurisy, pericarditis)

Raynaud's
phenomenon

Blood
> anaemia
> leucopenia
> thrombocytopenia

Arthralgia

Neuropsychiatric problems

Cardiac involvement

Renal disease

Spontaneous abortion
Postpartum exacerbation

Livedo reticularis

Fig 8 Manifestations of systemic lupus erythematosus. This figure illustrates the widespread potential manifestations of this multisystem disease.

> history of miscarriage

> drugs – some, eg hydralazine, can precipitate a lupus-like illness.

Examination

Once again it is important to make an initial assessment as to how ill the patient is (see Section 1.5.1), but the details given here do not indicate that the patient is in extremis. Examination, as always, should be focused on confirming or refuting diagnoses suggested by the history, hence – apart

from checking vital signs – look for the following.

> Signs of PE / deep venous thrombosis:

> raised JVP, palpable right ventricle, loud P2, right ventricular gallop, pleural rub and pleural effusion

> warm swollen leg

> hypoxia (<94%) on pulse oximetry.

> Signs of pericarditis / pericardial fluid:

> pericardial rub – raised JVP and/or pulsus paradoxus (a fall in systolic

BP of >10 mmHg on inspiration) if there is sufficient pericardial fluid to cause haemodynamic compromise.

> Signs suggesting SLE:

> skin – typically facial butterfly rash and/or alopecia; also livedo reticularis

> fingers and toes – are there signs of ischaemia caused by severe Raynaud's phenomenon?

> joints – are these swollen or tender? Small joints are typically involved in SLE in a symmetrical and (usually) non-deforming manner

> cardiovascular – cardiac murmurs and peripheral oedema

> neurological, including ocular fundi – neuropsychiatric lupus can present in a wide variety of ways: cranial nerve palsy, peripheral neuropathy, cerebrovascular accident, movement disorder and transverse myelitis.

Investigation

Exclusion of PE

Although it seems very likely that this woman has SLE, it would be unwise to completely dismiss PE on clinical grounds. A normal D-dimer would be reassuring, but an abnormal result – which would be very likely in the case described and almost certainly be non-specific – should be followed by appropriate imaging, either with lung ventilation/perfusion (V/Q) scanning or CT pulmonary angiography.

Urinalysis

Around 10% of adults presenting with SLE have protein or blood in their urine, which indicates renal involvement. Proteinuria should be quantified, most usually by measurement of urinary albumin:creatinine ratio (ACR) or protein:creatinine ratio (PCR). Red cell casts confirm active glomerulonephritis.

Biochemistry

Check renal function (to ensure no further acute deterioration in this case) and liver function tests. SLE can affect any organ, but liver involvement is unusual. Patients may have low serum albumin as a result of proteinuria, active inflammation and/or chronic disease.

Key point

Renal involvement is common in SLE but does not cause symptoms, so it is very important to perform urinalysis, measure serum creatinine and estimate glomerular filtration rate (GFR).

Haematology

Check FBC, blood film, reticulocyte count, direct antiglobulin test (Coombs test), clotting screen, lactate dehydrogenase (LDH) and haptoglobins. SLE often causes anaemia, which is usually normochromic and normocytic but can be haemolytic. Haemolysis is suggested by polychromasia,

reticulocytosis, low haptoglobin levels and a raised unconjugated plasma bilirubin. A positive Coombs test would suggest autoimmune haemolysis. The presence of fragmented red blood cells on the blood film would indicate a microangiopathic process, as can be seen in SLE (Fig 9). Up to two-thirds of SLE patients have leukopenia, with the main deficit being lymphopenia; there may also be mild thrombocytopenia. This contrasts with the primary systemic vasculitides, which usually cause high white cell and platelet counts. Abnormalities of the clotting screen may be associated with antiphospholipid antibodies.

Inflammatory and serological markers

Check erythrocyte sedimentation rate (ESR), C-reactive protein (CRP), anti-nuclear antibodies (ANAs), anti-double stranded DNA (dsDNA) antibodies and complement levels – the typical pattern of active SLE is a raised ESR with a low CRP, low levels of complement C3 and C4, ANAs and

antibodies to dsDNA. There may be other autoantibodies, especially antiphospholipid antibodies such as lupus anticoagulant, which prolong the activated partial thromboplastin time (APTT) but paradoxically predispose to thrombosis.

Other investigations

> Renal ultrasonography – to confirm that the patient has two anatomically normal kidneys.

> Renal biopsy – to make a precise renal diagnosis, determine prognosis and inform treatment decisions (see Section 2.7.5).

Management

The management of SLE is complex and depends on the precise clinical situation. Current recommendations are that all patients should receive supportive and psychological therapy, but disease specific therapy is dictated by the degree of disease activity.

> no major organ involvement (ie skin, joint or haematological changes only) – hydroxychloroquine or other antimalarials, low-dose steroids and antimetabolites such as azathioprine or mycophenolate mofetil

> major organ involvement – intravenous corticosteroids, cyclophosphamide, mycophenolate mofetil, biological agents such as belimumab (anti-B-cell activating factor (BAFF) antibody, which depletes B cells and has been recently licensed) or clinical trial entry, eg for alternative B-cell-targeted therapies.

The renal response to treatment depends on the class of lupus nephritis, assessed on histological appearances,

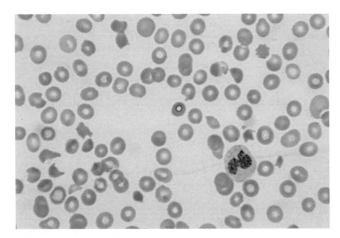

Fig 9 Blood film of microangiopathic haemolytic anaemia (MAHA). This blood film shows the typical features of a MAHA with abnormally shaped red blood cells and red blood cell fragments. Aside from systemic lupus erythematosus, this picture can be caused by pre-eclampsia or eclampsia, disseminated intravascular coagulation, prosthetic heart valves (especially if they are leaking or infected), thrombotic thrombocytopenic purpura, haemolytic–uraemic syndrome, accelerated phase hypertension and scleroderma. (Courtesy of Dr JA Amess, St Bartholomew's Hospital.)

with classes I–IV representing increasing severity of glomerular lesions (see Fig 10 and Section 2.7.5). Classes I and II are usually treated with oral therapy (steroids and for example mycophenolate mofetil). Classes III and IV usually require intravenous induction therapy with cyclophosphamide or biological agents. Class V (membranous nephropathy) is treated with optimal antiproteinuric treatment (eg ACE inhibitors) and control of BP, but there is evidence that biological agents and immunosuppressants may improve outcomes.

All treatments for SLE have potential side effects, many of which are particularly difficult for the predominately young, female patients that SLE usually affects.

Cyclophosphamide toxicity includes haemorrhagic cystitis, infection, bone marrow suppression, suppression of ovarian function and tumours. The use of 2-mercaptoethane sulphonate (mesna) helps protect against bladder toxicity. Drug toxicity should be discussed with the patient and, when practicable, storage of gametes should be considered before therapy is started. The interest in biologics has grown in part as a means of reducing drug toxicity and minimising long-term side effects.

Treatment of BP is important. Dialysis and/or renal transplantation may be required if the kidneys fail completely.

Further comments

Joint pains, pleuritic chest pain and renal abnormalities should always raise the possibility of SLE. Renal involvement in SLE is common and potentially very serious, so all patients with SLE should have BP monitoring, together with regular urinalysis and serum creatinine testing.

SLE is unpredictable; it can remit and relapse frequently. It can be a mere nuisance or it can be a devastating illness. This is worrying for patients; uncertainty is difficult for them, their family and friends, and also for their doctors. Many of the treatments used are of limited efficacy and all have side effects. All these issues need to be frankly discussed with the patient at the beginning.

With women, discuss the interplay between pregnancy and SLE (and hypertension or renal impairment if present, see Section 1.1.2 and Section 1.3.1). SLE can be exacerbated during pregnancy and for the first 2-months postpartum, and women with SLE have an increased incidence of miscarriage, perinatal death and preterm delivery.

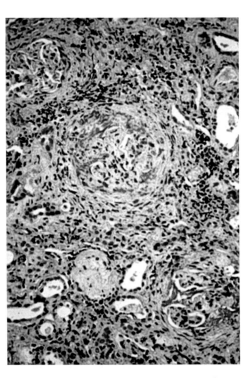

Fig 10 Glomerulonephritis in systemic lupus erythematosus (SLE). This is a section of a renal biopsy showing a severe crescentic glomerulonephritis (class IV lupus nephritis). The central glomerulus is full of inflammatory cells and shows a clear crescent caused by inflammatory cells in Bowman's space. (Courtesy of Dr JE Scoble, Guy's Hospital.)

1.5.4 Renal impairment and fever

Case history

A 22-year-old man with no significant previous history presented to the emergency department. He reported a 4-day history of fever, aching muscles and a rigor. His temperature was 39°C. Urinalysis showed proteinuria and haematuria. Laboratory blood test results included serum creatinine 275 µmol/L (normal range 60–110).

Introduction

What do you want to know next to guide your immediate management? There are three key pieces of information.

> The state of the patient's circulation. The renal impairment may be due to circulatory shock. What are his vital signs?

> How much urine he is passing? Acute kidney injury (AKI) is usually associated with oliguria or anuria. If he is passing <0.5 mL/kg/hour his creatinine is likely to be rising rapidly and renal replacement therapy (RRT) may be necessary within 24–48 hours. If he is unwell and it is not clear that he is producing good volumes of urine then a catheter should be inserted to enable continuous monitoring of urine output (UO).

> What are today's blood results, in particular his serum potassium – hyperkalaemia may be life-threatening (see Section 1.5.1) – and what is happening to his creatinine?

The possible causes of AKI can usefully be considered by thinking through the process of blood perfusing the glomeruli, generating a primary filtrate, which is then modified by the tubular epithelium and passes through the ureters, bladder and urethra:

> pre-renal disease – hypotension or reduced intravascular volume

> renovascular disease

> glomerular disease

> renal vasculitis

> tubular and interstitial disease

> post-renal obstruction – potentially in the renal pelvises, ureters, bladder or urethra.

Which possible causes of AKI are most likely in this case?

> The short history and prominent constitutional features in a previously fit man suggest he could have reduced renal perfusion due to a severe systemic illness. The commonest cause of AKI in this context would be acute tubular necrosis (ATN) (see Section 1.5.2). However, the presence of proteinuria and haematuria would not be expected in a diagnosis of ATN and they raise the possibility of a renal inflammatory process – an acute glomerulonephritis, a vasculitis or a tubulointerstitial nephritis.

> Another possibility to be considered is that he has unsuspected chronic renal impairment accounting for his raised creatinine and an unrelated acute illness.

What would you consider a normal glomerular filtration rate (GFR) for a 22-year-old man, and what do you estimate this man's GFR to be?

> A normal GFR in a man of this age would be 80–150 mL/min. If his creatinine were stable at 275 μmol/L, this would give an estimated GFR of about 25 mL/min. But his current GFR could be 0 mL/min – you only have a single value of creatinine, which may be climbing rapidly.

> **Key point**
> Even when glomerular filtration has stopped completely, serum creatinine will rise only by about 200 μmol/L per day.

History of the presenting problem

Assuming the patient is not *in extremis*, you will clearly start to take the history along the lines of 'what did you first notice', but key issues to probe are:

> 'How long have you been unwell?' 'When were you last completely well?' – He says he became unwell 4 days ago, but the point is important enough to pursue; 22 year olds may be rather dismissive of more subtle symptoms and patients with systemic vasculitis have usually been unwell for weeks or months.

> Possibility of infection – has he had contact with anyone else who has been unwell, and has he been travelling recently (which brings in a wider infective differential)?

Other relevant history

Ask specifically about the following:

> Possibility of multisystem disorder – skin rash, arthralgia, trouble with ears or sinuses, pins and needles / numbness / focal weakness (mononeuritis) and haemoptysis (suggestive of pulmonary haemorrhage).

> Sore throat – may suggest IgA nephropathy or post-streptococcal glomerulonephritis, but both are unlikely in the scenario described.

> Drugs (prescribed or non-prescribed) – some can trigger interstitial nephritis or (less commonly) vasculitic reactions. Ask about recreational drugs; many of the new 'legal highs' have unexpected side effects and can cause renal impairment.

Examination: general features

Look for signs that the patient is very unwell, as described in Section 1.5.1. If they are peri-arrest, call for ICU help immediately – do not wait for cardiac arrest.

Next, on a quick head-to-toe screen, look for potential sources and signs of sepsis, for signs to support a diagnosis of vasculitis (skin rash – typically 'palpable purpura' – and splinter haemorrhages) and perform a full physical examination.

Your examination reveals a temperature of 39°C and pulse 110 beats per minute, regular. The patient's peripheries are strikingly warm and his BP is 90/60 mmHg. There are infarcts around his fingertips (Fig 11) and widespread muscle tenderness. What are you considering now?

These findings are very worrying indeed. They would be most unusual in a systemic vasculitis, as would the abrupt onset and the rigor. The picture is more suggestive of a septicaemic illness: nail-fold infarcts suggest acute endocarditis; and aching and tender muscles are common in *Staphylococcus aureus* septicaemia – which should lead you back to take further history about 'recent infections, trouble with boils or spots, an abscess anywhere, bad toothache or a visit to the dentist'. Following such prompts, this man recalls that he had a spot on his elbow, which burst a week earlier. Examination suggests an infected olecranon bursa.

The possibility of staphylococcal endocarditis now leads you to repeat the cardiovascular examination – the pulse is too rapid to be sure of its character, but is there a decrescendo murmur?

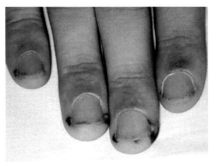
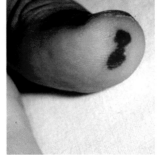

Fig 11 Fingertip infarcts.

> **Key point**
> Severe acute aortic regurgitation may not be accompanied by an obvious diastolic murmur.

> **Key point**
> Making a diagnosis in a sick patient often involves:

> taking a history
> physical examination
> reviewing investigations
> repeating elements of the history
> repeating elements of the physical examination
> re-reviewing investigations
> and so on repeatedly.

Plan for investigation and management

Your clinical diagnosis is acute endocarditis, probably staphylococcal. You need to confirm the diagnosis, institute appropriate supportive treatment and start empirical antibiotic treatment. AKI in this context is likely to be mainly due to hypotension and the sepsis syndrome, but it is probable that there is also an active glomerulonephritis, as indicated by the proteinuria and haematuria. Bacterial endocarditis can be associated with glomerulonephritis (similar to post-infectious glomerulonephritis histologically), acute interstitial nephritis and embolic events.

Investigations

Laboratory tests show a low platelet count, a neutrophil leucocytosis and CRP 300 mg/L. The high CRP and neutrophil leucocytosis are consistent with bacterial infection or systemic vasculitis, but the low platelet count is a typical feature of sepsis and would be uncommon in systemic vasculitis (where the platelet count is often elevated).

What investigations would you arrange?

> to pursue the diagnosis of bacterial endocarditis – three sets of blood cultures, taken separately, and an echocardiogram (which revealed aortic vegetations in this case)

> to assess severity and monitor for complications and progress – FBC, clotting screen, electrolytes, creatinine, liver/bone function tests and CRP; arterial blood gases; chest radiograph; and an ECG

> to consider vasculitic disease – ANAs, complement levels (C3 and C4), anti-neutrophil cytoplasmic antibodies (ANCA).

Hazard

Misleading serological results

> The indirect immunofluorescence test for ANCA is not uncommonly positive in endocarditis and other infective conditions – the specific tests for antibodies against serum proteinase 3 (PR3) and myeloperoxidase (MPO) are much less likely to mislead.

> C3 and C4 levels are commonly low in infection-related glomerulonephritis.

Management

Key point

Keep the relatives informed – they need to know that this man is extremely unwell and could die.

In a life-threatening situation such as this, it is often essential to start treatment before the diagnosis is confirmed. The following are appropriate here:

> Supportive care – transfer him to the ICU / high-dependency unit and ensure he gets a urinary catheter, close haemodynamic monitoring (central venous line and arterial line) and oxygen therapy if appropriate (if sats <94% or hypoxic on arterial blood gases). Ventilatory and inotropic support may also be required.

> Specific treatment – appropriate antimicrobials (initially the patient must be started on broad-spectrum cover, but given the suspicion of staphylococcal disease this must include high-dose flucloxacillin or vancomycin) and consideration of valve replacement (Fig 12).

Key point

AKI occurs in many severe illnesses. It is crucial to consider underlying diagnoses such as sepsis at an early stage. About one-third of a series of 200 patients with bacterial endocarditis developed AKI, which was more common in the older patients and those with an *S aureus* infection.

1.5.5 Renal impairment and haemoptysis

Case history

A 66-year-old man presented with a 5-week history of malaise, myalgia, arthralgia and increasing breathlessness. In the week leading up to admission he began to cough up blood and his GP performed blood tests that revealed creatinine 580 μmol/l (normal range 60–110) and haemoglobin 84 g/L (normal range 130–180). On receipt of these results he immediately went to the patient's house to reassess him, noticed a purpuric rash and organised emergency admission.

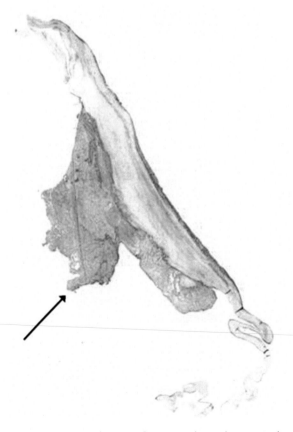

Fig 12 Low-power view of section through resected aortic valve leaflet showing adherent vegetation (arrow).

Introduction

This man almost certainly has a pulmonary renal syndrome, which is defined as a combination of diffuse pulmonary haemorrhage and glomerulonephritis. If not treated urgently this is usually fatal, and, despite aggressive treatment, mortality remains in the region of 25–50%.

Pulmonary–renal syndromes are usually caused by immunological diseases, mostly by the following:

> vasculitis, which is often anti-neutrophil cytoplasmic antibody (ANCA) positive – microscopic polyangiitis (MPA) or granulomatosis with polyangiitis (GPA, previously termed Wegener's)

> anti-glomerular basement membrane (anti-GBM) disease

> systemic lupus erythematosus (SLE).

Other causes of acute kidney injury (AKI) can be complicated by pulmonary oedema, infection or an increase in capillary permeability that may not be easy to distinguish from pulmonary haemorrhage. Patients with severe pneumonia can develop AKI as part of a sepsis syndrome, and these also need to be distinguished because their treatment is radically different.

Key point
AKI with blood/protein in the urine plus haemoptysis indicates a pulmonary–renal syndrome until proved otherwise – and this is a medical emergency.

History of the presenting problem

A detailed medical history is crucial. The presence of systemic symptoms and abnormalities in other organ systems may indicate a systemic vasculitis, SLE or an alternative diagnosis. The initial symptoms of many conditions, ranging from pneumonia to vasculitis, are relatively non-specific and include lethargy, fever, weight loss, arthralgia and a non-specific feeling of being 'unwell'. Probe for clues to the following diagnoses:

> Vasculitis – skin rash, abdominal pain and focal numbness or weakness (mononeuritis); this can be precipitated by some drugs, eg penicillamine or hydralazine, as well as recreational drugs.

> Granulomatosis with polyangiitis (GPA) (previously known as Wegener's granulomatosis) – sinus and upper respiratory tract symptoms, which may have been investigated in the past; also symptoms of generalised vasculitis.

> Anti-glomerular basement membrane disease (anti-GBM disease) (previously known as Goodpasture's disease) – can be triggered by inhaled hydrocarbons; pulmonary haemorrhage occurs almost exclusively in smokers.

> Eosinophilic granulomatosis with polyangiitis (eGPA, previously known as Churg–Strauss syndrome) – asthma, nasal polyps; also symptoms of generalised vasculitis.

> SLE – arthralgia, alopecia and pleurisy; more common in women and in those of African, Asian or African-Caribbean ethnicity.

> Pneumonia or other severe sepsis – any obvious symptoms suggesting infection, eg rigors or dysuria; always ask about travel history.

Examination

As always the first priority is to make an overall assessment of the patient: are they well, ill, very ill or peri-arrest? See Section 1.5.1 for discussion. This man sounds as though he might be very ill or worse: if he is, call for help from the ICU immediately. In addition to features indicative of the severity of his illness, note the following:

> signs of active vasculitis – palpable purpura (Fig 13), splinter haemorrhages, uveitis, mononeuritis multiplex and Roth spots; a collapsed nasal bridge is very suggestive of GPA but is extremely rare

> signs of SLE – alopecia, butterfly rash, arthritis and vasculitic skin lesions

> chest – there may be few abnormalities despite significant pulmonary haemorrhage.

Investigations

Blood and other routine tests

> to assess severity and monitor for complications and progress – FBC, clotting screen, electrolytes and creatinine, liver/bone function, CRP and ESR, and an ECG

> to make a diagnosis of vasculitis / autoimmune disease – ANCA, anti-GBM antibodies, ANAs, anti-dsDNA antibodies and complement (C3 and C4)

> to make a diagnosis of an infection-related syndrome – blood cultures and antistreptolysin O titre (ASOT)

> to support treatment – blood group and save (± cross match, which may take longer in patients with autoantibodies).

Lung investigations

A chest radiograph should clearly be a first-line investigation in this case, looking for appearances suggesting diffuse alveolar haemorrhage (Fig 14). Consider the following, depending on the fitness of the patient and clinical suspicion:

> Lung function tests – if the patient is well enough (which he may not be), looking for an elevated transfer coefficient (K_{CO}) indicating pulmonary haemorrhage.

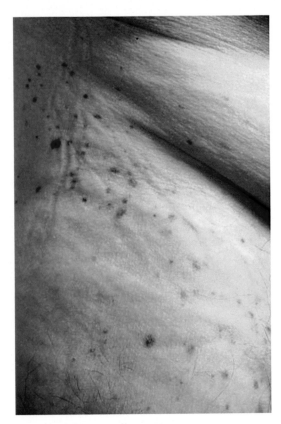

Fig 13 Typical vasculitic rash in the axilla of a patient with microscopic polyangiitis.

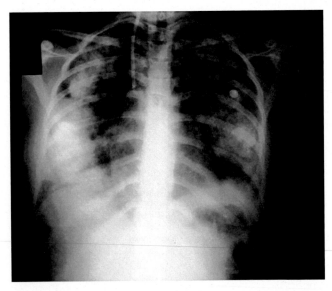

Fig 14 Chest radiograph showing pulmonary haemorrhage in a case of pulmonary–renal syndrome.

> CT scan of the chest – this may show appearances characteristic of alveolar bleeding; it is also good for demonstrating other pathology, eg pneumonia.

> Bronchoscopy and bronchoalveolar lavage – if infection is strongly suspected.

Renal investigations

Urine dipstick testing for proteinuria and haematuria, and urine microscopy for red cell casts are urgently required because they can establish the diagnosis of a renal inflammatory lesion. Urinary tract ultrasonography will be needed to demonstrate the presence of two normal-sized (and unobstructed) kidneys prior to renal biopsy, which will almost certainly be required to establish a definitive diagnosis of the particular type of pulmonary renal syndrome. Key things to look for on the renal biopsy are:

> Vasculitis – glomeruli that contain crescents (cells/material within Bowman's space and outside the glomerular capillary tuft, which they may compress – hence 'crescentic glomerulonephritis') and areas of necrosis (pink, amorphous material within the glomerular tuft on a standard haematoxylin and eosin stain, hence 'necrotising glomerulonephritis'), but no immunoglobulins or complement in the glomeruli (hence 'pauci-immune glomerulonephritis'). Not all glomeruli may be affected (hence 'focal glomerulonephritis'), and within a glomerulus not all parts may be involved (hence 'segmental glomerulonephritis') (Fig 15).

> Linear immunoglobulin (Ig) G deposition along the capillary basement membrane – anti-GBM disease.

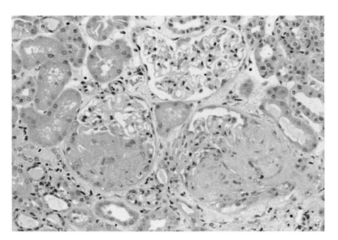

Fig 15 Renal histology in microscopic polyangiitis showing focal, segmental, necrotising glomerulonephritis with crescent formation.

> Widespread deposition of immunoglobulins and complement in the glomeruli – SLE/post-streptococcal glomerulonephritis.

Management

If you suspect a pulmonary–renal syndrome, early discussion with (and review by or transfer to) your local renal unit is essential.

Supportive care

Patients with pulmonary haemorrhage are often very ill and require:

> respiratory support – oxygen (high flow via reservoir bag if needed) to maintain adequate PO_2 levels (saturation >94%); ventilation if hypoxia does not respond to other measures

> haemostatic support – blood transfusion(s) if anaemic; correction of clotting abnormalities

> treatment of infection – low threshold for administration of antibiotics if infection is suspected

> RRT – haemodialysis or haemofiltration if appropriate (see Section 1.5.1), and without heparin if possible.

Specific treatments

If pulmonary haemorrhage is secondary to vasculitis, anti-GBM disease or SLE, management should be directed by an appropriate specialist, but the most commonly used initial treatment is the combination of:

> Steroids – usually initiated as intravenous methylprednisolone and then oral prednisolone.

> Immunosuppressant – cyclophosphamide or biological agents such as rituximab – particularly useful in cases where patients have coincident infection, which might be worsened by cyclophosphamide.

> Plasma exchange / plasmapheresis – this is definitely indicated for the treatment of anti-GBM disease with pulmonary haemorrhage, where the antibody is directly pathogenic. It is also used in pulmonary haemorrhage due to ANCA-associated vasculitis and SLE in some centres/cases.

Further comments

Anti-GBM disease (Goodpasture's) is almost always a 'one-hit' condition and does not relapse. By contrast, ANCA-positive vasculitis and SLE have a high incidence of relapse, and maintenance treatment is usually continued for years after diagnosis. Repeated episodes of pulmonary haemorrhage can cause pulmonary fibrosis.

1.5.6 Renal colic

Case history
A 47-year-old man presented to the emergency department with a 6-hour history of acute colicky loin pain, nausea, vomiting and haematuria.

Introduction

The diagnosis of renal colic is not usually difficult – typically there is very severe, colicky pain radiating from the flank. Sensory nerves from the ureter and renal pelvis enter the spinal cord at T11, T12, L1 and L2, and pain is referred to these dermatomes. Stones can lodge in the ureter at the pelviureteric junction, at the pelvic brim or at the ureterovesical junction. The renal pelvis refers pain to the loin and back, the lower ureter to the ipsilateral testis or labium majus, and the lowest pelvic part of the ureter to the tip of the penis or perineum (Fig 16).

The priorities are:

1 organise appropriate analgesia

2 confirm the suspected diagnosis of a ureteric stone

3 look for obstruction or infection.

The possibility of an underlying tendency to form stones needs to be considered after the acute problem has been dealt with.

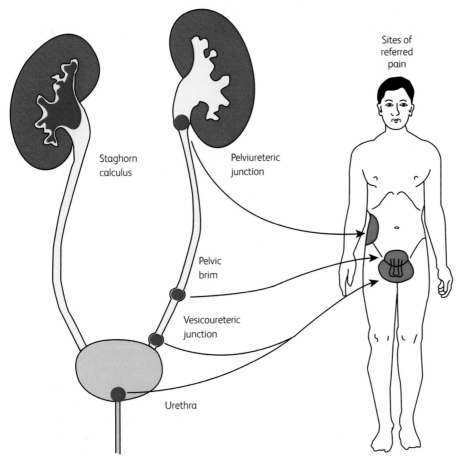

Labels on figure:
- Staghorn calculus
- Pelviureteric junction
- Pelvic brim
- Vesicoureteric junction
- Urethra
- Sites of referred pain

Fig 16 Sites where stones can lodge. This figure shows the common sites at which urinary tract stones can lodge as they pass down the urinary system.

History of the presenting problem

Ask about the following:

> Radiation of the pain – does this follow the pattern typical of renal/ureteric colic? Is the pain relieved by a particular position (normally not in renal colic)?

> Haematuria (present in this case).

> Passage of grit, gravel or stones in the urine, which clearly would confirm the diagnosis.

> Fevers, sweats and rigors – could there be infection? Combined with obstruction this can be a very dangerous combination.

> Are they continuing to pass urine – bladder stones can halt urine flow suddenly, with penile or perineal pain that is sometimes relieved by lying down.

The presence of haematuria in this case makes it nearly certain that the diagnosis is a urinary stone; but if there is no history of blood in the urine and if the pain does not radiate in a typical manner, then consider:

> Musculoskeletal pain – not usually so severe; not typically associated with nausea or vomiting; may be exacerbated by movement; and may be possible to get into a comfortable position.

> Biliary colic – typically felt in the right upper quadrant and epigastrium; may be precipitated by fatty food; and is also associated with nausea and vomiting, a past history of indigestion, dark urine and pale stools.

Other relevant history

Has the patient had any similar episodes previously? Ask carefully about predisposing factors: family history, recurrent UTIs, previous bowel surgery, dehydration (eg diarrhoea, marathon running) and use of antacids or vitamin-D-containing compounds. Also other medical conditions can increase the risk – diabetes, obesity, gout and hypertension.

Examination: general features

Once again it is important to make an initial assessment as to how ill the patient is (see Section 1.5.1), but the details given here do not indicate that the patient is likely to be very ill. Note particularly:

> Evidence of infection – is there a fever? Is the kidney tender?

> Are there any physical signs that might suggest a different diagnosis?

> Spine and back: does movement exacerbate the pain? Is there local tenderness?

> Upper abdomen: is there right upper quadrant or epigastric tenderness? Is this gall bladder pain?

Investigation

Blood and urine tests
Urine dipstick (if there is not at least a trace of haematuria, then the diagnosis of renal colic is in doubt) and culture; also electrolytes, creatinine, liver/bone function tests, FBC, inflammatory markers and blood culture (if there is clinical suspicion of infection).

Imaging

To confirm the diagnosis of urinary stone disease, to demonstrate the site of any stone, to detect evidence (if any) of obstruction and to look for the presence of other stones. First-line investigation is a non-contrast abdominal CT to both confirm the diagnosis (stones are visible in the majority of cases) and identify the site of obstruction. CT has a high sensitivity for detection of stones, although stones <2 mm are not always visible.

A plain abdominal film should only be used where CT is not available, and ultrasonography is reserved for those who should avoid radiation, eg pregnant women.

Key point

Urate stones are radiolucent on abdominal film, but visible on CT. Only stones associated with HIV protease inhibitors, particularly indinavir, cannot be seen on a non-contrast CT. If this is suspected, a contrast CT is required.

Management

Immediate priorities are to:

> Give adequate analgesia and antiemetics – the pain of renal colic is very severe: NSAIDs such as diclofenac are often used (often rectally if the patient is vomiting), alone or with opioids. Try to avoid NSAIDs if there is significant renal impairment.

> Maintain adequate hydration – if necessary with intravenous fluids.

> If infected – treat quickly with broad-spectrum antibiotics.

Obstruction without infection

This is usually diagnosed when CT (or ultrasonography) demonstrates dilatation of the pelvicalyceal system but there are no clinical or laboratory features to suggest infection. Stones smaller than 6 mm in diameter usually pass spontaneously, but stones larger than 1 cm will probably not. If the patient's pain is controlled and the stone is small, observe carefully. Alpha-blockers such as tamsulosin can help stone passage. If there is no progress over a few days or if the stone is large, then the obstruction must be relieved – a range of techniques is available to urologists to do this: extracorporeal shock wave lithotripsy (first choice, successful in 75% of cases) and endoscopic, percutaneous, laparoscopic or (rarely) open surgical removal (Fig 17).

Obstruction with infection

This is an emergency requiring urgent (same-day) relief of obstruction – usually by anterograde percutaneous nephrostomy – and broad-spectrum intravenous antibiotics pending culture results. Early urological input is mandatory.

Further comments

See Section 2.6.2 for details of the approach to making the diagnosis of the specific type of urinary stone and preventive treatment.

1.5.7 Backache and renal impairment

Case history

A 60-year-old man was referred to the medical admissions unit with general malaise and lower backache. On examination he was dehydrated and there was tenderness over his lumbar spine. Initial investigations revealed serum calcium 3.2 mmol/L (normal range 2.20–2.60) and creatinine 275 µmol/L (normal range 60–110).

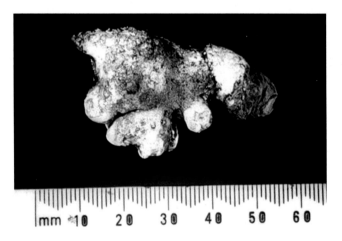

Fig 17 A huge staghorn calculus that was surgically removed. (Courtesy of Dr JE Scoble, Guy's Hospital.)

Introduction

The priorities with hypercalcaemia are to rehydrate the patient, control the hypercalcaemia and establish a diagnosis. The main causes of hypercalcaemia are shown in Table 15. In this case, myeloma seems the most likely diagnosis (Fig 18), but other malignancies with lumbar metastases should also be considered.

History of the presenting problem

Hypercalcaemia can cause many symptoms, as listed in Table 16. Ask about these as they may give a clue as to how long ago problems began.

Key point

Chronically high serum calcium levels cause neurological, GI and renal symptoms (depressive moans, abdominal groans and renal stones).

Other relevant history

Ask in particular about:

> weight loss – a general feature of malignancy

> pointers to a primary tumour, eg haemoptysis, rectal bleeding

> drug history – including over-the-counter medications (antacids and 'white medicine') and vitamin supplements (cod liver oil / vitamin D), which many patients do not regard as drugs.

Examination: general features

As always in an acute context it is vital to make an initial assessment as to how ill the patient is (see Section 1.5.1), but the details given here do not indicate that the patient is likely to be very ill. Note particularly:

> Fluid status – the details given state that the patient is dehydrated, but is there clear evidence of intravascular

Common	Other
Malignancy – myeloma or metastases from solid tumour (eg bronchial, prostate) Primary hyperparathyroidism Sarcoid or other granulomatous conditions	CKD with tertiary hyperparathyroidism Vitamin-D excess Thiazide diuretics Immobilisation Thyrotoxicosis

Table 15   Causes of hypercalcaemia

CKD, chronic kidney disease.

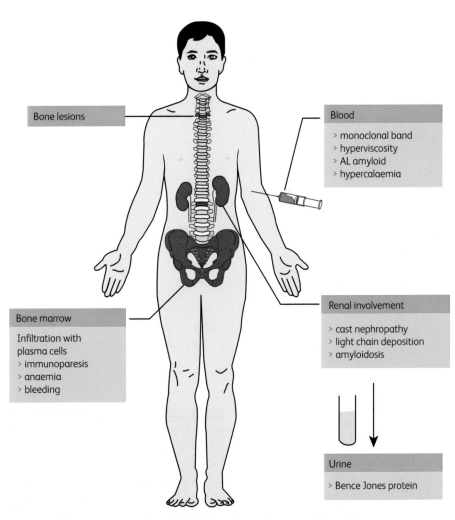

Fig 18 Clinical features of myeloma. This figure illustrates the different ways in which myeloma can affect the patient. AL, amyloid light-chain.

volume depletion (postural drop in BP and low JVP) and/or dehydration (reduced skin turgor and dry mucous membranes / axillae)?

> Evidence of malignancy, in particular – are any lymph nodes palpable? Are there any chest signs? Feel carefully

for any abdominal mass or hepatomegaly, and do not forget rectal examination for rectal or prostate malignancy. Look for localised bone deformity or tenderness. In a woman, perform a breast examination.

Table 16   Symptoms and signs of hypercalcaemia

	Symptom	Sign
Neurological	Drowsiness Lethargy Weakness Depression	Coma
GI	Constipation Nausea Vomiting Anorexia Peptic ulceration	
Renal	Nephrogenic diabetes insipidus and dehydration Urinary stones	Nephrocalcinosis / urinary stone
Cardiac		Shortening of the QT interval, sometimes with broad T waves and atrioventricular block
Others		Corneal calcification Tissue calcification may be detectable radiographically

GI, gastrointestinal.

Key point

Hypercalcaemia increases urinary sodium and water loss – this causes dehydration and a fall in glomerular filtration rate (GFR), which further reduces urinary calcium excretion.

Investigation

Blood and urine tests

> FBC and blood film: is there anaemia? Are there rouleaux suggesting myeloma? See Fig 19.

> Electrolytes and creatinine (to monitor for deterioration or improvement).

> Bone function tests and parathyroid hormone (PTH) – both to monitor calcium levels and look for causes (PTH will be suppressed by any cause of hypercalcaemia other than hyperparathyroidism, when it will be high or inappropriately – given hypercalcaemia – at the upper limit of the normal range).

> Liver function tests (may give clue to malignancy).

> Screening tests for myeloma – immunoglobulins, serum and urinary electrophoresis (looking for monoclonal band in serum – found in 97% of patients with myeloma, Bence Jones protein in urine, and immune paresis – all suggesting

myeloma), plus serum free light chains (SFLCs) (3% of patients have non-secretory myeloma, when the monoclonal protein can be detected by SFLC assay only, and levels are useful to monitor response to treatment once myeloma diagnosed).

> Serum ACE (if sarcoid is suspected).

> Dip the urine and ask for microscopy looking for casts.

> Septic screen (blood, urine, inflammatory markers) if indicated.

Imaging
Depending on your clinical findings, imaging may be used to investigate for causes of hypercalcaemia (eg chest radiograph for lung primary and bony secondaries), or for consequences (CT for urinary stones and nephrocalcinosis). Begin with simple investigations such as an ultrasound of the renal tract and chest radiograph, but most patients will require further imaging for both diagnosis and staging of disease, unless there is a clear non-malignant cause (eg hyperparathyroidism).

Other investigations, as clinically indicated
Examination of bone marrow: should be performed in all patients suspected of

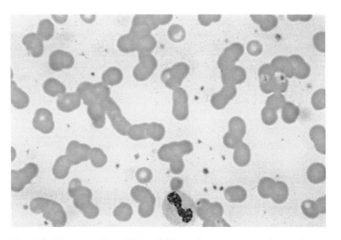

Fig 19 The peripheral blood film of a patient with myeloma. The red blood cells have formed stacks known as rouleaux. (Courtesy of Dr JA Amess, St Bartholomew's Hospital.)

myeloma – including aspiration and biopsy, to diagnose (excess plasma cells, see Fig 20) and stage (with immunophenotyping, fluorescence *in situ* hybridisation and cytogenetics).

Plain radiographic or CT skeletal survey: assist diagnostic evaluation in suspected myeloma.

Renal biopsy: sometimes appropriate in myeloma with renal impairment to provide additional diagnostic information, plus establish the nature and chronicity of damage, and hence the potential for reversibility.

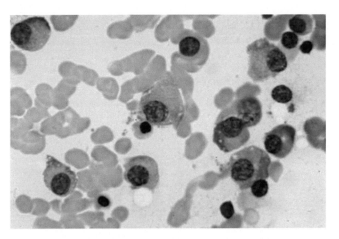

Fig 20 Bone marrow appearances in myeloma. There are multiple nucleated plasma cells infiltrating the bone marrow. (Courtesy of Dr JA Amess, St Bartholomew's Hospital.)

Key point

Hypercalcaemia and myeloma

> Hypercalcaemia occurs in about 25% of patients with myeloma.

> Myeloma cells secrete osteoclast mobilising and stimulating cytokines, and osteoclasts secrete interleukin 6, which is a growth factor for myeloma cells.

> Bone destruction is caused by osteoclasts related to collections of myeloma cells.

> Osteoblastic activity is reduced, so bone scans are usually negative in myeloma. If there is doubt about the extent of bony disease, then CT, positron emission tomography (PET)/CT or magnetic resonance imaging (MRI) can be useful.

Management

Fluid

Whatever the cause of hypercalcaemia, initial management is to correct volume depletion while carefully monitoring the patient and their urine output (UO) to ensure that you do not overload them in the (relatively unlikely) event that their renal function does not pick up with volume expansion.

> Correct volume depletion – this may require several litres of intravenous 0.9% saline: give 1 L over 1–2 hours and then reassess clinically; repeat until signs of hypovolaemia have been corrected (no postural drop in BP and JVP easily seen).

> Consider giving a loop diuretic (eg furosemide 40–80 mg IV) to increase urinary volume and calcium excretion if UO is <100 mL/hour (probably of little benefit if the patient is polyuric).

After restoration of circulating volume, further fluid management should be dictated by urinary output.

> UO satisfactory (>100 mL/hour) – ensure that fluid input (oral or intravenous) is enough to sustain a UO of 3 L/day, but monitor this closely and reduce input if UO not maintained.

> UO not satisfactory – this indicates that volume depletion is not the sole explanation for renal impairment (pre-renal acute kidney injury (AKI) and other pathological processes are involved (eg myeloma kidney, acute tubular necrosis (ATN) or urinary obstruction) and further investigations are required.

Key point

Fluid management in the patient with renal impairment

> Ensure adequate filling – no volume depletion (no postural BP drop, no low JVP) and no volume overload (breathless, high JVP and basal crackles).

> Give input equal to all measured outputs plus 500–1,000 mL/day for insensible losses.

> Examine patient at least once a day for signs of volume depletion or overload and adjust input as appropriate.

> Check electrolytes, calcium and renal function at least daily to assess response.

Other treatments for hypercalcaemia

If the patient's serum calcium remains very high (<3.0 mmol/L) or they continue to be symptomatic from hypercalcaemia, further therapy for hypercalcaemia might include bisphosphonates or steroids.

> Bisphosphonates – the P–O–P bond of pyrophosphate is cleaved by

a phosphatase during bone mineralisation and in osteoclastic bone resorption. Bisphosphonates contain a P–C–P bond that is resistant to cleavage; they bind tightly to any calcified bone matrix, impairing both mineralisation and resorption. Zoledronate (4 mg over 15 minutes) or pamidronate (60–90 mg slowly) are commonly used to treat hypercalcaemia, but require 2–4 days for full effect.

> Steroids, eg prednisolone 20 mg daily – are very effective in hypercalcaemia caused by sarcoidosis but may be of more limited use in hypercalcaemia caused by vitamin-D intoxication or myeloma. They reduce calcium absorption in the gut, reduce the production of osteoclast-activating cytokines and can induce tumour lysis. They usually take 1–2 days to act.

Management of myeloma
Note that patients requiring long-term dialysis for myeloma-associated end-stage renal failure (ESRF) have a poor prognosis, but newer treatments, such as bortezomib, can improve outcomes.

Further comments

Does renal impairment need investigation if there is hypercalcaemia? If renal impairment does not completely correct with rehydration and other measures to lower the serum calcium, then it is essential to try to find out why. See Section 1.5.2 for further discussion, but the key elements are:

> Dipstick of urine and urine microscopy – proteinuria and haematuria would almost certainly indicate kidney myeloma, but could also indicate another renal inflammatory lesion, eg malignancy-associated glomerulonephritis.

> Renal ultrasonography – what is the renal size? Is there obstruction?

> Daily check of fluid input, UO and patient weight – with appropriate fluid management to ensure that the patient does not become fluid deplete or volume overloaded.

> Daily measurement of renal function and serum calcium.

1.5.8 Renal impairment and coma

Case history
A 34-year-old man was found collapsed at home 18 hours after spending a night on a drinking binge with friends. He was brought in to the resuscitation room. No other history was available.

Examination

Your initial assessment as for anyone in coma:

> Airway, Breathing and Circulation (ABC).

> Disability (neurological assessment) – Glasgow Coma Scale (GCS) and pupillary responses. Blood glucose measurement.

> Exposure – signs of injury, muscle damage, needle marks, chronic disease?

This assessment revealed:

> airway is patent; he is breathing spontaneously with a respiratory rate of 12 breaths per minute; and his arterial oxygen saturation, measured by pulse oximetry, is 97% on room air

> heart rate 120 beats per minute, with BP 87/45 mmHg

> GCS 10/15 – eyes 2, voice 3 and motor 5 = total 10/15

> pupils – normal size, equal and reactive.

> blood glucose – 5.6 mmol/L.

What is your next step? ABCD is followed by E, Exposure – make a thorough examination of the patient, which reveals that he:

> looks dehydrated

> has tender, tense swelling of the right arm: the hand is discoloured but warm with palpable pulses (Fig 21).

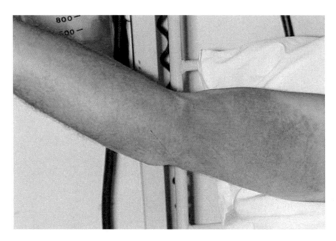

Fig 21 Swollen arm caused by muscle damage. If ischaemic compression is suspected, an urgent orthopaedic opinion should be sought as fasciotomy or debridement may be limb saving.

More information becomes available:

> He is catheterised by one of the nursing staff and passes a small quantity of dark-brown urine.

> The laboratory phones through the results of urgent blood tests, which demonstrate potassium 7.2 mmol/L (normal range 3.5–4.9), urea 15 mmol/L (normal range 2.5–7.0), creatinine 430 µmol/L (normal range 60–110), phosphate 3.6 mmol/L (normal range 0.8–1.4) and corrected calcium 1.85 mmol/L (normal range 2.20–2.60).

The diagnosis is clear – rhabdomyolysis is responsible for his renal impairment, with muscle breakdown originating from the right arm, which was injured by ischaemic compression during his coma. The electrolyte results are typical: hyperkalaemia, hypocalcaemia and hyperphosphataemia. The causes of rhabdomyolysis are shown in Table 17: excess alcohol and drug overdose are common contributors, as seems very likely in this case.

Key point
Rhabdomyolysis

> Suspect it in unexplained acute kidney injury (AKI), particularly if associated with coma.

> Look carefully for evidence of muscle damage or limb ischaemia.

Investigation

As in Section 1.5.1, with particular note of:

> ECG – hyperkalaemia is often severe in AKI associated with rhabdomyolysis.

> Urine dipstick and microscopy – with rhabdomyolysis the urine looks brown (like a cola drink) and registers strongly positive for haem on stick testing, although there are no red cells visible on microscopy.

Table 17	Causes of rhabdomyolysis	
Frequency	**Cause**	**Example**
Common	Crush injury	Trauma or coma with compression
	Ischaemic injury	Femoral artery thrombosis or embolism
	Prolonged epileptic fits	
	Severe exercise	
	Snake bite (commonest cause in some parts of the world)	
Rare	Infections	Viral necrotising myositis and coxsackievirus
	Inflammatory myopathies	Polymyositis
	Metabolic myopathies	McArdle's syndrome
	Malignant hyperpyrexia	Statins
	Drugs	
	Hypothyroidism	

> Creatine kinase – measure whenever rhabdomyolysis is suspected: a grossly elevated value (>10,000 U/L, with a normal upper limit of 180–200 U/L) establishes the diagnosis, a less elevated value is consistent with it but not diagnostic.

> Arterial blood gases – metabolic acidosis is expected.

> Toxicology – in the comatose patient and/or where drug overdose is a possibility.

Key point
> In rhabdomyolysis serum potassium rises rapidly and can be life-threatening.

> Phosphate rises rapidly and calcium is usually low.

> Creatinine kinase is massively elevated, as are other muscle enzymes (aminotransferase and lactate dehydrogenase (LDH)).

Management

Close clinical monitoring – aside from regular checks of vital signs and urine output (UO), keep a careful watch on the arm. Apart from the swollen, tender muscles, examination should look for distal neurovascular compromise: skin colour and temperature, capillary refill, pulses and sensation (if and when the patient regains consciousness).

Close biochemical monitoring – regular measurement (at least every 12 hours) of electrolytes and renal function tests. Hyperkalaemia can develop rapidly in this context.

The following are the immediate issues:

> standard measures to manage the unconscious patient

> initial management of hyperkalaemia (see Section 1.5.1)

> monitor hourly UO (via urinary catheter)

> aggressive fluid resuscitation to correct intravascular volume depletion, with the aim of achieving a UO of >100 mL/hour (as described in Section 1.5.7)

> get surgical/orthopaedic help quickly – urgent fasciotomy or debridement may be needed to treat compartment syndrome and save the ischaemic limb – compartment syndrome refers to ischaemic compression, created by swelling within a muscle group that is constrained by fascial planes and resulting in necrosis of the muscle with or without compromise of the distal limb circulation.

Further comments

What about urinary alkalinisation?

Myoglobin is more soluble in alkaline urine (pH >6.5) and urinary alkalinisation has frequently been used in patients with rhabdomyolysis. This is achieved by intravenous infusion of isotonic (1.26%) sodium bicarbonate as part of the fluid regimen, but there is no controlled trial evidence that this is better than resuscitation and maintenance of diuresis with 0.9% saline. However, bicarbonate infusion can worsen both hypocalcaemia and fluid overload, and is best reserved for hyperkalaemic, volume-replete patients with an adequate UO, who are closely monitored on high-dependency units with access to regular electrolyte assessment, eg with an arterial line for blood gases.

When does the patient need dialysis?

Standard indications for dialysis apply (see Section 1.5.1), but note that metabolic disturbances can worsen more rapidly in patients with rhabdomyolysis than with other sorts of AKI, so consult renal services sooner rather than later. Dialysis does not remove myoglobin, so cannot treat the underlying cause, just the metabolic disturbance.

Who should be investigated for an underlying muscle disorder?

An underlying muscle disorder should be considered if the patient presents without a clear precipitant, if there is a preceding history of increasing or intermittent muscle fatigue, or if there is a clinical picture suggestive of an inflammatory process. Diagnosis is usually by muscle biopsy.

2 Diseases and treatments

2.1 Major renal syndromes

2.1.1 Acute kidney injury

Abnormal renal function, identified by a rising creatinine or oliguria (<0.5 mL/kg/hour), is frequent and caused by a wide range of processes. The term acute kidney injury (AKI) rather than acute renal failure is now used because small decrements in kidney function that do not result in 'failure' are still of clinical importance and associated with increased morbidity and mortality. AKI leads to electrolyte imbalance (most notably hyperkalaemia, which can be fatal), retention of urea and other toxic waste products, fluid retention and acidosis.

Aetiology/pathophysiology

AKI can be caused by a problem anywhere from the renal artery to the urethra. It is useful to classify on the basis of where the principal problem is – pre-renal (or volume dependent), renal or post-renal (Fig 22).

Epidemiology

Transient renal dysfunction occurs in up to 5% of hospital admissions, and 5–20% critically ill hospital patients. In the UK, severe AKI (a reversible increase in creatinine >500 µmol/L) has an incidence of about 140 per million members of the population per year.

Clinical presentation

Usually AKI is diagnosed on the basis of rising plasma creatinine, or when oliguria develops in a patient whose urine output (UO) is being monitored reliably (eg catheterised). Sometimes the presentation will be a direct

consequence of the renal failure (eg fluid overload or acidosis), but usually features of the underlying condition predominate.

Immediate consideration must be given to whether dialysis (or another intervention) is required urgently. A circulatory assessment is essential. The medication chart should be reviewed to ensure that any nephrotoxic medication is stopped and that drug dosages are appropriate for the degree of renal impairment.

In glomerulonephritis, there may be a nephritic presentation – meaning the combination of oliguria, hypertension, oedema and haematuria.

Key point

Renal failure does not usually cause specific symptoms. Have a high index of suspicion for any patients who are unwell for any reason (especially those who have risk factors for AKI such as those with chronic kidney disease (CKD), diabetes, hypertension, heart failure and sepsis). You should have a low threshold for measuring plasma creatinine.

Investigations

To assess severity/danger, the following are appropriate in all cases of AKI:

> serum potassium and ECG (hyperkalaemia)

> blood gases (PO_2 and pH; oxygenation and acidosis)

> chest radiograph (pulmonary oedema and others).

To determine the cause of the renal failure check the following:

> examine the urine (urine dip for blood, protein (if present may indicate intrinsic renal disease), signs of infection)

> renal ultrasonography (exclude obstruction)

> obtain results of any previous blood tests to prove that renal impairment is acute

> further investigations will be guided by the clinical setting. Some cases of AKI will merit renal biopsy to establish the diagnosis, especially if an intrinsic renal cause is suspected, eg glomerulonephritis or vasculitis. In these cases, it is imperative to seek specialist nephrological opinion early.

Note the following points about specific diagnoses:

> Acute tubular necrosis (ATN) – often the cause of AKI is pre-renal/ATN. A renal biopsy will be performed only if there is doubt about the diagnosis.

> Obstructive uropathy will usually be diagnosed on ultrasonography, but be aware that obstruction does not always cause hydronephrosis, eg if there is rapid onset of obstructive uropathy, especially if the patient is volume deplete, or if the kidneys are encased (eg retroperitoneal malignancy). Consider plain abdominal CT if the history fits with obstruction but this is not evident on ultrasound.

> Suspected renovascular disease / occlusion or renal vein thrombosis – magnetic resonance angiography or CT renal angiography is the preferred investigation if a case of renal failure might be the result of a renal artery

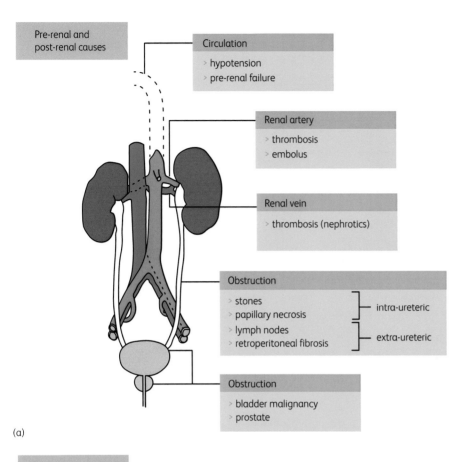

(a)

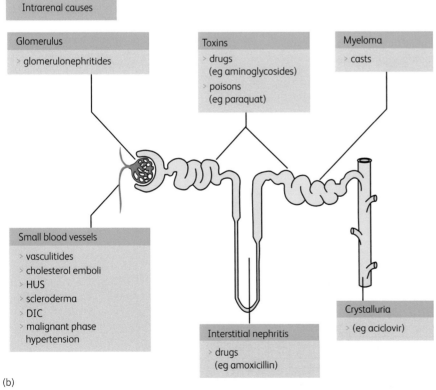

(b)

Fig 22 Selected causes of acute kidney injury **(a)** pre-renal and post-renal; **(b)** intrarenal. DIC, disseminated intravascular coagulation; HUS, haemolytic–uraemic syndrome.

occlusion/stenosis or renal vein thrombosis (usually in a patient with nephrotic syndrome).

> Blood tests will be helpful in certain settings, and in some circumstances will mean that a biopsy is not required, eg haemolytic–uraemic syndrome (HUS), disseminated intravascular coagulation and rhabdomyolysis.

AKI scoring systems

RIFLE criteria (2004): state that changes should have occurred within the past 7 days.

> Risk: serum creatinine increased to >1.5 × baseline, or glomerular filtration rate (GFR) fall by >25%, or UO <0.5 mL/kg/hour for 6 hours.

> Injury: serum creatinine increased to >2 × baseline, or GFR fall by >50%, or UO <0.5 mL/kg/hour for 12 hours.

> Failure: serum creatinine increased to >3 × baseline, or GFR fall by >75%, or UO <0.3 mL/kg/hour for 24 hours, or anuria for 12 hours.

> Loss: complete loss of kidney function for 4 weeks.

> End-stage renal disease: loss of function for 3 months.

> This has been correlated with prognosis – a systemic review showed a stepwise increase in the relative risk of death from 2.4 to 4.15 to 6.37 through risk to failure, respectively.

The Kidney Disease: Improving Global Outcomes (KDIGO) guidelines (2012) included the Acute Kidney Injury Network (AKIN) scoring criteria.

> Stage 1: Increase in creatinine to 1.5–1.9 × baseline, or increase in serum creatinine by >0.3 mg/dL (26.5 µmol/L), or reduction in UO to <0.5 mL/kg/hour for 6–12 hours.

> Stage 2: Increase in creatinine by 2.0–2.9 × baseline, or reduction in UO to <0.5 mL/kg/hour for 12 hours.

> Stage 3: Increase in creatinine by 3 × baseline, or increase to >4 mg/dL (353.6 µmol/L), or reduction in UO <0.3 mL/kg/hour for 24 hours, or anuria for 12 hours or initiation of renal replacement therapy (RRT).

Future scoring systems may well include the use of biomarkers that are currently in development.

Treatment

Urgent attention is given to maintaining oxygenation and circulation. Determine whether immediate renal replacement is required.

Key point

Indications for RRT

> hyperkalaemia (K^+ >6.5 mmol/L) – seriousness best evaluated by ECG (Fig 23)

> fluid overload not responsive to diuretic

> acidosis

> generally if urea >40 mmol/L (certainly if >50 mmol/L)

> uraemic encephalopathy.

Key point

AKI is frequently a manifestation of a very serious systemic illness. Sometimes – for instance, in the setting of disseminated malignancy – dialysis is technically feasible but may not be appropriate.

Supportive treatment

> optimise the circulation (if the lungs are clear on auscultation give fluid rapidly as boluses until the JVP is seen easily, then stop and review the situation)

> treat infection

> avoid further renal insults (eg hypotension and nephrotoxic drugs)

> exclude obstruction – catheterise

> monitor fluid balance (input/output charts and daily weighing)

> monitor renal function: biochemistry and UO

> maintain nutrition (enteral or parenteral if necessary)

> renal replacement if necessary.

Treat underlying cause
See individual diagnoses in Sections 2.3–2.7.

Prognosis

If a patient has single organ failure, mortality is 10%. This rises to 50% in the context of multi-organ failure requiring ICU admission. If a patient with multi-organ failure requires RRT, mortality approaches 80%. It is imperative to recognise and treat AKI early.

Prevention of AKI

Care should be taken to try and prevent AKI. Simple measures should include:

> recognising 'at risk' groups – older patients, diabetics, patients with cardiac failure

> pre-emptively stopping potentially nephrotoxic (or at least non-beneficial) medications – eg ACE inhibitors, ARBs, diuretics, NSAIDs, other antihypertensives – when patients are unwell (eg gastroenteritis, pneumonia) – and when admitted for elective procedures (eg major surgery, angiography)

> measuring renal function proactively in 'at-risk' patients when unwell.

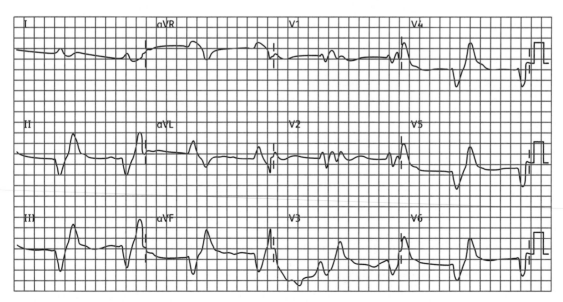

Fig 23 An electrocardiogram (ECG) showing changes of severe hyperkalaemia. Widened QRS complexes slur into tall, tented T waves. There are no P waves. Cardiac arrest will occur soon if appropriate action is not taken immediately (see Section 1.5.1).

2.1.2 Chronic kidney disease

Chronic kidney disease (CKD) is the irreversible loss of glomerular filtration rate (GFR). This is important for two main reasons:

> There may be direct consequences of impaired renal function.

> Loss of GFR tends to be progressive, ultimately leading to end-stage renal failure (ESRF).

Normal young adults have a much higher GFR (approximately 10-fold) than that needed for life, so substantial decrements in GFR often cause few (if any) symptoms.

Key point

Do not dismiss a slightly elevated creatinine level as a minor problem.
In CKD, lost nephrons cannot be recovered and an elevated creatinine score represents a loss of about 50% of the GFR.

Aetiology/pathophysiology

Diverse primary processes result in the loss of GFR (see Sections 2.3–2.7). The following are the most common causes in the UK:

> diabetes mellitus

> glomerulonephritides (most common is IgA nephropathy)

> congenital dysplasia / chronic pyelonephritis / reflux nephropathy

> obstructive uropathy

> autosomal dominant polycystic kidney disease

> vascular disease / hypertension.

Loss of renal function tends to be progressive, probably from the following:

> continuing loss of nephrons from the primary process (eg glomerulonephritis)

> glomerular hypertension in remaining glomeruli – this increases GFR per nephron, but in doing so leads to loss of further nephrons (the hyperfiltration hypothesis).

Epidemiology

Around 6–7% of the UK population have CKD stages III–V. The prevalence is likely higher as the condition is often underdiagnosed. Normal GFR in the population varies with age (Fig 24), falling as patients get older. Although muscle bulk (and thus creatinine production) also decreases with age, the normal range for plasma creatinine remains the same. An elevated creatinine will be outside the normal range of GFR at any age, and usually represents a loss of about 50% of GFR. In older people, a slightly elevated creatinine may represent a GFR of only 30 mL/min. In 18–25-year-olds, the prevalence of CKD stage III is <1%, but in those over 75 years this rises to 30–35%. CKD is more likely to be recognised in older people as they are more likely to present to health services (due to higher levels of morbidity) and so have blood tests.

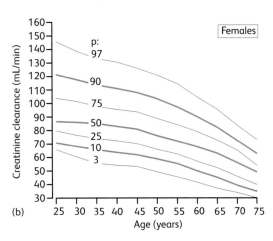

Fig 24 Percentiles (p:) of creatinine clearances according to age and sex, calculated using the method of Cockcroft and Gault. (Redrawn from Elseviers MM *et al. Lancet* 1987;i:457.)

Table 18 Stages of chronic kidney disease (CKD[1]) as defined in the American Kidney Diseases Outcome Quality Initiative (KDOQI)

CKD stage	Definition: GFR mL/min/1.73 m^2	Interventions
I	≥90 with urinary markers or imaging indicating kidney damage	Control blood pressure and cardiovascular risk factors
II[2]	60–89 with urinary markers or imaging indicating kidney damage	Control blood pressure and cardiovascular risk factors
III	30–59	Control blood pressure and cardiovascular risk factors
IV	15–30	Plan for RRT if appropriate; likely to need erythropoietin, dietary restriction of phosphate and potassium, and vitamin-D analogue
V	≤14	Likely need to commence RRT (or conservative management if RRT is inappropriate)

1 'Chronic' is defined as markers of kidney damage or GFR <60 mL/min/1.73 m^2 persisting for at least 3 months. In all cases consideration should be given to identifying any potentially treatable cause of continuing renal damage (eg systemic vasculitis and tubulointerstitial nephritis).
2 Note that a patient should *not* be described as having CKD stage II just on the basis of having a GFR in the range 60–89 mL/min/1.73 m^2.
CKD, chronic kidney disease; GFR, glomerular filtration rate; RRT, renal replacement therapy.

Investigation and interventions need to be considered in those who are outside the normal range for GFR and have risk factors for progression (hypertension or proteinuria), or when renal function is changing – even if the absolute value lies within the normal range (Table 18). Prevention of progression is clearly most effective if started early, well before there are any symptoms attributable to renal failure.

Presentation

> Most often with the incidental finding of a raised creatinine, abnormal urinalysis or hypertension.

> Sometimes with symptoms related to underlying process (eg haematuria or outflow obstruction).

> Symptoms/findings attributable to loss of renal function are often present in those with more severe renal impairment, but they are relatively non-specific, eg fatigue, anaemia and disturbed taste.

> A significant number of patients will have previously unrecognised ESRF at presentation.

Hazard

Signs and symptoms pointing to chronic renal impairment rather than AKI are commonly quoted but are very unreliable. Assume that any patient has acute (ie potentially reversible) renal impairment until you can prove that it is chronic – for example by finding a blood test showing a similar level of renal function months or years previously, or reduced renal size.

Key point

Symptoms attributable to loss of renal function usually only occur when there is severe renal impairment (GFR <25 mL/min). This has two implications:

> check creatinine in high-risk populations (people with diabetes or hypertension, or those with protein or blood on a dipstick test)

> in patients with moderately elevated creatinine (<300 mmol/L), symptoms need another explanation.

Investigations

To guide interventions
Check bloods:

> biochemistry (potassium, creatinine, calcium and phosphate)

> haematological parameters.

Identify cause of renal impairment
If possible identify the cause of renal impairment, especially treatable conditions. All patients should have:

> urinalysis and microscopy

> urinary albumin:creatinine ratio (ACR) (if dipstick urinalysis demonstrates proteinuria)

> renal ultrasonography.

Further tests are guided by these and the probable underlying cause in the particular patient. The choice of tests is also influenced by whether or not a treatable condition could be identified.

> Autoimmune screen (ANA, dsDNA, C3/4, ANCA, anti-GBM antibodies, ESR, rheumatoid factor) – indicated in those with symptoms of vasculitis or autoimmune disorders.

> Myeloma screen – appropriate in older patients with proteinuria (Fig 25).

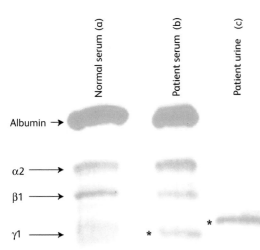

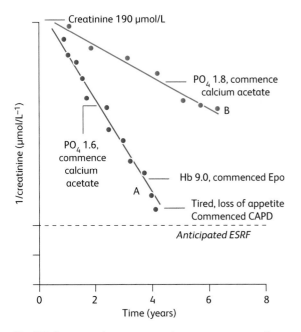

Fig 25 Electrophoretic analysis of proteins in serum and urine. In the normal serum sample **(a)** there is a broad gamma band containing IgA, IgG and IgM. In the sample from the patient **(b)**, there is a monoclonal band (indicated by *), which is an IgG κ paraprotein. In the urine **(c)**, there is a band which represents free κ light chain. (Courtesy of Dr S Marshall, Oxford Radcliffe Hospitals.)

Fig 26 Reciprocal creatinine plots against time for two patients with progressive chronic renal failure disease (CRF). Patient A had IgA nephropathy with protein excretion 3 g/24 hours. Patient B had autosomal dominant polycystic kidney disease. CAPD, continuous ambulatory peritoneal dialysis; Epo, erythropoietin; ESRF, end-stage renal failure.

> Renal biopsy – likely to be indicated in patients with normal-size, unobstructed kidneys without scars; by contrast, patients with small kidneys (ie <9 cm in length) should usually not be biopsied – the hazards are substantial and little useful information can be obtained.

Hazard

Misleading elevation of serum creatinine

Some drugs (eg trimethoprim and cimetidine) decrease creatinine secretion, causing a reversible rise in plasma creatinine, which can be mistaken for deterioration in renal function.

Key point

Plotting progress of CKD

Often a reciprocal plot of creatinine against time is linear (Fig 26), representing a constant rate of loss of GFR. This plot is useful in:

> predicting when ESRF is likely to be reached

> seeing whether a new value of creatinine is consistent with the expected trend. If a new value indicates a faster than expected deterioration, it may prompt a search for another cause (eg prostatic obstruction, urinary tract infection (UTI) or an NSAID).

Complications and treatment

Aims are to:

> prevent the progression of CKD

> prevent secondary complications.

Where possible, the underlying cause of the renal damage should be treated or corrected (eg myeloma, systemic lupus erythematosus (SLE)).

Progression of CKD

As stated previously, irrespective of cause, there is a tendency for CKD to progress.

Key point

The amount of proteinuria correlates well with the risk of progression of CKD (Fig 27).

Many interventions alter the course of CKD in animal models, but antihypertensives, in particular ACE inhibitors and angiotensin-receptor blockers (ARBs), are the only treatment that has been proved to influence the progression of CKD in convincing clinical trials in humans (see below).

In diabetics, good glycaemic control should be encouraged. Successful pancreatic transplantation has been shown to reverse the histological changes of diabetic nephropathy.

Key point

Antihypertensive agents

Diabetes

In the Captopril Diabetes study (1993) 409 patients with type 1 diabetes were randomised to captopril or placebo. Other antihypertensives (but not calcium channel blockers (CCBs) or other ACE inhibitors) could be added. After 4 years of similar blood pressure (BP) control, the group given captopril had a slower rate of increase in plasma creatinine, reduced proteinuria and less likelihood of ESRF or death (combined primary end point). In those with creatinine above 132 µmol/L, the rate of rise in the placebo group was 123 µmol/L/year versus 53 µmol/L/year in the captopril group. Importantly, there was benefit in normotensive patients.

In nephropathy due to type 2 diabetes, two large trials (RENAAL and IDNT) published in 2001 compared ARBs to placebo and showed a benefit beyond BP control with no increase in serious adverse effects.

The DETAIL trial (2004) showed that there was no difference between ACE inhibitor and ARBs in patients with early diabetes, and the ONTARGET trial (2013) showed that there was no benefit to adding ARB to ACE inhibitor treatment and there were increased risks of hypotension, hyperkalaemia and acute need for dialysis.

Non-diabetic chronic renal failure

The Modification of Diet in Renal Disease was a 2 × 2 study of 840 patients that examined the effect of protein restriction; it also compared aggressive and standard BP control. Achieved mean arterial pressure in the groups was 91 and 96 mmHg (corresponding to 125/75 and 130/80, respectively). The benefit was greatest in those with more proteinuria (>3 g/day) and moderate renal impairment (see Fig 27).

Subsequent large randomised trials show that ACE inhibitors offer greater protection of renal function compared to placebo or other antihypertensive agents in patients with significant proteinuria (eg the Ramipril Efficiency In Nephropathy trial) with a 50% reduction in GFR decline in those with >3 g/day proteinuria.

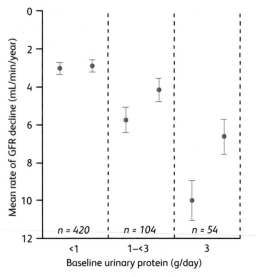

- ● Intensive blood pressure lowering
- ● 'Normal' blood pressure lowering

Fig 27 Rate of loss of renal function (mL/min/year) in a randomised study comparing a target mean arterial pressure of 107 mmHg with one of 92 mmHg. The patients were categorised according to the amount of proteinuria (g/24 hours). GFR, glomerular filtration rate.

Key point

Control of BP

This is the only intervention that has been proved to slow the progression of CKD in humans. In patients with heavy proteinuria (>3 g/24 hours) a BP of 125/75 mmHg can be more beneficial than one of 130/80 mmHg (see Fig 27), but not all studies have confirmed such advantage. The National Institute for Health and Care Excellence (NICE) blood pressure guidelines for CKD suggest a target blood pressure of 140/90 mmHg, reduced to 130/80 mmHg if a patient is diabetic or has a urine ACR >70 mg/mmol.

Hypertension

A high proportion of patients with CRF (80% as ESRF approaches) will have hypertension. Treating hypertension slows CRF progression, especially in those with proteinuria (see above), and is also presumed to reduce cardiovascular risk.

Treatment strategy

When planning, remember:

> Most patients are salt sensitive so it is appropriate to decrease salt intake.

> Many patients will require multiple antihypertensive drugs. The first-choice antihypertensive is an ACE inhibitor (based on animal studies and studies of people with diabetes) – except in those with renovascular disease.

> Loop diuretics (eg furosemide) are useful adjunctive agents, especially if there is evidence of sodium overload.

> In patients with proteinuria >3 g/24 hour or diabetes, the target BP should be <130/80 mmHg.

Hyperkalaemia

Hyperkalaemia will cause symptoms only at near lethal levels. Serum potassium should be monitored by blood tests (not symptoms!) and, acutely, ECG.

Treatment strategy

As follows:

> dietary restriction of potassium intake (Table 19)

> avoid potassium-sparing diuretics

> consider changing from ACE inhibitor / angiotensin receptor antagonist

> correct acidosis with oral sodium bicarbonate

> in diabetes, improve diabetic control

> for emergency management, see Section 1.5.1.

Acidosis

Metabolic acidosis is usually a clinical problem only at or near ESRF, and may contribute to feelings of malaise and breathlessness. It is identified and monitored by measuring venous bicarbonate.

Treatment strategy

Remember:

> to avoid excessive protein intake

> to consider oral sodium bicarbonate, but a sodium load may exacerbate hypertension

> that some patients will need dialysis.

Bone and mineral metabolism

As CKD progresses, phosphate excretion is insufficient and plasma phosphate rises, stimulating parathyroid hormone (PTH) secretion (Fig 28). Also, 1-alpha-hydroxylation of vitamin D (proximal tubule mitochondria) is impaired, which:

> reduces inhibition of PTH secretion (by 1,25-Vit D)

> reduces calcium absorption thus lowering serum calcium, further stimulating PTH.

Consequences of elevated PTH

In normal individuals this produces marked phosphaturia. However, in those with CRF this does not occur and phosphate rises as a result of the increased bone turnover, further stimulating PTH. This results in the following:

> renal osteodystrophy: a complex combination of skeletal abnormalities – this includes osteomalacia which results from the lack of vitamin D and leads to loss of bone mineralisation

> progressive parathyroid hyperplasia, and eventual autonomy

> itching and calcinosis cutis

> pyrophosphate arthropathy.

Treatment strategy

This should include:

> Dietary restriction of phosphate.

> Phosphate binders, eg calcium acetate before food. The use of calcium is often limited by hypercalcaemia. Aluminium compounds are effective, but can cause toxicity as a result of accumulation. These are now rarely used. Sevelamer hydrochloride or carbonate and lanthanum carbonate are relatively new treatments which

Table 19 Foods and drinks high in potassium and some of their alternatives	
Foods and drinks high in potassium	**Alternatives**
Coffee	Tea
Fruit juice	Squashes
Beer, cider, sherry and wine	Spirits
Bananas, grapes and oranges	Apples, pears and satsumas
Chips / French fries and jacket potatoes	Rice and pasta
Baked beans, mushrooms and tomatoes	Carrots, cabbage and lettuce
Chocolate	Boiled sweets
Crisps and nuts	
Salt substitutes (eg Lo Salt)	

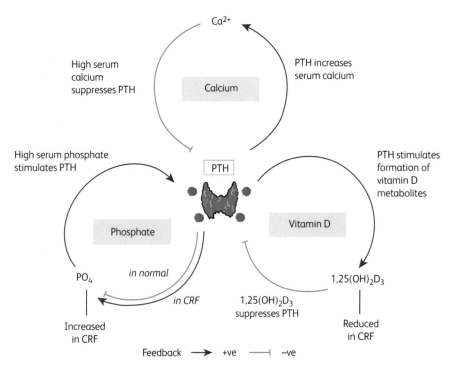

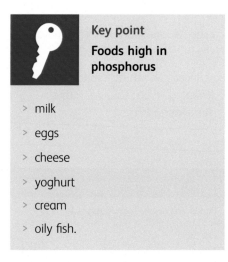

Fig 28 The central role of the parathyroid gland in bone and mineral homeostasis, and the principal effects of chronic renal impairment. CRF, chronic renal failure; PTH, parathyroid hormone.

do not produce a calcium load but they are more expensive. They have equivalent effects on phosphate lowering. Sevelamer is not absorbed and may have positive effects on vascular calcification and bone disease.

> Alfacalcidol or calcitriol: corrects deficiency in activated vitamin D (Fig 29). Its use may be restricted by hypercalcaemia, and it also tends to increase plasma phosphate.

> Cinacalcet (calcium-receptor agonist): stimulates the calcium-sensing receptor, leading to decreased PTH secretion. This is used to treat tertiary hyperparathyroidism when there is loss of responsiveness of PTH to low phosphate and raised calcium.

> Avoidance of oversuppression of PTH, which can lead to adynamic bone disease, hence careful monitoring of PTH is needed.

Key point

Foods high in phosphorus

> milk

> eggs

> cheese

> yoghurt

> cream

> oily fish.

Anaemia

In renal disease, the renal cortical and outer medullary fibroblasts produce less erythropoietin for a given haematocrit. Consequently, the haemoglobin set point falls as GFR falls. The resulting anaemia is normochromic and normocytic (Fig 30). Always consider other contributory factors, eg iron

deficiency or ongoing inflammation. Haematinics should be checked as concomitant vitamin B_{12} or folate deficiency is common. Consequences include fatigue and left ventricular hypertrophy (LVH).

Treat with recombinant erythropoietin, which is usually not necessary until creatinine >400 µmol/L. Aim to maintain haemoglobin 100–120 g/L (higher values are associated with increased cardiovascular mortality).

Cardiovascular risk and LVH

There is a high cardiovascular mortality in those with CKD – even after correction for conventional cardiovascular risk factors such as diabetes, age, sex and race, it is at least 10 times greater than that of the general population once ESRF has been reached. Additional aetiological factors include inflammation, albuminuria, anaemia, vascular calcification and elevated homocysteine.

LVH is an independent risk factor for cardiovascular mortality and, as renal impairment progresses, the percentage of patients with LVH rises to 45% when GFR is <25 mL/min. Major factors are hypertension and anaemia.

Treatment strategy

This should include:

> Attention to other cardiovascular risk factors (smoking cessation, weight loss, exercise, reducing salt intake).

> Aspirin – used as secondary prevention but may increase risk of bleeding.

> Meticulous treatment of hypertension (also important in preventing progression of CKD).

> Lipid-lowering therapy – should be started if the 10-year cardiovascular risk is >20% according to the Joint British Society guidelines. The Study of Heart and Renal Protection (SHARP) trial (2011) showed that

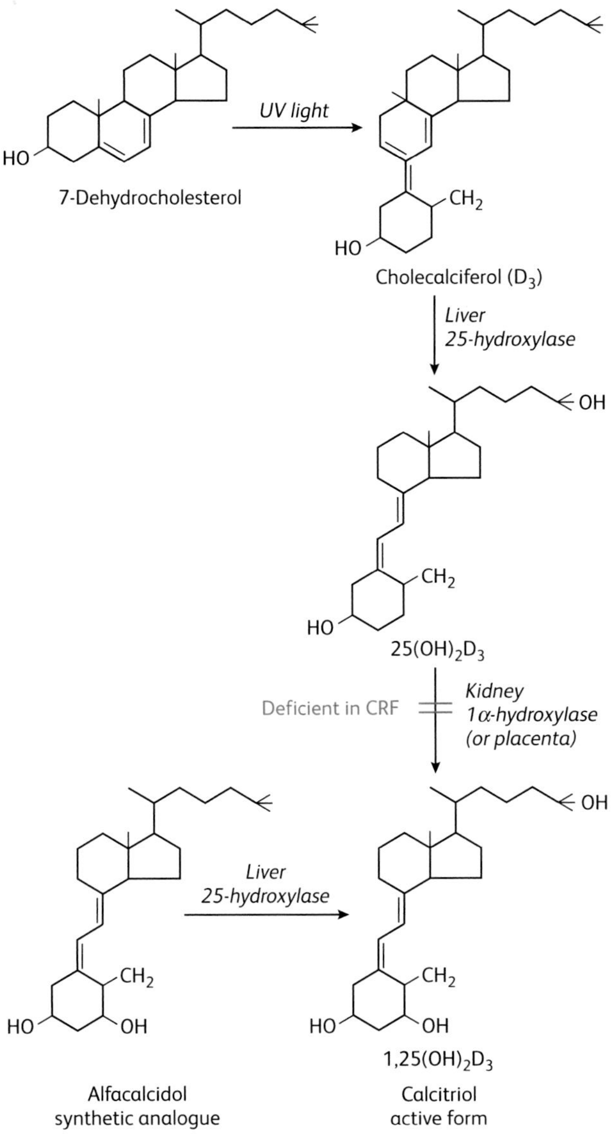

Fig 29 Principal pathway of vitamin D metabolism. Alfacalcidol or calcitriol are used to treat patients with renal impairment.

there was a reduction in major atherosclerotic events in patients with CKD on simvastatin and ezetimibe compared to placebo over 5 years of follow up.

Gout

Gout is common. Reduced urate excretion and diuretics are the major factors. It is often confused with pseudogout (pyrophosphate). Generally treat acute episodes with colchicine or medium-dose oral steroids (avoiding NSAIDs). Prevention with allopurinol (if urate is high or after an episode).

> **!** **Hazard**
> Remember to reduce the dose of allopurinol in those with renal impairment.

Pregnancy in chronic kidney disease

As renal function declines, so does the ability to conceive and to carry a pregnancy successfully. In some women with CKD, pregnancy results in an additional deterioration in renal function superimposed on top of the predicted course of their chronic renal impairment.

The chance of successful fetal outcome and risk to maternal renal function can be stratified on the basis of renal impairment, hypertension and proteinuria. Normal pregnancy is rare with a creatinine >275 µmol/L. See Section 2.7.11 for further discussion.

Drugs

Dose adjustments are required for many medications. Take care to avoid nephrotoxic drugs. If in doubt look in the *British National Formulary* or the *Renal drug handbook*.

> **!** **Hazard**
> Patients on ACE inhibitors, ARBs or diuretics should be informed about 'sick-day rules' – if they become severely unwell or dehydrated, they should stop these medications immediately and seek urgent medical review. A combination of CKD, dehydration and ACE inhibitors / ARBs significantly increases the risk of acute kidney injury (AKI).

Preparation for renal replacement therapy

Once it is clear that the patient will develop ESRF, preparation for renal replacement therapy (RRT) should be made well in advance. Patients should be referred to a multidisciplinary predialysis clinic so that they can receive appropriate information to guide their choice of dialysis modality. They can also have access created in a timely fashion (eg arteriovenous fistula (AVF)). Transplant assessment should be considered early in appropriate patients as this could take place pre-emptively prior to commencing RRT (within 6 months of the need for dialysis).

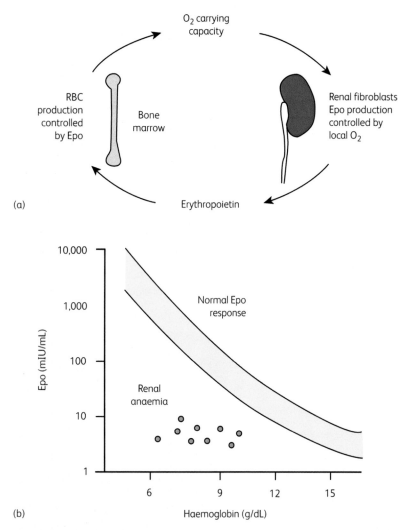

(a)

(b)

Fig 30 (a) Control of erythropoietin secretion. **(b)** Patients with renal impairment (red dots) have a relative deficiency in erythropoietin secretion, with reduced levels of circulating erythropoietin compared to the normal response for a given level of haemoglobin. Epo, erythropoietin; RBC, red blood cell.

Prognosis

The effect of CKD on morbidity and mortality is uncertain. The tendency to progress correlates closely with the following:

> the amount of proteinuria

> the amount of interstitial damage on the renal biopsy

> it is higher in men than in women.

The likelihood of ESRF obviously increases as functional reserve decreases. The most useful guide is the trend in eGFR.

2.1.3 End-stage renal failure

End-stage renal failure (ESRF) is the point at which an individual's renal function is no longer sufficient for normal life as a result of an irreversible loss of renal function, ie the point at which renal replacement therapy (RRT) should be commenced (if appropriate for the patient).

Aetiology/pathophysiology/pathology

At a certain level of glomerular filtration rate (GFR), the accumulation of molecules that are usually excreted by the kidney reaches a level at which they prevent or endanger normal physiological functions. The principal problems are:

> potassium

> salt and water

> hydrogen ions

> uraemic toxins.

The term 'uraemic toxins' refers to the vast numbers of chemicals that accumulate in the blood as the kidneys fail. Urea and creatinine are the two measured in clinical practice, but they do not correlate very strongly with uraemic symptoms (those made better by dialysis). Older people and those with less muscle mass will have a lower GFR for any given creatinine than is normal, and will reach ESRF with a lower creatinine (eg 450 µmol/L as opposed to 850 µmol/L).

> **Hazard**
>
> As patients approach ESRF, they frequently become malnourished because of loss of appetite, resulting in muscle wasting and deceptively low creatinine. The correct treatment is dialysis and attention to nutrition.

Epidemiology

The take-on rate for RRT in the UK is approximately 110 per million population (pmp) per year. The prevalence has increased over the past few years, with a rate of 888 pmp in 2013 compared to 523 pmp in 2000. The mean prevalent age has also increased from 58.4 in 2013 compared to 55 in 2000. There is an increasingly older population on dialysis, with those over the age of 70 accounting for 25%

in 2013 compared to 19.2% in 2000. Given that these patients often have other significant comorbidities they are rarely suitable for transplantation and so are often on dialysis for the rest of their lives. ESRF is much more common in older than in young people, but the relative risk of death on RRT is much higher in the younger population – 28.6 × that of the general population in 30–34-year-olds, but only 2.7 × over the age of 85. Causes are the same as for chronic kidney disease (CKD) – the most common are diabetes, glomerulonephritis and hypertension.

Clinical presentation

Symptoms are sensitive, but not very specific:

> tiredness and difficulty concentrating

> loss of appetite

> nausea and vomiting

> shortness of breath (fluid overload)

> pruritus.

If these symptoms are present in a patient with a creatinine above 450 μmol/L, serious consideration should be given to commencing dialysis unless there is another cause (eg anaemia contributing to tiredness). In severe/late cases, presentation may be with pericarditis, uraemic encephalopathy or neuropathy. In other instances, the need for dialysis will be precipitated by acidosis, hyperkalaemia or fluid overload resistant to diuretics and sodium restriction.

Key point
Monitoring patients with renal impairment as they approach ESRF should enable them to have access created in a timely manner and be commenced on dialysis at a time when symptoms are minimal, but they will feel a clear benefit.

Key point
Early referral to a renal unit enables emphasis to be placed on delaying the progression to ESRF, avoiding complications, and making the appropriate physical and psychological preparations for RRT.

Physical signs

> Commonly, there are no physical signs when a patient reaches ESRF.

> Signs of fluid overload may be present.

> Less commonly, pericardial rub or metabolic flap may be present.

> Peripheral neuropathy, uraemic frost and fits are rare.

Investigations

> Identify the cause of the renal damage if possible (as for CKD).

> Establish that the diagnosis is CKD: look for small scarred kidneys on ultrasonography with loss of corticomedullary differentiation and evidence of previous renal impairment. If kidneys are normal size and not obstructed, a renal biopsy will usually be indicated.

> Consider whether there is a reversible factor causing acute-on-chronic renal failure: volume depletion or hypotension, nephrotoxic drugs (eg NSAIDs), or prostatic obstruction.

> Test for hepatitis B and C, and HIV: potentially infectious patients will require special dialysis arrangements. Those not already immune should be immunised against hepatitis B.

Treatment

> Commence RRT – if the need is urgent, haemodialysis will usually be used initially but peritoneal dialysis can also be used.

> If there is cardiovascular instability, haemofiltration may be preferred to begin with, which is usually available only in a high-dependency setting.

> Emergency treatment for hyperkalaemia (see Section 1.5.1) may be indicated pending transfer for dialysis.

Key point
It is unwise to defer dialysis – if in doubt, dialyse first and ask questions later.

Key point
It is important to appreciate that dialysis is equivalent only to a low level of GFR – in the region of 10–15 mL/min for thrice weekly haemodialysis. Although sometimes patients (and occasionally their doctors) will suggest dialysis in the context of less severe renal impairment, this would represent a relatively small increment in clearance compared with the patient's own renal function. This is unlikely to lead to clinical benefit, would be at considerable financial cost, and would also be a major inconvenience to the patient. Most patients commence dialysis with a GFR of approximately 8–10 mL/min – the IDEAL study showed there is no benefit to initiating dialysis at higher levels of GFR.

Complications

These are as listed for chronic renal impairment (Section 2.1.2). The following are particular problems in patients with end-stage renal disease treated by dialysis:

> increased cardiovascular mortality (Fig 31)

> autonomous hyperparathyroidism, requiring parathyroidectomy (Fig 32)

> accumulation of beta-2 microglobulin amyloid with carpal tunnel syndrome and arthropathy (Fig 33)

> there are also specific complications of the renal replacement therapies (see Section 2.2).

Prognosis

In appropriate patients dialysis can usually be performed relatively smoothly and safely, especially when adequate practical and psychological preparation is made.

Survival of incident patients on RRT continues to improve, although mortality is much higher than in a population matched for age and comorbidity. The median life years on dialysis for those aged 25–29 is 18.5 years, but only 2.4 years for those over the age of 75. The most common causes of death are cardiovascular disease, infection and withdrawal from treatment.

Prevention

> Measures to prevent progression of CKD (see Section 2.1.2).

> If there is sufficient advance planning, transplantation before ESRF is reached – either from a living or cadaveric donor – may avoid the need for dialysis.

2.1.4 Nephrotic syndromes

Nephrotic syndrome is the combination of:

> proteinuria – the traditional definition of nephrotic syndrome requires 24-hour urine protein excretion

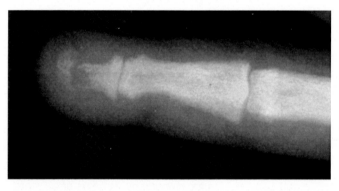

Fig 31 Annual mortality in the general population and dialysis patients (data from the United States Renal Data System 1994–1996). Mortality is increased over 100-fold in younger dialysis patients.

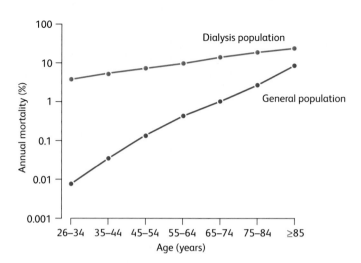

Fig 32 Radiograph of the finger of a haemodialysis patient with severe hyperparathyroidism. There is subperiosteal resorption and osteo-acrolysis.

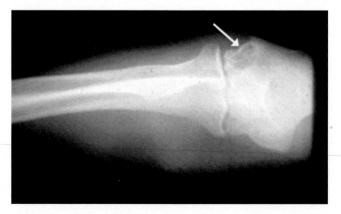

Fig 33 Radiograph of the wrist of a long-standing haemodialysis patient. The radiolucent area (arrow) is an amyloid deposit.

>3 g, but this test is now rarely performed: equivalent values are albumin:creatinine ratio (ACR) >200 mg/mmol and protein:creatinine ratio (PCR) >300 mg/mmol

> hypoalbuminaemia (<35 g/L)

> oedema.

Aetiology/pathophysiology/pathology
Proteinuria
The underlying defect is increased glomerular permeability to protein. Some of the leaked protein is absorbed and catabolised by the tubular cells; the remainder is passed in the urine. The normal glomerulus selects which molecules can pass from the circulation to the tubular space based on size and electrical charge.

> Size selectivity – relates to fenestrae in the endothelium, pores in the basement membrane, and slit diaphragms between the foot processes of the epithelial cells (podocytes).

> Charge selectivity – is the result of electrostatic repulsion of negatively charged proteins by negative charge on the basement membrane and endothelium.

The podocyte is the main target in diseases that cause nephrotic syndrome, which include membranous nephropathy, minimal change disease and focal segmental glomerulosclerosis (FSGS). Heavy proteinuria without oedema or a low serum albumin is more likely due to secondary FSGS. The most common abnormalities seen on biopsy in these conditions is podocyte foot process effacement, disruption to the slit diaphragms or depletion of podocytes. Some patients with congenital nephrotic syndrome have mutations in podocyte proteins (eg nephrin or podocin) that are important in the maintenance of the slit diaphragm or that affect the integrity of the podocyte cytoskeleton (alpha-actinin-4).

Hypoalbuminaemia
The circulating albumin concentration does not correlate tightly with the proteinuria as a result of the variable extent of tubular catabolism. The amount of compensatory increase in hepatic synthesis is also variable.

Oedema
An attractive hypothesis was that the oedema is driven by hypovolaemia caused by reduced plasma oncotic pressure, resulting in compensatory sodium retention. However, this simple explanation cannot be sustained in adults, although it may apply in children with minimal change disease. Plasma volume is not reduced in untreated sodium-retaining adult nephritis; sodium retention does not correlate well with renin–angiotensin activation; and converting enzyme inhibitors are not natriuretic.

Epidemiology
The underlying histological diagnosis varies with age (Fig 34). Not included are large numbers of people with diabetes who are technically late in the course of diabetic nephropathy, but in whom a renal biopsy would not be appropriate.

Most children with nephrotic syndrome are steroid responsive (minimal change disease or FSGS). For patients under the age of 10, it is therefore usual to treat with steroids and only biopsy non-responders.

Clinical presentation

> Usually with peripheral oedema, which may be of gradual or sudden onset.

> Ranges from trivial to a major problem resistant to diuretics, etc.

> Some children present with abrupt onset of massive proteinuria, hypovolaemia and even collapse.

> Older patients with minimal change disease may present with acute kidney injury (AKI).

> Sometimes the patient will notice frothy urine (Fig 35) – but often not reveal this unless asked directly.

Investigations
Investigations aim to do the following:

> confirm that the patient is nephrotic

> assess the severity of the protein leak

> obtain a precise diagnosis, often requiring histological diagnosis of the glomerular abnormality.

Investigations should include the following:

> Serum albumin and creatinine.

> Urinalysis and microscopy: the presence of some red cells does not rule out minimal change, but makes it less likely.

> Urine ACR or PCR is more reproducible and less cumbersome for the patient than a 24-hour urine collection, which is now rarely (if ever) used. A PCR of 100 mg/mmol or ACR of 70 mg/mmol is approximately equal to 1 g of protein per 24 hours. An ACR has a greater sensitivity for low levels of proteinuria (see Section 3.1).

> Renal ultrasonography: scars suggest reflux nephropathy. Biopsy is relatively contraindicated if there is a single kidney.

> Renal biopsy: adults (and children over the age of 10) will almost always require a renal biopsy.

Other conditions that may need to be sought are:

> Systemic lupus erythematosus (SLE) – characterised by positive antinuclear factor (ANA), antibodies to double stranded (dsDNA) and low complement levels; to be considered particularly in any young woman presenting with the nephrotic syndrome.

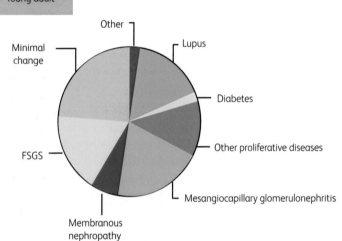

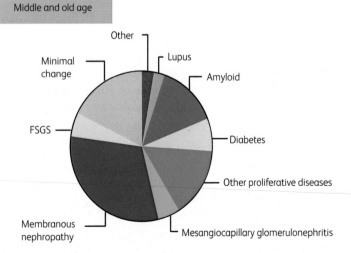

Fig 34 Histological diagnoses of renal biopsies of 1,000 patients at Guy's Hospital, London, 1963–1990. FSGS, focal segmental glomerulosclerosis. (Redrawn with permission from Cameron JS. In: Davison AM *et al* (eds). *Oxford textbook of clinical nephrology*, 2nd edn. Oxford: Oxford University Press, 1998.)

> Amyloidosis – this is a consideration, particularly in any older patient: check protein electrophoresis of urine and serum.

> Primary membranous nephropathy – anti-phospholipase A2 receptor antibody is (virtually) diagnostic.

> Hepatitis B – associated with membranous nephropathy.

> Hepatitis C – associated with cryoglobulinaemia and mesangiocapillary glomerulonephritis.

> Malignancy – particularly in the older patient with membranous nephropathy; check chest radiograph and have a low threshold for investigating digestive/abdominal symptoms.

Differential diagnosis

> Oedema commonly results from other factors (eg congestive cardiac failure (CCF), hepatic failure).

> Proteinuria: dipstick testing of the urine is very sensitive and minor proteinuria occurs in many situations (eg CCF and fever).

> Hypoalbuminaemia is common in other circumstances (liver disease and chronic illness).

Treatment

Oedema

The success of symptomatic treatment is best monitored by daily weighing; aim to reduce the patient's weight by 0.5–1.0 kg/day.

To achieve negative sodium balance, do the following:

> Restrict dietary sodium and fluid intake.

> Diuretics will almost always be necessary, usually furosemide/ bumetanide. Large doses are often required (partly because the drugs are sequestered by filtered protein in the tubular lumen). In resistant

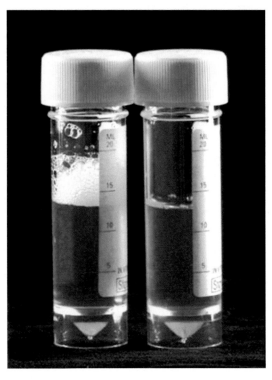

Fig 35 Urine from a nephrotic patient with a protein content of 5 g/L (left) and a normal sample (right).

cases, additional diuretics that act synergistically, eg metolazone, may be needed, also potassium supplements and/or amiloride.

> Severe cases may be treated with the combination of intravenous 20% albumin and diuretics, or haemofiltration/haemodialysis.

Reduction of proteinuria

> Where appropriate the underlying process is treated, eg steroids in minimal change.

> ACE inhibitors reduce proteinuria and slow deterioration in glomerular filtration rate (GFR), although their use may be restricted by hypotension.

> Refractory cases: NSAIDs or ciclosporin are sometimes used to reduce proteinuria in refractory cases. The effect results mainly from a reduction in GFR. Such cases should be distinguished from the use of

calcineurin inhibitors to treat the underlying condition (relapsing minimal change or membranous glomerulonephritis). Nephrectomy and renal replacement therapy (RRT) are rarely justified in exceptional cases of refractory oedema.

Complications

Hyperlipidaemia

> Over half of nephrotic patients have cholesterol >7.5 mmol/L.

> High-density lipoprotein is often decreased.

> Low-density lipoprotein synthesis is increased and catabolism decreased.

It is not clear what impact hyperlipidaemia has on cardiovascular risk, but concern is obviously increased with the increased duration of nephrotic syndrome. 3-Hydroxy-3-methylglutaryl coenzyme A reductase inhibitors do lower cholesterol in this group and are considered on the basis of the overall risk profile (see Section 1.5).

Thrombosis

Between 10% and 40% of patients with the nephrotic syndrome develop deep venous thrombosis or renal vein thrombosis (Fig 36). This is probably less common in minimal change disease. Prothrombotic abnormalities include reduced antithrombin III (urinary losses). Renal vein thrombosis may present with:

> pulmonary emboli (Fig 37)

> decrease in GFR

> flank pain and haematuria.

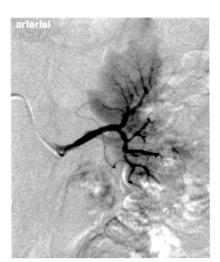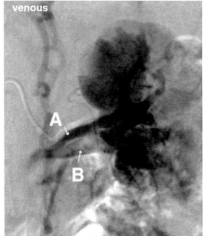

Fig 36 Digital subtraction angiography in a patient with membranous nephropathy. On the venous phase (right-hand image) there is normal filling of the superior renal vein (A), but defective filling of the inferior renal vein (B), resulting from renal vein thrombosis.

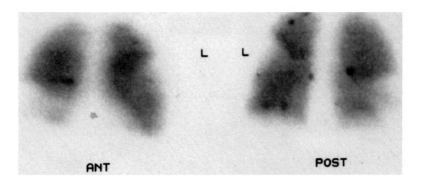

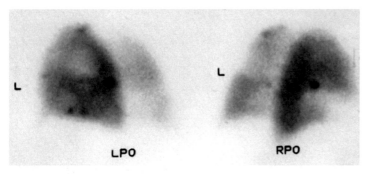

Fig 37 Lung perfusion scan of the same patient as in Fig 36 showing multiple defects consistent with pulmonary emboli.

Diagnosed on selective venography, venous phase of renal angiogram (see Fig 36), CT or MRI.

Prevention of thrombosis

> Primary prevention: oral anticoagulants may be considered in ambulant patients with severe nephrotic syndrome (usually those with a serum albumin <20 g/L who are not expected to respond rapidly to treatment).

> Secondary prevention: after an episode of thrombosis, anticoagulation should continue as long as the patient remains nephrotic.

Infections

> Primary peritonitis (usually with *Streptococcus pneumoniae*) can occur in children. Low concentrations of complement factor B (55 kDa), which is necessary for alternative pathway activation, might explain this propensity. Most adults are probably protected by antibodies

to capsular antigens. Consider prophylactic penicillin in children or the pneumococcal vaccine.

> Cellulitis is frequent, presumably as a result of immunological factors and skin fragility / oedema.

Deterioration in renal function
Minimal change disease does not lead to chronic deterioration in renal function. Other histological categories carry a substantial risk of progressive loss of GFR, which varies according to histological diagnosis (see Section 2.3).

Other complications

> protein malnutrition

> hypovolaemia

> acute kidney injury (AKI).

Prognosis
This varies with the histological diagnosis (see Section 2.3).

2.2 Renal replacement therapy

Renal replacement therapy (RRT) is necessary in order to sustain and/or maintain quality of life once renal function is no longer sufficient to do so. There are three available modalities of RRT:

> haemodialysis

> peritoneal dialysis

> renal transplantation.

2.2.1 Choice of treatment modality

Whatever the ultimate treatment modality, patients with chronic kidney disease (CKD) in whom progression to end-stage renal failure (ESRF) is predictable (ie patients with late stage IV and stage V CKD) should be managed in a 'pre-dialysis' or 'low clearance' clinic. Multidisciplinary support should consist of a nephrologist, specialist renal nurses and renal dieticians. The aim should be to help patients and their families make an informed decision about future therapy, and to ensure that patients are prepared for RRT. This would include:

> transplantation work-up and listing, including assessment of potential living donors

> timely creation of arteriovenous fistulae (AVF) and insertion of peritoneal dialysis catheters.

The clinic will also manage the complications of stage IV–V CKD – anaemia, bone disease, acidosis and fluid overload.

Renal transplantation is the modality of choice for most patients because both quality of life and survival are improved compared to dialysis. Transplantation is, however, restricted by the suitability of patients to undergo the transplant operation and the availability of donor

Table 20   Advantages and disadvantages of haemodialysis and peritoneal dialysis

	Advantages	Disadvantages
Haemodialysis	Intermittent, allowing 'time off treatment' Responsibility lies with renal staff Dialysis is separate from home environment Higher clearances of toxins may be achievable than with peritoneal dialysis	Requires transport to/from the dialysis unit Requires vascular access Attached to a machine Imposes restrictions on travel Haemodynamically stressful; patients may feel unwell after treatments Bacteraemia – particularly if dialysing over a line
Peritoneal dialysis	In control of own treatment, more independence Simple apparatus Much less frequent visits to hospital Ease of travel Can usually be integrated into work Haemodynamically gentle compared to haemodialysis	Daily treatment May be unsuitable for patients with previous abdominal surgery or large body mass Episodes of acute peritonitis Sclerosing peritonitis is uncommon but very serious Technique survival is shorter than for haemodialysis

organs, and carries risks associated with long-term immunosuppression.

Relative advantages and disadvantages of haemodialysis and peritoneal dialysis are outlined in Table 20.

Some of the problems with haemodialysis (particularly transport and inflexibility) can be avoided by performing the treatment at home (which may also allow patients to increase the time spent dialysing each week), hence patients should ideally be offered a choice between 'home'- and 'hospital'-based dialysis treatment.

Conservative management

Haemodialysis and peritoneal dialysis are poorly tolerated by some patients. In those with frailty and/or substantial comorbidity the burden of RRT may be greater than the benefit. If possible, this should be discussed with the patient (and any family members the patient wishes to involve) well before they reach end-stage renal disease. Conservative management to alleviate symptomatic complications of renal failure may include erythropoietin, management of fluid balance with diuretics, and (to prolong life) potassium restriction. With more advanced renal failure a symptomatic approach is taken, similar to that given to patients with any other terminal illness.

2.2.2 Haemodialysis

Principle

Haemodialysis involves circulating the patient's blood through an extra-corporeal circulation where it is exposed to an isotonic-buffered dialysis solution across a semipermeable membrane. The patient's blood is obtained via a form of vascular access.

The removal of toxins occurs principally through diffusion (Fig 38). Waste products that are at a high concentration in the patient's blood travel down a concentration gradient across the semipermeable membrane into the dialysis solution.

Removal of fluid occurs principally by ultrafiltration (Fig 39). Water moves from the circulation down a pressure gradient across the semipermeable

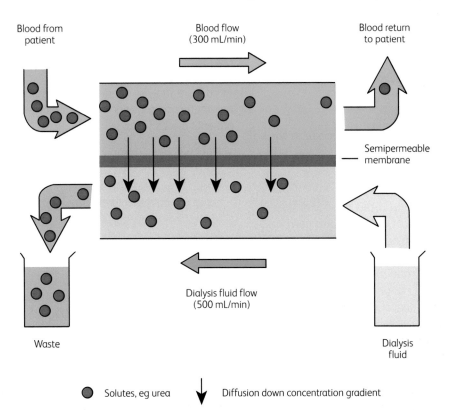

Blood from patient   Blood flow (300 mL/min)   Blood return to patient

Semipermeable membrane

Dialysis fluid flow (500 mL/min)

Waste   Dialysis fluid

● Solutes, eg urea   ↓ Diffusion down concentration gradient

Fig 38 Haemodialysis: clearance of toxins by diffusion.

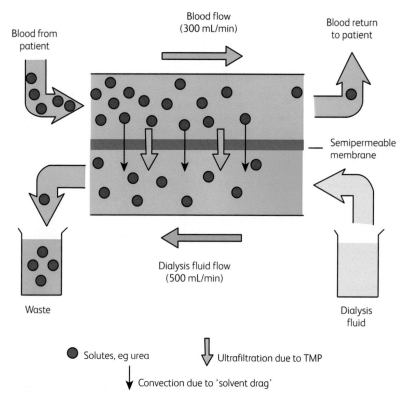

Blood from patient

Blood flow (300 mL/min)

Blood return to patient

Semipermeable membrane

Dialysis fluid flow (500 mL/min)

Waste

Dialysis fluid

● Solutes, eg urea

⬇ Ultrafiltration due to TMP

↓ Convection due to 'solvent drag'

Fig 39 Haemodialysis: ultrafiltration (fluid removal) is driven by the transmembrane pressure (TMP) across the semipermeable membrane.

membrane into the dialysis solution. Dialysis machines control fluid removal by regulating transmembrane pressure. Some solute molecules move with water by convection.

Practical details

The basic haemodialysis circuit is shown in Fig 40.

Most patients in the UK receive three treatments of about 4 hours each week. There is evidence for a threshold amount of dialysis below which morbidity and mortality increase. There are national targets for measured dialysis adequacy based on urea (small molecule) clearance. Increasing dialysis delivery for a patient requires either an increase in their time on dialysis or greater dialysis efficiency. Improved dialysis efficiency may be achieved by using dialysis membranes with a larger surface area, by increasing

blood flow through the dialysis circuit (where possible), or by increasing the convective removal of small solutes (eg haemodiafiltration).

Apart from dialysis adequacy, the major parameters to consider in haemodialysis patients are as follows:

> Fluid balance – removal of salt and water during dialysis to achieve a target 'dry' weight. Blood pressure control should ideally be obtained by manipulation of 'dry' weight in dialysis patients.

> Electrolyte balance – different dialysis solutions are available in which the concentration of sodium, potassium, calcium and bicarbonate varies.

> Removal of larger 'middle' molecules – high-flux dialysis membranes and haemodiafiltration clear middle molecules such as beta-2 microglobulin with greater efficiency.

Vascular access

Haemodialysis requires vascular access, with the preferred form being an AVF (Fig 41). Formation of an AVF requires an operation in which (most typically) the radial or brachial artery is anastomosed to a vein, which is not always possible or successful. An AVF must 'mature' (involving an increase in flow arterialisation of the vein) before it can be used: this takes at least 6 weeks and the operation should therefore be planned well before dialysis is required. Other forms of vascular access, all of which are less good than AVF, are as follows:

> Temporary dialysis catheter – large bore dual lumen catheters inserted into the internal jugular (Fig 42) or femoral veins. Used for acute inpatient dialysis, but not suitable for outpatient use.

> Tunnelled dialysis catheter – large bore dual lumen catheters inserted into the internal jugular vein and tunnelled subcutaneously to an exit point on the chest wall (Fig 43). A Dacron cuff that sits in the 'tunnel' reduces infection rates, however, infection remains a very significant problem. Suitable for outpatient use. Can also be placed in subclavian veins, femoral veins or the inferior vena cava.

> Polytetrafluoroethylene graft – if native veins are unsuitable for anastomosis to an artery, then a graft can be used, but there are risks of anastomotic stenosis and infection if this route is chosen.

Blood circulating in the extracorporeal system requires anticoagulation (usually with heparin), and many nephrologists prescribe regular low-dose aspirin for patients with an AVF as prophylaxis against thrombosis.

Complications of haemodialysis

Table 21 shows the major complications of dialysis.

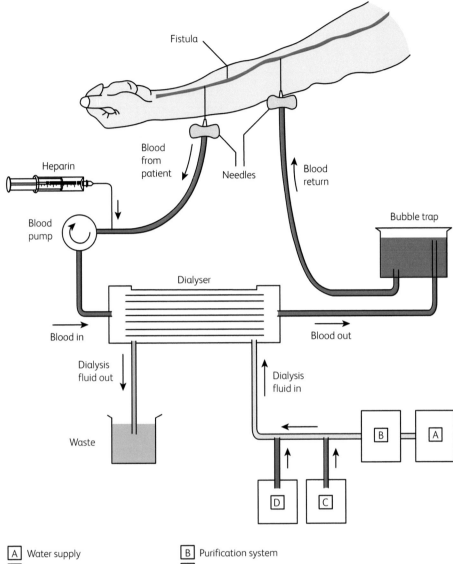

A Water supply   **B** Purification system
C Dialysis solution concentrate   **D** Bicarbonate concentrate

Fig 40 Basic haemodialysis circuit.

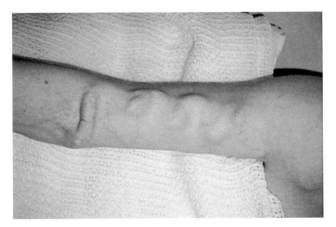

Fig 41 Well-developed brachial arteriovenous fistula.

2.2.3 Peritoneal dialysis

Principle

As with haemodialysis, peritoneal dialysis exposes the patient's blood to a buffered dialysis solution across a semipermeable membrane. However, the blood remains within the body and the semipermeable membrane is the peritoneum. Dialysis fluid is introduced via a peritoneal dialysis catheter (Fig 44).

Removal of toxins occurs through diffusion and convection. Small molecules diffuse across the peritoneal membrane down the concentration gradient between the blood and the intraperitoneal dialysis fluid. Larger molecules tend to move through convection associated with the movement of fluid.

Removal of fluid (ultrafiltration) occurs through osmosis. Water moves to equilibrate the osmolalities between the two compartments (Fig 45). Peritoneal dialysis fluids are manufactured to be hyperosmolar, using dextrose as the usual osmotic agent. Different concentrations of the osmotic agent enable control of fluid removal.

The rate at which solutes cross the peritoneal membrane varies, and depends on the individual characteristics of a patient's membrane. Broadly patients fall into two groups (Fig 46):

> Low transporters – have a slow rate of solute removal and so require long dwell times (ie continuous ambulatory peritoneal dialysis (CAPD)).

> High transporters – have a fast rate of solute removal and therefore require short dwell times. High transporters tend to rapidly absorb the dextrose, thus losing the osmotic gradient and leading to poor ultrafiltration. Best suited to automated peritoneal dialysis (APD).

With more time on peritoneal dialysis the peritoneum tends to move towards higher transport. Similar numbers of patients receiving peritoneal dialysis in the UK are on CAPD and APD.

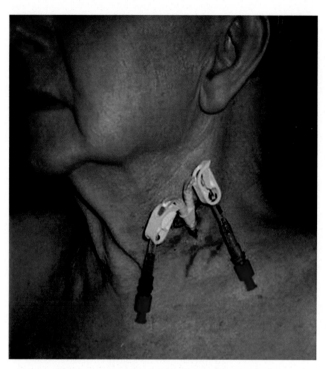

Fig 42 Temporary dialysis line inserted in the left internal jugular vein.

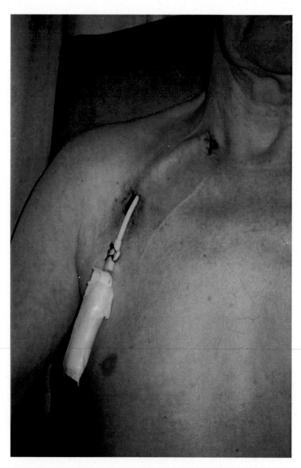

Fig 43 Semipermanent dialysis line inserted into the right internal jugular vein.

Practical details

Relative contraindications to peritoneal dialysis include previous major abdominal surgery, diverticulitis, the presence of hernias or chronic respiratory disease, and an inability to learn to perform the technique.

CAPD is illustrated in Fig 47. There are usually four exchanges of 1.5–3.0 L per day.

APD is illustrated in Fig 48. The regimen involves continuous cyclic peritoneal dialysis with several exchanges of 2–2.5 L overnight, each with short dwell times. After the last cycle, fluid is left in during the daytime. Often one additional manual daytime exchange is necessary.

As in haemodialysis, clearance on peritoneal dialysis can be measured, and below a certain minimum level mortality appears to be increased. Increasing the amount of dialysis on CAPD usually involves exchanging five times daily (ie an additional daily exchange), but many patients cannot achieve adequate dialysis with CAPD as their residual renal function declines. Some achieve targets by switching to APD, but most require a switch to haemodialysis.

A recent advance is specialised fluid using polymerised dextran (icodextrin) instead of glucose. The polymer is not transported across the peritoneum, so ultrafiltration is greatly improved in fast transporters.

Patient survival on peritoneal dialysis is probably equivalent to that with haemodialysis, but technique survival is markedly inferior to haemodialysis. The following factors are frequently involved in the failure of peritoneal dialysis:

> ultrafiltration failure – may be due to increased peritoneal membrane permeability (convert to APD) or membrane sclerosis (convert to haemodialysis)

> recurrent peritonitis

Table 21 Major complications of haemodialysis

Timing	Nature of complication
Acute	Hypotension Access related: infection, thrombosis, inadequate flow for dialysis and steal syndrome related to reduced distal flow Haemorrhage: may be related to anticoagulation
Chronic	Accelerated cardiovascular disease (the usual cause of death in dialysis patients)

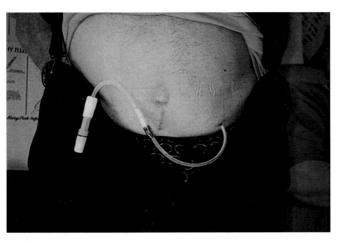

Fig 44 Tenckhoff dialysis catheter.

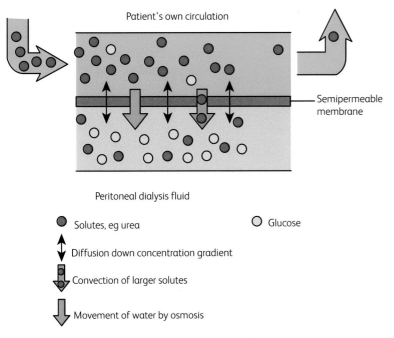

Fig 45 Mechanisms underlying peritoneal dialysis.

> inability to achieve dialysis adequacy – may develop as residual renal function declines.

Complications of peritoneal dialysis

Table 22 shows the major complications of peritoneal dialysis.

2.2.4 Renal transplantation

Principle

The principle is to implant a functioning healthy kidney that may be from the following sources:

> Living related donor – sibling to sibling and parent to child are the most common pairings. Long-term graft survival is better with living than cadaveric kidneys.

> Living unrelated donor (eg spouse or friend) – becoming more common in the UK.

> Cadaveric – heart-beating donors who satisfy the criteria of brain death (donation after brain-stem death (DBD)). Historically this has been the main source of organs in the UK.

> Cadaveric – non-heart-beating donors (donation after circulatory death (DCD)). Long-term results are similar to DBD, but there are higher initial rates of delayed graft function.

Practical details and complications

The possibility of renal transplantation should be considered in nearly all patients requiring RRT. Suitability for transplantation depends on the following:

> Patient survival issues – for example, coronary artery disease is common in patients with ESRF, may be asymptomatic, and is associated with a high risk of early postoperative mortality. It should be sought in high-risk patients and (if appropriate) intervention should take place prior to transplantation.

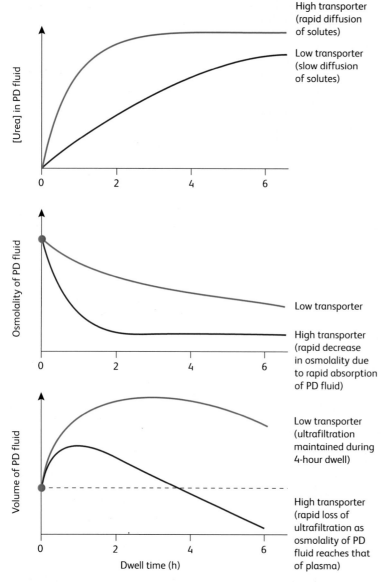

Fig 46 Solute transport properties of the peritoneal membrane. High transporters rapidly clear toxins, but also quickly experience a fall in dialysis fluid osmolality as a result of the rapid uptake of glucose, which leads to poor ultrafiltration. Low transporters take longer to clear toxins, but their ultrafiltration is good because glucose uptake from the dialysis fluid is slower. PD, peritoneal dialysis.

> Graft survival issues – for example, there is a significant risk of disease recurrence and graft loss in patients with focal segmental glomerulosclerosis (FSGS).

There is a UK transplant register managed by NHS Blood and Transplant onto which all potential transplant recipients are enrolled. Allocation from the national pool of organs is on a points system (human leukocyte antigen (HLA) matching, donor/recipient relative age and time on waiting list etc). Preoperatively, recipient serum and donor lymphocytes are cross-matched to detect preformed antibodies that would preclude transplantation.

Surgical technique
The transplant kidney is placed extraperitoneally in the iliac fossa and vessels are anastomosed, usually to the external iliac artery and vein. The ureter is implanted into the bladder, with a J-J stent usually placed to protect the anastomosis between the donor ureter and bladder. This stent is typically removed after 6 weeks.

Immunosuppression
Various immunosuppression regimens are used to prevent rejection of the donor kidney by the recipient's immune system. Most units tailor immunosuppression regimens according to the perceived risk of transplant rejection. Increasingly a depleting monoclonal antibody may be given at the time of transplantation as induction therapy. Nearly all regimens contain steroids initially, but many units now withdraw steroids within the first year. A standard immunosuppression regimen would include a calcineurin inhibitor (tacrolimus or ciclosporin), steroids and an inhibitor of purine synthesis (azathioprine or mycophenolate mofetil).

Other medical treatments
Other therapies may include aspirin to reduce the risk of thrombosis, co-trimoxazole prophylaxis against *Pneumocystis jirovecii* pneumonia, and valganciclovir prophylaxis against cytomegalovirus (CMV) (when donor is CMV positive).

The complications of renal transplant are summarised in Table 23.

Outcomes
The UK 5-year graft survival rate is 86% for first cadaveric transplant and 92% after first living donor kidney transplant. Graft and patient survival with live donor transplantation is superior to that with cadaveric transplantation regardless of HLA matching. Median patient survival with a functioning transplant is approximately 13 years for a deceased-donor kidney, and 20 years for a live-donor kidney.

There is a definite survival benefit with transplantation compared to remaining on the transplant waiting list, although there is an initial increase in mortality in the first year after transplantation. Relative to remaining dialysis dependent, patients with diabetes benefit the most from transplantation despite poorer absolute survival than other patients groups following transplantation.

2.3 Glomerular diseases

Although many different diseases act on the glomeruli, the effects of glomerular damage are limited and include the following:

> reduced glomerular filtration

> proteinuria and haematuria

> hypertension

> sodium retention, causing oedema.

Glomerular diseases can seem confusing, partly because they can be classified (and hence named!) according to clinical features, the histopathological appearance or the underlying disease process, and sometimes a combination eg membranous nephropathy (histological diagnosis) causing nephrotic syndrome (clinical features).

Glomerular disease can affect one or more of the components of the glomerulus, which are:

> glomerular basement membrane (GBM)

> glomerular cells

> intraglomerular vessels

> mesangium.

Important pathological terms describing histopathological appearances are:

> Proliferative disease – there is proliferation of cells within the glomerulus. In severe cases, proliferation of cells, especially

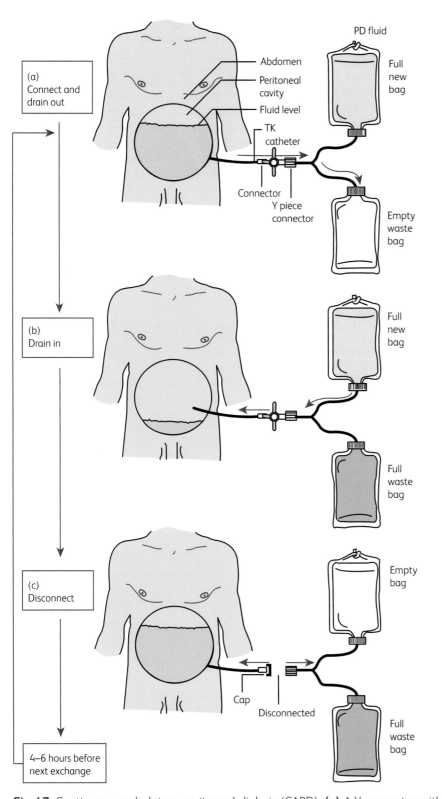

Fig 47 Continuous ambulatory peritoneal dialysis (CAPD). **(a)** A Y connector with an empty waste bag and a bag with fresh dialysis fluid is attached to the Tenckhoff (TK) catheter. Dialysis fluid is drained into the waste bag. **(b)** The Y connector is switched to drain in the fresh dialysis fluid. **(c)** The Y connector is removed. The patient is free to do whatever they like until the next exchange in 4–6 hours.

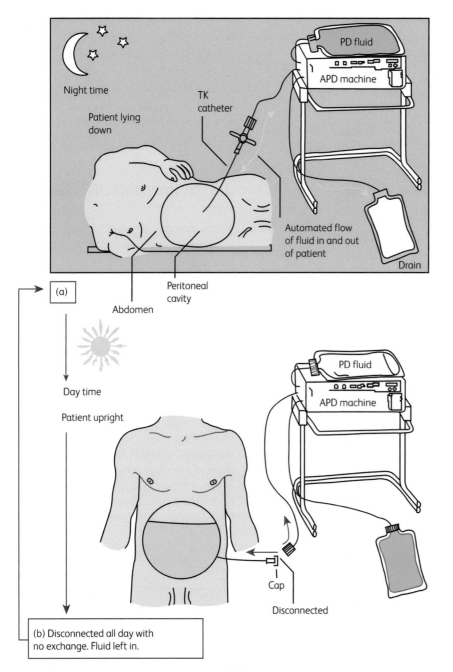

Fig 48 Automated peritoneal dialysis (APD). **(a)** At bedtime the patient connects to the machine with sufficient dialysis solution for the night. The machine delivers and drains fluid automatically throughout the night. **(b)** In the morning the patient disconnects. Fluid is left inside the peritoneal cavity. The patient may need to do one manual exchange in the daytime, but is otherwise free until bedtime.

macrophages within Bowman's capsule, causes an appearance known as a crescent.

> Mesangial disease – there is excess production of mesangial matrix.

> Membranous disease – the GBM is damaged and thickened.

> Membranoproliferative disease – there is both thickening of the GBM and cellular proliferation, usually of mesangial cells.

The pattern of glomerular involvement is further classified on the basis of whether all glomeruli are involved, and whether the whole of each glomerulus is involved.

Key point

> Focal disease affects only some glomeruli.
> Diffuse disease affects all the glomeruli.
> Segmental disease affects only part of the glomerulus.
> Global disease affects the whole glomerulus.

2.3.1 Primary glomerular disease

Minimal change nephropathy

Aetiology/pathophysiology/pathology
The cause is unknown, but it is associated with atopy. The signs are:

> light microscopy and immunofluorescence are normal or nearly normal

> electron microscopy shows glomerular epithelial podocyte foot process fusion (Fig 50).

Epidemiology
This constitutes 80% of childhood nephrotic syndromes, and 25% of adult nephrotic syndromes, with an incidence of two per 100,000. The peak age of incidence is between the age of 2 and 7 years, but all ages can be affected.

Clinical presentation
Nephrotic syndrome often follows upper respiratory tract infection. In older people minimal change disease may be associated with acute kidney injury (AKI). Patients may complain of swelling and frothy urine.

Physical signs

> oedema

> often facial swelling in children.

Medical Masterclass Third edition

Table 22	Complications of peritoneal dialysis
Timing	**Nature of complication**
Acute	> Peritonitis, the main acute problem associated with peritoneal dialysis Commonest organisms are Gram positive (coagulase-negative staphylococci and *Staphylococcus aureus*). Occurs about once per 18 patient months or less. Usually responds to intraperitoneal antibiotics > Poor drainage of dialysis fluid, usually due to constipation or poorly positioned catheter > Hernias are relatively common > Fluid leak, typically through the diaphragm causing pleural effusion
Chronic	> Accelerated cardiovascular disease (as in haemodialysis) > Sclerosing peritonitis, usually diagnosed more than 5 years after commencement of peritoneal dialysis. Poorly understood, very limited response to treatment and sometimes fatal. Some nephrologists advocate a switch from peritoneal to haemodialysis at around 5 years for all patients to prevent this complication

Table 23	Short- and long-term complications of renal transplantation
Timing	**Nature of complication**
Short term	Surgical problems: eg renal venous or arterial thrombosis, ureteric necrosis or stenosis, and lymphocoele Delayed graft function: occurs in up to 30% of patients. More common in non-heart beating donor kidneys (DCD) Acute rejection: occurs in up to 30% of patients and its presence probably reduces long-term graft survival. Usually reversible Infection: CMV is the commonest major problem. Infection of renal tubular cells by the human polyomavirus, BK, results in progressive graft dysfunction and may be stabilised by reducing immunosuppression (Fig 49b). Fungal pathogens are uncommon but frequently fatal
Long term	Cardiovascular disease: very common Diabetes: develops in up to 10% of patients, and in an even higher proportion of those receiving an immunosuppression regimen containing tacrolimus and steroids Chronic allograft nephropathy: involves immunological and non-immunological mechanisms. Average graft survival is about 10–12 years and has not increased in recent years Malignancy: skin cancers are very common. PTLD is a particular concern, and is related to the intensity of immunosuppression. It is frequently driven by EBV-positive B-cell proliferation, and is most common in the first year after transplantation. The incidence of most solid tumours is also significantly increased

CMV, cytomegalovirus; DCD, donation after circulatory death; EBV, Epstein–Barr virus; PTLD, post-transplant lymphoproliferative disorder.

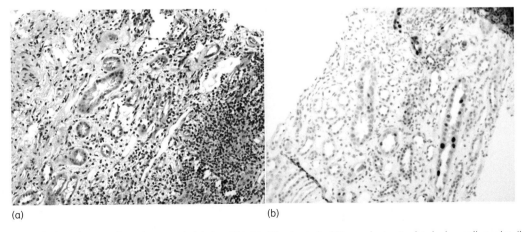

(a) (b)

Fig 49 Renal transplant biopsy. **(a)** interstitial infiltrate, tubulitis and atypical tubular cell nuclei (haematoxylin and eosin staining (H&E)); **(b)** immunohistochemistry showing a BK protein (brown staining) in the tubular cell nuclei.

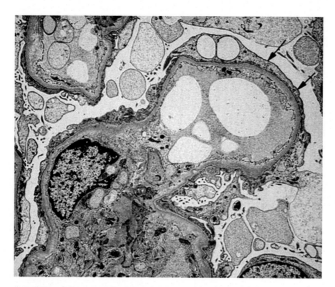

Fig 50 Electron micrograph of glomerular changes in minimal change disease (magnification ×6,200). Note the fusion of epithelial cell foot processes (arrowed).

Investigations

> Urinalysis: check urine albumin: creatinine ratio (ACR) or protein: creatinine ratio (PCR).

> Bloods: check for hypoalbuminaemia and hyperlipidaemia.

> Renal biopsy – NB children with nephrotic syndrome are often given a trial of steroids without a biopsy (Fig 50) given the high frequency of minimal change disease.

Differential diagnosis

The differential diagnosis includes other causes of the nephrotic syndrome – especially focal segmental glomerulosclerosis (FSGS) and membranous nephropathy, amyloidosis, diabetic nephropathy, systemic lupus erythematosus (SLE) and (rarely) congenital nephrotic syndrome.

Treatment

> Steroids: most adults respond rapidly to high-dose oral steroids (eg 60 mg prednisolone/day) and will enter disease remission (see below).

> If there are frequent relapses or a poor response, then cyclophosphamide, ciclosporin or tacrolimus can be useful. Rituximab has also been given with some anecdotal success.

> Diuretics for oedema. Consider ACE inhibitor or ARB if hypertension persists.

> Lipid-lowering drugs (usually statins), if there is prolonged nephrotic syndrome with hyperlipidaemia.

> Penicillin prophylaxis may be given to prevent streptococcal infection due to loss of immunoglobulins in the urine.

Complications

Complications are those of the nephrotic syndrome (see Section 2.1.4).

Prognosis

Nearly all patients (98% of children and 80–95% of adults) respond to steroids (although response in adults is slower): 10–20% of these relapse several times, of whom 40–50% relapse frequently. Long-term steroid dependence is not uncommon in adults (25–30%), in which case steroid-sparing agents (azathioprine, mycophenolate mofetil) may be of use.

Disease associations

> lymphoma

> NSAID use.

Focal segmental glomerulosclerosis

Aetiology/pathophysiology/pathology

Can be primary or secondary.

> Primary FSGS – this is of unknown aetiology, apart from rare familial cases due to mutations in defined genes (*NPHS2*, encoding podocin; *ACTN4*, encoding alpha-actinin-4; and *TRPC6* encoding a cation channel). Minimal change nephropathy and FSGS share similarities and may be different points on the spectrum of a disease process.

> Secondary FSGS – as FSGS is a histological description, the lesions can be seen in other disease processes, and is classified as secondary if in association with HIV-associated nephropathy, diabetes, obesity, glomerular damage for other reasons (IgA nephropathy, vasculitis, SLE, toxins such as heroin, and drugs such as interferon) and renal vascular disease. Secondary FSGS presents more insidiously and usually with non-nephrotic range proteinuria.

In both primary and secondary FSGS damage to the glomerular filtration barrier causes protein leak and (eventually) the nephrotic syndrome. The histological findings are:

> Light microscopy – focal and segmental glomerular sclerosis (Fig 51) – although given the focal nature, this may be missed by sampling error.

> Immunofluorescence – may show non-specific IgM and C3 in sclerotic lesions.

> Electron microscopy – glomerular epithelial podocyte foot process fusion (characteristic and diagnostic) in primary disease. Podocyte foot process effacement is seen in secondary FSGS.

Epidemiology

This accounts for 15% of adult nephrotic syndrome. It is also a common finding in individuals with non-nephrotic proteinuria and can occur if there is hyperfiltration due to any

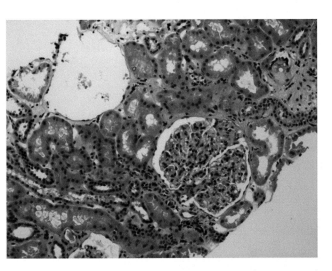

Fig 51 Renal biopsy showing a glomerulus with segmental sclerosis. Note that the sclerosis is at the tip of the glomerulus – opposite the vascular pole near the origin of the proximal tubule. This 'tip variant' of focal segmental glomerulosclerosis (FSGS) generally responds well to steroids.

cause, eg renal agenesis, surgical removal of kidney tissue (rare unless >50% removed).

Clinical presentation
Clinical presentations may include:

> proteinuria
> nephrotic syndrome
> hypertension
> chronic renal impairment.

Physical signs

> hypertension
> oedema if nephrotic.

Investigations

> urinalysis: protein ± blood
> bloods: hypoalbuminaemia and renal impairment
> renal biopsy.

Differential diagnosis
The differential diagnosis is other causes of nephrotic syndrome, and biopsy is therefore required.

Treatment

> Steroids will induce a remission in many nephrotic individuals with FSGS, but the time to remission is longer than in minimal change disease.

> Calcineurin inhibitors or cyclophosphamide may be beneficial in patients with a partial response to steroids.

> Symptomatic treatment is given to all: diuretics, ACE inhibitors or ARBs to control BP and reduce proteinuria, and lipid-lowering agents if required. Consider anticoagulation if proteinuria is nephrotic range, albumin is <20 g/L or there are other risk factors for thrombosis.

> In patients with primary FSGS, it has been postulated that there is a circulating factor causing damage, although no clear candidate has been identified. This is supported by the observation that proteinuria can occur rapidly in kidneys transplanted into patients with renal failure due to FSGS, and such proteinuria may respond to plasmapheresis.

Complications
Complications are those of the nephrotic syndrome and chronic kidney disease (CKD) (see Section 2.1.2). Often recurs in transplanted kidneys.

Prognosis
Between 40% and 60% of patients develop end-stage renal disease within 10 years of being diagnosed with FSGS.

Up to 40% of both adults and children remit in response to steroids: those who do respond have a much better prognosis for renal survival.

Disease associations
FSGS is associated with obesity and also occurs at increased frequency in black ethnic groups, those who are HIV-infected and intravenous drug users.

Membranous nephropathy
Aetiology/pathophysiology/pathology
Membranous nephropathy can be characterised as primary (idiopathic, up to 75% of cases) or secondary (usually associated with SLE, drugs, viral infection such as hepatitis B virus, or malignancy). Until recently the aetiology of primary membranous nephropathy was unknown. However, the discovery of autoantibodies directed against the phospholipase A2 receptor (anti-PLA2R antibodies) in up to 80% of patients with primary membranous nephropathy strongly suggests that this is an antibody-mediated autoimmune disease. Circulating anti-PLA2R antibodies are not found in secondary membranous nephropathy, patients with other causes of nephrotic syndrome, or healthy individuals.

Whether primary or secondary, damage to the glomerular filtration barrier causes protein leak and nephrotic syndrome. The histological findings are:

> light microscopy – thickening of the glomerular basement membrane (GBM)

> immunofluorescence/ immunohistochemistry – antibodies bound to the PLA2R (IgG4 subclass) can be identified in primary membranous nephropathy, and occasionally secondary, although in secondary these antibodies are not IgG4. In both primary and secondary disease a diffuse, granular pattern of IgG and C3 is seen along the GBM

> electron microscopy – subepithelial electron-dense membrane deposits.

Epidemiology

This is one of the most common causes of nephrotic syndrome in older Caucasian patients. The peak age of presentation is 30–50 years and it is more common in males than females. While membranous nephropathy is seen in all racial backgrounds, FSGS is a more common cause of nephrotic syndrome in those of African-American and Hispanic ethnicity.

Clinical presentation

Clinical presentations may include:

> nephrotic syndrome

> chronic renal impairment

> asymptomatic proteinuria

> hypertension.

Physical signs

> oedema if nephrotic

> hypertension.

Investigations

> urinalysis: protein ± blood

> bloods: hypoalbuminaemia, renal impairment

> renal biopsy (Fig 52)

> consider anti-PLA2R antibodies in those with a histological diagnosis of membranous nephropathy and no obvious secondary cause.

Differential diagnosis

The differential diagnosis is from other causes of nephrotic syndrome or renal impairment (if present). Exclude SLE and causes of secondary membranous nephropathy. Screening for viral infection and taking a detailed history of drugs and symptoms of malignancy should be routine for all patients presenting with nephrotic syndrome. Screening for malignancy should be carried out in older patients or those with risk factors (eg heavy smoking history) or unexplained symptoms, eg weight loss).

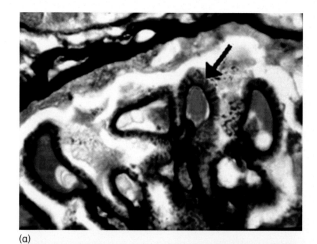

(a)

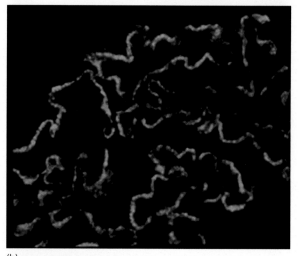

(b)

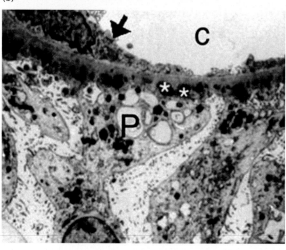

(b)

Fig 52 Characteristics of membranous nephropathy. **(a)** Silver-stained section: the basement membrane is widened, with spikes. **(b)** Immunofluorescence for IgG: part of the glomerulus is shown and there is granular fluorescence along the basement membrane. **(c)** Electron micrograph of capillary loop: the basement membrane is seen adjacent to the capillary (C) lined by an endothelial cell (arrow); within the basement membrane are electron-dense deposits (*); and a podocyte (P) is also visible. (Courtesy of Dr D Davies, Oxford Radcliffe Hospitals.)

Treatment

Choice of treatment depends on the risk of progression of disease. Patients can be divided into low risk of progression (<4 g/day proteinuria, normal renal function), moderate risk (proteinuria 4–8 g/day, normal or near-normal renal function, and minimal symptoms) or high risk (>8 g/day proteinuria, abnormal renal function, uncontrolled symptoms, eg of oedema).

All patients should receive symptomatic treatment – diuretics, ACE inhibitors or ARBs to control BP, and lipid-lowering agents. Specific treatments include:

> In secondary membranous nephropathy, treat the underlying cause.

> In patients who are anti-PLA2R antibody positive, studies are ongoing with treatments targeting B cells, and early results show good responses in patients with >4 g/day of proteinuria.

> In patients who are not eligible for clinical trials, current best practice for patients with a moderate risk of progression is to provide supportive therapy for 6 months and then – if there is no spontaneous remission – commence immunosuppressive therapy. The preferred regimen is alternating steroids and cyclophosphamide (chlorambucil has also been used but has a worse toxicity profile and no additional benefit) or, in those wanting to avoid cyclophosphamide, calcineurin inhibitors. Both regimens show reasonable success (Fig 53). Immunosuppressive therapy may be initiated before 6 months in high-risk patients.

Complications

Complications are those of the nephrotic syndrome, CKD and hyperlipidaemia if present. Venous thromboembolism can occur.

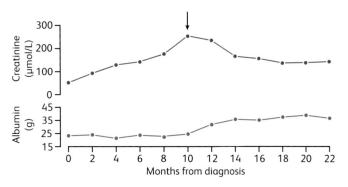

Fig 53 Creatinine and albumin in a patient with membranous nephropathy. Renal function deteriorated progressively over the 10 months following diagnosis and the patient was then treated with immunosuppression (alternating chlorambucil and prednisolone for 6 months). This resulted in remission of the nephrotic syndrome and the creatinine returned to normal.

Prognosis

Roughly the 'rule of thirds': 20–30% of patients remit spontaneously, 40% have a partial remission or remain stable, and around 30% develop progressive renal impairment.

Disease associations

> hepatitis B (and rarely hepatitis C)

> malignancy

> SLE

> drugs and toxins (anti-tumour necrosis factor (TNF) therapy, NSAIDs, gold, penicillamine).

Immunoglobulin A nephropathy

Aetiology/pathophysiology/pathology

The aetiology is unknown: is associated with abnormal glycosylation of the hinge region of IgA, but several mechanisms are likely to be responsible. Abnormal IgA forms immune complexes, which deposit in the kidney and may trigger complement-mediated damage. The histological findings are:

> light microscopy – mesangial matrix expansion and mesangial cell proliferation, which can be focal or, more commonly, diffuse (Fig 54)

> immunofluorescence – IgA deposits in mesangium (Fig 55).

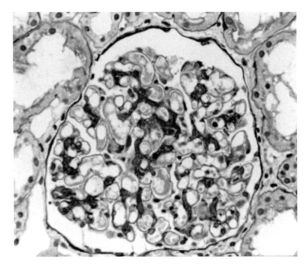

Fig 54 Light microscopy of a glomerulus. The section has been stained by the periodic acid–Schiff method, and shows expansion of the mesangium.

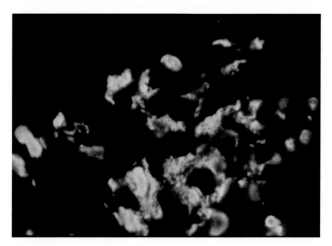

Fig 55 Immunofluorescence of part of a glomerulus for IgA: there is mesangial deposition of IgA.

Epidemiology

Key point

IgA nephropathy is the commonest glomerulonephritis worldwide.

The prevalence of overt nephropathy is approximately two per 10,000 individuals, with the peak incidence in the second and third decades. The male to female ratio is 2:1. Post-mortem studies have revealed mesangial IgA deposits in 3–16% of the total population, suggesting IgA deposition is much commoner than overt nephropathy.

Clinical presentation

There may be haematuria at the same time as, or 1–2 days after, a sore throat (synpharyngitic haematuria). Most patients will have non-visible haematuria, hypertension is common, and there may be renal impairment (all three = nephritic syndrome). There may be a vasculitic skin rash (Henoch–Schönlein purpura). Less common presentations include nephrotic syndrome (in 10% of cases) and, rarely, rapidly progressive glomerulonephritis.

Physical sign

> hypertension

Investigations

> urinalysis: blood and protein (rarely nephrotic range)

> bloods: check renal function, and immunoglobulins, IgA is raised in 50% of cases

> renal biopsy.

Differential diagnosis

The differential diagnosis is other forms of glomerulonephritis (eg SLE, poststreptococcal glomerulonephritis and anti-neutrophil cytoplasmic antibody (ANCA)-associated vasculitis).

Treatment

The role of specific treatment is unclear and depends to an extent on clinical presentation. Strict BP control, typically with ACE inhibitors or ARBs, reduces the risk of progression of renal impairment. Hypercholesterolaemia should be controlled with statins. There may be a small benefit from fish oils, although this is controversial. Remember:

> Steroids may be given if nephrotic, or progressive renal impairment.

> Aggressive disease with crescent formation may be treated with steroids, cyclophosphamide or other immunosuppressants such as mycophenolate mofetil.

> Other treatments: diuretics for oedema, ACE inhibitors to control BP, and lipid-lowering agents.

Complications

Complications are those of the nephrotic syndrome or CKD (if present).

Prognosis

Highly variable. Ranges from spontaneous clinical remission (although often with intermittent relapses) to rapid progression to end-stage renal disease: 15% of patients develop end-stage renal disease within 10 years of diagnosis; 20–30% develop it by 20 years.

Disease associations

> cirrhotic liver disease: alcoholic and viral hepatitis

> HIV

> coeliac disease.

Mesangiocapillary glomerulonephritis (also known as membranoproliferative glomerulonephritis)

Aetiology/pathophysiology/pathology

There are two main pathological processes leading to mesangiocapillary glomerulonephritis (MCGN), and the classification system has recently been modified to better reflect this. It is based on the appearances seen on immunofluorescence microscopy.

> Immune complex mediated – is driven by circulating immune complexes, which deposit in the kidney and cause activation of complement via the classical pathway (see haemolytic–uraemic syndrome (HUS) below). An underlying cause is usually found, eg SLE, chronic infection (especially hepatitis B and C (the latter associated with cryoglobulinaemia)), dysproteinaemia, although it can be idiopathic.

> Complement mediated – much less common. This pathway involves constitutive activation of the alternative pathway of complement activation, and patients often have

systemic manifestations. Often associated with antibodies to complement components, eg C3 nephritic factor. Some familial forms have been described.

On histology all forms show mesangial expansion and mesangial cell proliferation along with thickening of the GBM. Immune-complex-mediated disease tends to show deposition of immunoglobulins and complement on immunofluorescence, but complement mediated shows only complement components.

Epidemiology
This is declining in developed countries; and 80% of the cases that do occur are immune complex mediated. MCGN accounts for 10–20% of biopsies performed for presumed primary glomerulonephritis.

Clinical presentation
Presentation varies from asymptomatic haematuria or proteinuria to acute nephritic syndrome or severe nephrotic syndrome.

Physical signs
> hypertension
> oedema.

Investigations
> urinalysis: blood and protein
> bloods: renal impairment, hypoalbuminaemia and low complement levels – especially C3. In complement-mediated disease there may be antibodies to complement components (C3 nephritic factor). In immune-complex-mediated disease there may be indicators of the underlying disease process, eg anti-dsDNA antibodies in SLE
> renal biopsy.

Differential diagnosis
The differential diagnosis is from other causes of chronic renal impairment and of nephrotic syndrome (if present). Both

post-infectious glomerulonephritis and SLE also cause renal disease and hypocomplementaemia.

Treatment
Immune-complex-mediated disease usually remits after treatment of the underlying cause, if identified. In the absence of a treatable underlying cause, the degree of renal impairment and proteinuria can dictate whether purely symptomatic treatment (diuretics, ACE inhibitors to control BP, lipid-lowering agents) will be sufficient, or whether a trial of immunosuppression is indicated.

Complement-mediated disease can be treated with immunosuppression if autoantibodies are detected; glucocorticoids and rituximab have been trialled with some success. Genetic mutations leading to MCGN can respond to complement targeted therapies such as eculizumab. All patients should receive symptomatic treatment.

Complications
Complications are those of the nephrotic syndrome or CKD (if present). There is a high recurrence rate in renal transplantation (19–48%).

Prognosis
Fifty per cent of patients develop end-stage renal disease within 10 years of diagnosis; 90% develop it by 20 years.

Disease associations
> infection, especially with hepatitis B and C viruses, but also chronic infections such as endocarditis
> autoimmune disease, especially SLE
> complement deficiency: partial lipodystrophy is associated with type II disease
> hypogammaglobulinaemia
> monoclonal gammopathies: monoclonal gammopathy of undetermined significance (MGUS), myeloma.

Diffuse proliferative glomerulonephritis (post-streptococcal glomerulonephritis)

Aetiology/pathophysiology/pathology
This is a histological description, suggesting that >50% of glomeruli are involved in the disease process. Typical histology (Fig 56) includes:

> light microscopy: endothelial and mesangial cell proliferation, and glomerular infiltration with neutrophils and monocytes

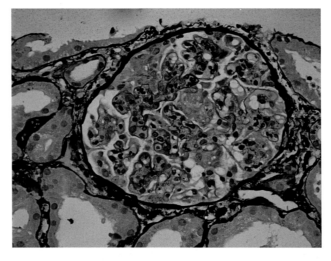

Fig 56 Post-streptococcal glomerulonephritis. Glomerulus showing endocapillary hypercellularity with numerous neutrophils. This silver stain shows a small extraglomerular crescent at 11 o'clock. (Courtesy of Dr V Bardsley, Addenbrooke's Hospital, Cambridge.)

> immunofluorescence: complement and immunoglobulin deposition

> electron microscopy: subepithelial deposits.

There are several causes for this histological appearance, and in patients presenting acutely unwell with nephritic syndrome or nephrotic syndrome with renal impairment, this is often seen on biopsy. Common associations include infection (post-streptococcal glomerulonephritis), discussed below, and autoimmune disease (SLE, vasculitis), which is discussed in Sections 2.7.5 and 2.7.6.

Post-streptococcal glomerulonephritis is caused by infection with nephritogenic strains of group-A beta-haemolytic *Streptococcus* and thought to be a reaction to streptococcal antigens being deposited in the GBM, leading to antibody binding and hence local complement activation and inflammation.

Epidemiology
Post-streptococcal glomerulonephritis is declining, and is now only common in developing countries. It is most often seen in the 5–12-year age group, although it is also seen in those >60 years. It is rare below 3 years. There may be isolated cases, but epidemics of group-A *Streptococcus* can lead to clusters of cases.

Clinical presentation
Presentation is typically 1–2 weeks after a streptococcal throat infection or 3–6 weeks after a streptococcal skin infection. It varies from asymptomatic non-visible haematuria to acute nephritic syndrome with visible haematuria, oedema, hypertension and oliguria.

Physical signs

> hypertension

> oedema

> signs of preceding infection.

Investigations

> urinalysis: blood (all cases), sometimes protein and often red blood cell casts

> bloods: impaired renal function; and serological evidence of infection such as raised antistreptolysin O titres (ASOT) and anti-DNase B. Also low complement levels, especially C3.

Differential diagnosis

> mesangiocapillary glomerulonephritis – symptoms/signs persist for longer

> SLE – if both C3 and C4 are low, or there are systemic signs, consider SLE

> IgA nephropathy – shorter latency (approximately 5 days after infection), recurrent episodes.

Treatment

> Ensure that any persistent focus of infection is eradicated (eg antibiotics).

> Symptomatic treatment: loop diuretics, treat hypertension.

> Dialysis is rarely required – spontaneous diuresis usually begins within a week of presentation.

Complications
Complications are those of any ongoing infection (although this is rare), uncontrolled oedema (particularly respiratory compromise) or hypertension (encephalopathy is rare but serious).

Prognosis

> Good: only 0.1–1% of patients have progressive renal impairment, although proteinuria can persist for months to years.

Anti-glomerular basement membrane disease (previously known as Goodpasture's disease)

Aetiology/pathophysiology/pathology
In anti-glomerular basement membrane (anti-GBM) disease, autoantibodies to the basement membrane in glomeruli and alveoli cause renal and pulmonary damage. The antigen is usually part of the non-collagenous domain of the alpha-3 component of type IV collagen. The histological findings are:

> Light microscopy – focal segmental proliferative glomerulonephritis, often with necrosis and crescents. All the glomerular lesions are of a similar age, unlike ANCA-associated vasculitis where the lesions tend to be of differing ages (Figs 57 and 58).

> Immunofluorescence – linear antibody deposition (usually IgG) along the GBM.

Epidemiology
This is rare: 0.5–1 per million. It occurs mainly in Caucasians, with a slight male preponderance. Respiratory involvement is more common in smokers.

Clinical presentation
The presentation is with lung haemorrhage in 50–70% of patients, causing cough, haemoptysis or shortness of breath. Renal involvement is initially asymptomatic, but can cause loin pain, visible haematuria, oliguria and AKI.

Physical signs

> Lung signs resemble pulmonary oedema or infection.

Investigations

> urinalysis: blood and protein, and red cell casts

> bloods: renal impairment and anti-GBM antibodies

> chest radiography: diffuse pulmonary haemorrhage may resemble pulmonary oedema or infection. CT of the chest may help

> lung function: gas transfer (K_{CO}) is raised by the absorption of carbon monoxide by the blood in the alveoli if haemorrhage has occurred recently

> renal biopsy.

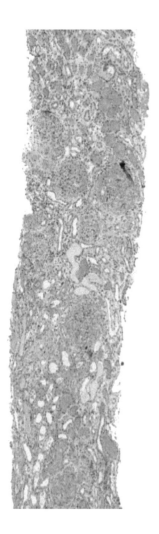

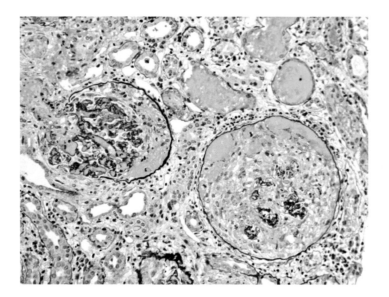

Fig 58 The silver stain shows two involved glomeruli: the one on the left shows a rupture in Bowman's membrane (incomplete black line from 7–11 o'clock) with fibrinoid necrosis and a developing crescent. The glomerulus on the right shows a massive cellular crescent engulfing a collapsed tuft (only remnants of the basement membrane are visible – staining black). Both lesions are of similar age. (Courtesy of Dr V Bardsley, Addenbrooke's Hospital, Cambridge.)

Fig 57 Medium power view of core biopsy showing that all the glomeruli are abnormal, with cellular crescents and surrounding haemorrhage. Many tubules also show fresh intraluminal haemorrhage. (Courtesy of Dr V Bardsley, Addenbrooke's Hospital, Cambridge.)

Differential diagnosis

> systemic vasculitis

> another glomerulonephritis with pulmonary oedema or infection.

Treatment

Key point

If you think that a patient has anti-GBM disease, speak to your local renal unit immediately.

> Plasma exchange is used to remove the pathogenic antibody. This can be a life-saving treatment in those with pulmonary haemorrhage.

> Immunosuppression with steroids and cyclophosphamide is used to inhibit further antibody production and reduce inflammatory damage. Rituximab is an alternative if the patient is intolerant of cyclophosphamide or there is a contraindication to therapy. A week of plasma exchange and intravenous steroids is followed by rituximab, then a 48-hour break before plasma exchange is recommenced (to avoid removing the monoclonal antibody!).

> Antibodies typically take 6–9 months to fall: maintenance therapy with azathioprine ± steroids can be commenced after initial cyclophosphamide/rituximab therapy.

If the patient presents with dialysis-dependent renal failure but without pulmonary haemorrhage, there is a very low likelihood of renal recovery (around 8% at 1 year), and the risks of immunosuppression may outweigh the limited potential for benefit. However, in younger patients, who are more able to tolerate immunosuppression, or those with a very acute presentation where long-term outcomes are less predictable, a short trial of steroids and plasma exchange may be appropriate.

Complications

> respiratory failure; secondary pulmonary infection; and treatment toxicity.

Prognosis

Untreated, most patients die. Patients who require dialysis before treatment is started do not usually recover renal function and morbidity from immunosuppression is high (if it is given at all). Of those patients whose plasma creatinine is <600 μmol/L before treatment, 80–90% recover independent renal function.

Disease associations

There is a strong association with human leukocyte antigen (HLA)-DR15 and a weaker association with HLA-DR4. Pulmonary haemorrhage is more common if the patient is a smoker, has pulmonary infection or oedema, or there is exposure to other inhaled toxins.

Crescentic glomerulonephritis (or rapidly progressive glomerulonephritis, focal necrotising glomerulonephritis or renal microscopic polyangiitis)

Aetiology/pathophysiology/pathology

This is (also) a histological description with variable aetiology. The histological findings are:

> light microscopy – shows a proliferative glomerulonephritis with fibrinoid necrosis (often with crescents – inflammatory cells in Bowman's capsule) and may show small vessel vasculitis

> immunofluorescence – see below.

This condition is subclassified as follows:

> anti-GBM disease (see above)

> renal small-vessel vasculitis (pauci-immune) – immunofluorescence shows scant or absent immunoglobulins; serum anti-neutrophil cytoplasmic antibody (ANCA) is usually positive (see Section 1.5.5 and Section 2.7.6)

> complicating a pre-existing glomerulonephritis, a systemic disorder or an infection – immunofluorescence often shows immunoglobulin deposition (associations include SLE, Henoch–Schönlein purpura, IgA nephropathy, mesangiocapillary glomerulonephritis and post-infectious glomerulonephritis).

Epidemiology

This accounts for 2–5% of renal biopsies; age range, sex and racial preponderance are variable depending on cause.

Clinical presentation

Renal disease ranges from asymptomatic to oliguria and AKI. Manifestations of associated or underlying systemic diseases may be present, eg haemoptysis. There may be systemic symptoms such as fever, weight loss and general malaise.

Physical signs

Manifestations of systemic disease may be present, such as rashes or eye, upper respiratory tract or joint lesions.

Investigations

> urinalysis: blood, protein and red blood cell casts

> bloods: renal impairment; raised inflammatory markers such as C-reactive protein (CRP), erythrocyte sedimentation rate (ESR), white cell count and platelet count; and positive serological tests for associated systemic diseases – especially ANCA or anti-GBM antibody

> renal biopsy.

Differential diagnosis

> other forms of acute glomerulonephritis

> other causes of AKI.

Treatment

Rapidly progressive glomerulonephritis (GN) is, as the name suggests, a severe form of nephritis that progresses to end-stage renal failure (ESRF) over days to weeks if not treated. Treatment includes:

> Immunosuppression with prednisolone and cyclophosphamide – azathioprine may be substituted as maintenance therapy for cyclophosphamide after 3 months. Depending on the cause, rituximab has also been used in patients for whom cyclophosphamide is contraindicated or who are intolerant of it. Several trials have shown rituximab is at least as effective as cyclophosphamide in ANCA-associated vasculitis for both induction and maintenance of remission, and it has fewer side effects.

> Plasma exchange is used for anti-GBM antibody disease. Therapy for rapidly progressive glomerulonephritis is often supplemented with adjuvant methyl prednisolone or plasma exchange.

Complications

Complications are those of immunosuppression and AKI, as well as complications of the underlying disease process and any systemic manifestations.

Prognosis

For ANCA-associated vasculitis, remission is now achieved in 80–90% of patients, although relapse is common. Mortality has been steadily falling, thanks in part to less toxic treatment regimens and better supportive care. Approximately 15–40% of patients will develop ESRF, and prognosis is much worse for those presenting with dialysis-dependent renal failure, with mortality of 20–50% and 30–40% reaching ESRF.

Disease associations

See aetiology above.

2.3.2 Secondary glomerular disease

Glomerular disease can be secondary to many conditions, including those discussed in Section 2.7. Malignancy and infection-associated glomerular disease are considered here.

Aetiology/pathophysiology/pathology

Malignancy-associated glomerulonephritis

The mechanism is usually unclear (see MCGN above) but renal disease may improve with treatment of the malignancy. Most patterns of glomerulonephritis can occur.

Infection-related glomerulonephritis

The mechanism is usually unclear; pathogen antigens can trigger an aberrant immune response causing renal damage. Most patterns of glomerulonephritis can occur; some types are more common with certain infections.

Epidemiology

Malignancy-associated glomerulonephritis

Of patients with malignancy, 15–58% have urinary abnormalities. Up to 17% of patients with solid tumours have histologically evident glomerular changes. Membranous nephropathy is the most common histological type.

Infection-related glomerulonephritis

Significant glomerulonephritis can be associated with viral infection (hepatitis C, hepatitis B and HIV), bacterial infection (streptococcal and endocarditis) and other infections (malaria and syphilis).

Clinical presentation and physical signs

Malignancy-associated glomerulonephritis

This varies from asymptomatic urinary abnormality to nephrotic syndrome or AKI. Physical signs depend on the tumour and the renal pathology.

Infection-related glomerulonephritis

This is highly variable, depending on the infection and the associated renal disease.

Investigations

These are as for other glomerular disease (see Section 2.3.1). Investigations will also be directed towards the malignancy or infection.

Differential diagnosis

Malignancy-associated glomerulonephritis

The differential diagnosis is from either primary glomerulonephritis or other tumour-related causes of renal dysfunction, including obstruction, invasion of the renal tract, renal vein thrombosis, urate nephropathy, hypercalcaemia and drug toxicity.

Infection-related glomerulonephritis

Differential diagnosis is from unrelated primary glomerulonephritis. With chronic infection, amyloid A amyloidosis can occur. In treated infections, consider drug toxicity.

Treatment

> Treat the malignancy in malignancy-associated glomerulonephritis.

> Eradicate, where possible, the infection in infection-related glomerulonephritis.

> Supportive care (manage hypertension, oedema, dialysis if required).

Complications

Malignancy-associated glomerulonephritis

The complications are those of the malignancy and its therapy; and also of the nephrotic syndrome, hypertension or renal impairment if they are present.

Infection-related glomerulonephritis

The complications are those of the underlying infection; and also of the nephrotic syndrome, hypertension and renal impairment if they are present.

Prognosis

This depends on the infection or malignancy. Generally, renal involvement is associated with a worsened prognosis for the malignancy.

Disease associations

In infection-related glomerulonephritis these could potentially be:

> hepatitis B – membranous nephropathy, mesangiocapillary glomerulonephritis (immune complex mediated) and IgA nephropathy

> hepatitis C – mesangiocapillary glomerulonephritis (immune complex mediated) and mixed cryoglobulinaemia

> HIV – focal segmental glomerulosclerosis (FSGS)

> Epstein–Barr virus (EBV) – non-visible haematuria and proteinuria

> streptococcal infection – post-streptococcal (diffuse proliferative) glomerulonephritis

> staphylococcal infection (endocarditis, shunt infections and general sepsis) – diffuse proliferative glomerulonephritis, focal segmental proliferative glomerulonephritis or immune-complex mediated mesangiocapillary glomerulonephritis

> *Salmonella* infections – mesangiocapillary glomerulonephritis or IgA nephropathy

> tuberculosis – amyloidosis

> leprosy – amyloidosis, diffuse proliferative glomerulonephritis or mesangiocapillary glomerulonephritis

> malaria and syphilis – membranous nephropathy

> *Escherichia coli* and other enteric infections can cause haemolytic–uraemic syndrome (HUS) (see Section 2.7.3)

> leptospirosis causes an acute tubulointerstitial nephritis.

2.4 Tubulointerstitial diseases

2.4.1 Acute tubular necrosis

Aetiology/pathophysiology

Acute tubular necrosis (ATN) occurs when there is tubular cell injury and death. This usually results from renal hypoperfusion, referred to as ischaemic ATN. Drugs may also directly damage tubular cells, referred to as nephrotoxic ATN (eg contrast media and aminoglycosides).

In ischaemic ATN, reduced renal blood flow results in cortical vasoconstriction and medullary hypoxia (Fig 59). Cells of the proximal convoluted tubule and thick ascending limb of the loop of Henle have high oxygen requirements and are particularly susceptible to hypoxic damage. Thus cell necrosis results – mediated by oxygen free radicals and calcium – and cells are shed into the tubular lumen, forming casts that obstruct urine flow. Loss of tubular integrity produces backleak of glomerular filtrate and hence reabsorption of water and toxins. Vascular endothelial cells within the medulla are also damaged, further impairing blood flow.

When renal perfusion is compromised, exposure to NSAIDs will inhibit cyclooxygenases and further decrease perfusion. This is a common contributing factor to ATN in clinical practice.

Remarkably, the kidney can recover from ATN. Once blood supply and oxygen delivery are normalised, tubular cells still adherent to the basement membrane can divide and regenerate a functional epithelium. Glomerular filtration is reinitiated through mechanisms that are unclear. However, at this point tubular function may not have sufficiently recovered to enable fluid reabsorption, resulting in a 'polyuric phase' during recovery from ATN.

Epidemiology

Acute kidney injury (AKI) has been reported in 1–7% hospital admissions, with the incidence in the UK ranging from 170 cases per million population (pmp) to 630 pmp in more recent case series. Over 50% of these are caused by ATN. Older people are much more at risk.

Clinical presentation

> Presentation is usually in the context of an obvious illness (eg the initial presentation may be with pneumonia and dehydration).

> ATN is often part of the multi-organ failure syndrome and is common in patients on the intensive care unit (ICU).

> Occasionally patients present with acute renal failure due to ATN without an obvious episode of hypoperfusion.

> It may occur on the background of known or previously unrecognised chronic renal impairment (acute on chronic kidney disease (CKD)).

Investigations

> Urine may show low-grade (trace/1+) proteinuria and/or haematuria, but heavy proteinuria/haematuria and cellular casts raise doubt about the diagnosis.

> Ultrasonography shows normal-sized unobstructed kidneys.

> Renal biopsy is not usually necessary, but if performed shows tubular necrosis – sometimes with evidence of regeneration.

Treatment

> The first priority is treatment of life-threatening complications (see Section 1.5.1).

> Supportive treatments: maintain circulation and oxygenation, and avoid further nephrotoxic drugs.

> The precipitating condition must be treated vigorously.

> If the patient remains oliguric and renal function is not improving, discuss with renal services sooner rather than later.

Prognosis

Approximately 50% of all patients who require renal replacement therapy (RRT) for ATN will survive. Mortality is higher in those who require RRT in the context of multi-organ failure on the ICU. Of the survivors, 60% will regain full renal function, but 30% will have residual CKD

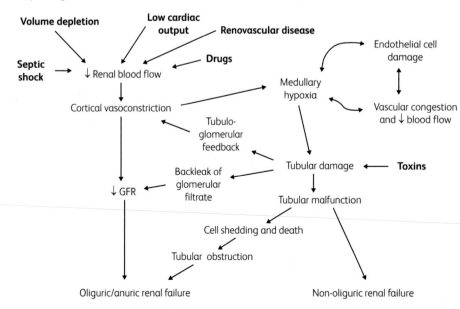

Fig 59 Pathophysiology of acute tubular necrosis (ATN). Reproduced with permission from Fry A, Farrington K. Management of acute renal failure. *Postgrad Med J* 2006;82:106–116. © BMJ Publishing Group Ltd.

and 10% will have end-stage kidney disease such that they need to remain on long-term dialysis. The likelihood of recovery is lower in older people.

2.4.2 Acute interstitial nephritis
Aetiology
Some cases are idiopathic, but a recognised precipitating cause (most often drugs, particularly NSAIDs) can be identified in most patients.

Key point
Causes of acute intestinal nephritis

> idiopathic

> drugs (70–75%) – eg NSAIDs (most common cause), penicillin, rifampicin, allopurinol, cephalosporins, sulphonamides, furosemide, thiazide diuretics, cimetidine and amphotericin

> infections – viral (eg hantavirus), bacterial (eg leptospirosis) and mycobacterial

> autoimmune conditions – eg systemic lupus erythematosus (SLE), sarcoidosis, Sjögren's syndrome

> tubulointerstitial nephritis with uveitis (TINU) syndrome.

Clinical presentation
This is usually with mild renal impairment and hypertension or, severe acute kidney injury (AKI), which is often non-oliguric. Systemic manifestations may include fever, arthralgia and skin rash (more so in drug-related cases). Patients with TINU present with interstitial nephritis, uveitis, abdominal pain, fever, fatigue and arthralgias.

Investigations

> Urinalysis – typically shows low-grade proteinuria and non-visible haematuria; urinary eosinophils may be present.

> Differential FBC may show an eosinophilia and serum IgE can be raised.

> Renal biopsy typically shows oedema of the interstitium with an acute inflammatory infiltrate (plasma cells, lymphocytes and eosinophils) (Fig 60).

Treatment

> Withdraw the causative agent (eg drugs).

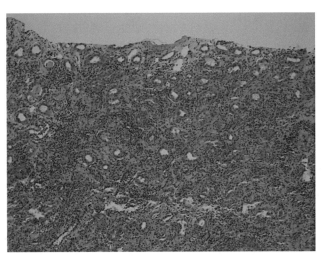
(a)

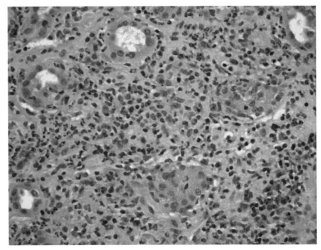
(b)

Fig 60 (a) Medium power and **(b)** high power images of acute tubulointerstitial nephritis (H&E). They both demonstrate a diffuse infiltrate of mixed leukocytes including numerous eosinophils, typical of a drug-induced / allergic-type interstitial nephritis. (Courtesy of Dr V Bardsley, Addenbrooke's Hospital, Cambridge.)

> Moderate-dose oral steroids (eg prednisolone 30 mg od) are commonly given.

Prognosis
Most patients make a complete renal recovery.

2.4.3 Chronic interstitial nephritis
Aetiology
Diverse systemic or renal conditions and drugs can result in chronic inflammation within the tubulointerstitium.

Key point

Causes of chronic intestinal nephritis

> immunological diseases – systemic lupus erythematosus (SLE), Sjögren's syndrome, rheumatoid arthritis and systemic sclerosis

> granulomatous disease – Wegener's granulomatosis, tuberculosis (TB) and sarcoidosis

> drugs – cyclosporin A, cisplatin, lithium, iron and analgesics

> haematological disorders – myeloma, light-chain nephropathy and sickle cell disease

> chronic infections – TB

> heavy metals – lead and cadmium

> hereditary disorders – nephronophthisis and Alport syndrome

> metabolic disorders – hypercalcaemia, hypokalaemia and hyperuricaemia

> endemic disease – Balkan nephropathy (aristolochic acid (AA) nephropathy)

> other – irradiation and chronic transplant rejection.

Clinical presentation

Patients present with chronic kidney disease (CKD) or end-stage renal failure (ESRF). Some patients may also manifest renal tubular acidosis (RTA) (usually type I) (see Section 2.4.4), nephrogenic diabetes insipidus or salt-wasting states.

Investigations

Renal biopsy shows a chronic inflammatory infiltrate within the interstitium, often with extensive scarring and tubular loss (Fig 61); the latter indicates irreversible renal damage.

Other histological features may be specific to the underlying disorder:

> tubular casts with myeloma or light-chain nephropathy

> granulomas in TB or sarcoidosis.

Treatment

Treat the underlying condition. Withdraw any drugs/toxins.

Prognosis

This depends on the cause and the severity of damage at the time of diagnosis. If the cause can be treated (eg connective tissue disorder) or removed (eg drugs), then progression of the CKD may be prevented. However, extensive tubulointerstitial fibrosis usually predicts a progressive decline to ESRF.

2.4.4 Specific tubulointerstitial disorders

Balkan nephropathy

Aetiology

There have been multiple causes proposed but the most likely is chronic low-level exposure to aristolochic acid (AA). This is a nephrotoxic alkaloid found in the plant *Aristolochia clematitis* and has also been associated with a more rapidly progressive nephropathy in patients (often young women) taking Chinese herbal slimming remedies.

Epidemiology

This is a chronic interstitial renal disease endemic in villages along the tributaries of the River Danube in south-eastern Europe (in the area thought of as the Balkans: Serbia, Romania, Bulgaria, Bosnia and Herzegovina, and Croatia).

Clinical presentation

This is slowly progressive and presentation is with often with chronic kidney disease (CKD) or end-stage renal failure (ESRF).

Physical signs

Patients have coppery-yellow pigmentation of the palms and soles.

Investigations

Imaging reveals small, smooth kidneys in later disease. A normochromic normocytic anaemia is observed early in the disease, progressing with disease severity.

Treatment

There is currently no specific treatment. Proceed with the appropriate treatment for CKD and renal replacement see Sections 2.1.2 and 2.1.3).

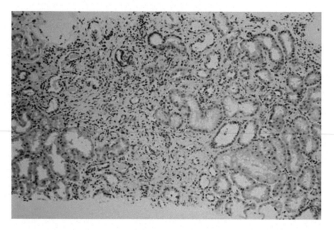

Fig 61 Histological appearance of chronic interstitial nephritis. Alongside the inflammatory infiltrate, there is evidence of chronic tubulointerstitial damage, with scarring and tubular atrophy (H&E; magnification ×80).

Complications

There is an increased incidence of transitional cell carcinoma of the renal pelvis, ureter and bladder (two to 10 times that of non-endemic areas). Regular surveillance with urine cytology may be advisable.

Analgesic nephropathy

Aetiology

Chronic analgesic usage (previously compound analgesics containing phenacetin, now NSAIDs).

Epidemiology

Between 1950 and 1970 analgesic nephropathy was the most common cause of CKD in parts of Europe and Australia. The prevalence has since declined substantially, especially since the withdrawal of phenacetin in the 1990s. It affects women more often than men. Most are over 45 years of age.

Clinical presentation

There is a history of chronic analgesic usage, eg for backache, pelvic inflammatory disease and headache. There may be loin pain associated with papillary necrosis. Presentation is often incidental with CKD found on blood tests or urinalysis or ESRF.

Investigations

The classic radiological appearance is of 'cup and spill' calyces, resulting from papillary necrosis, with renal scarring seen on an intravenous urogram (IVU) (Fig 62). Renal biopsy is not of diagnostic value. Ultrasound shows small kidneys with irregular outlines. CT may show calcification of the renal papilla.

Treatment

As for CKD (see Section 2.1.2) and ESRF (see Section 2.1.3). Complete cessation of analgesic consumption. Initiate prompt treatment of infection/obstruction.

Complications

The risk of urothelial malignancy is increased.

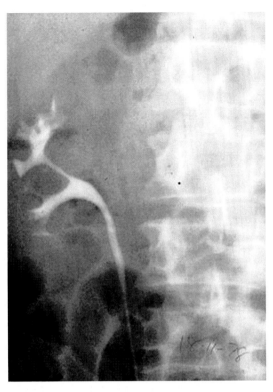

Fig 62 Intravenous urogram (IVU) of papillary necrosis. There is clubbing of right upper polar calyces with typical 'cup and spill' deformities.

Renal tubular acidosis

Aetiology

> Distal or type I renal tubular acidosis (RTA) results from impaired urinary acidification.

> Proximal or type II RTA is caused by a failure of bicarbonate reabsorption.

> Type IV RTA (hyporeninaemic hypoaldosteronism) describes a (usually mild) metabolic acidosis that is associated with hyperkalaemia and mild renal impairment (glomerular filtration rate (GFR) usually >30 mL/min).

> Type III RTA – a mixed picture, usually referring to carbonic anhydrase deficiency.

Epidemiology

> Distal RTA is fairly common and can complicate many renal parenchymal disorders.

> Proximal RTA is uncommon.

The causes of different forms of RTA are shown in Table 24.

Clinical presentation

> Distal RTA can present with normal anion gap (hyperchloraemic) metabolic acidosis, hyperventilation and muscular weakness (due to hypokalaemia). It is also associated with growth failure and rickets in children and osteomalacia in adults. Seventy per cent of people with distal RTA have nephrocalcinosis or urinary stones.

> Proximal RTA can present with growth failure and rickets (children), osteomalacia (adults) and proximal myopathy. Polyuria and polydipsia can be seen.

Physical signs

The diagnosis of RTA depends on demonstrating that in the presence of normal or near-normal GFR the renal tubules cannot excrete acid normally.

Table 24 Causes of RTA

Type of RTA	Causes
Distal RTA	Primary: genetic (dominant or recessive) or idiopathic Secondary to autoimmune diseases: SLE, rheumatoid arthritis and Sjögren's syndrome Tubulointerstitial disease: chronic pyelonephritis, transplant rejection, obstructive uropathy and chronic interstitial nephritis Nephrocalcinosis: medullary sponge kidney and hypercalcaemia Drugs and toxins: lithium, amphotericin and toluene
Proximal RTA	Occurring alone: idiopathic With Fanconi syndrome: Wilson's disease, cystinosis, fructose intolerance and Sjögren's syndrome Tubulointerstitial disease: interstitial nephritis, myeloma and amyloidosis Drugs and toxins: outdated tetracyclines, streptozotocin, lead and mercury (and other heavy metals), acetazolamide, topiramate and sulphonamides
Type IV RTA	Diabetic nephropathy Gouty nephropathy Urinary tract obstruction Drugs: NSAIDs or potassium-sparing diuretics

NSAIDs, non-steroidal anti-inflammatory drugs; RTA, renal tubular acidosis; SLE, systemic lupus erythematosus.

In many cases formal testing is not required because the patient is already acidaemic.

A formal acidification test involves determination of the minimum urinary pH after ingestion of a standardised dose of ammonium chloride. Urine pH should fall to less than pH 5.5. Specific signs are:

> Distal RTA – plasma bicarbonate tends to be very low (<12 mmol/L) and urinary pH is always >5.5. There may be severe hypokalaemia. Abdominal radiograph may show nephrocalcinosis / urinary stones.

> Proximal RTA – when plasma bicarbonate falls sufficiently, the urinary pH can fall to normal minimum (pH<5.5). Proximal RTA is almost always associated with Fanconi syndrome (phosphaturia, glycosuria, aminoaciduria and uricosuria). Nephrocalcinosis and urinary stones are not seen. Hypokalaemia is common.

Treatment

> Distal RTA: the acutely acidotic patient is usually very hypokalaemic.

Acutely, potassium should be given before bicarbonate. Chronic acidosis responds well to oral sodium bicarbonate (1–3 mmol/kg body weight/day)

> Proximal RTA: very large doses of oral sodium bicarbonate (3–20 mmol/kg body weight/day) are required, usually with potassium supplementation. Phosphate supplementation may be

needed to prevent metabolic bone disease.

Complications

> distal RTA: nephrocalcinosis (see Fig 63), calculi and growth failure

> proximal RTA: rickets and osteomalacia (caused by phosphate wasting).

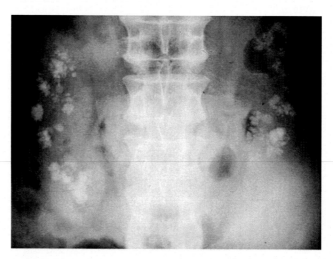

Fig 63 Nephrocalcinosis in a plain abdominal radiograph of a patient with renal tubular acidosis (RTA). There is gross calcification within the outer medullary and cortical regions of the kidneys.

Reflux nephropathy (or chronic pyelonephritis)

Aetiology
Childhood vesicoureteral reflux (VUR) and infection cause renal scarring and nephropathy (Fig 64). There is a genetic predisposition: children of parents with reflux nephropathy have an approximately 25% risk of VUR.

Epidemiology
> Common during the first 5 years of life (when almost all scarring occurs).

> Reflux diminishes with age.

> Accounts for about 15% of patients entering dialysis programmes.

Clinical presentation
> Young children – urinary tract infection (UTI) and/or pyelonephritis.

> Adults – hypertension, proteinuria or chronic renal impairment. Often there will be a history of bedwetting in late childhood and/or UTIs. Renal impairment due to reflux nephropathy is usually accompanied by proteinuria (less than nephrotic range). Haematuria is not expected and should prompt further investigation (eg cystoscopy).

Investigations
Scarring can be demonstrated by ultrasonography or ^{99m}Tc-dimercaptosuccinic acid (DMSA) scintigraphy. The presence of scars in an adult without another explanation is taken as evidence of childhood VUR and scarring. Further investigations are not usually performed. Reflux does not usually persist in adults.

An IVU is not usually necessary. The classical appearance is of 'cup and spill' calyces, resulting from papillary necrosis, with renal scarring (Fig 62).

It is recommended that offspring or siblings (if they are a child) of affected patients undergo screening for VUR. Diagnosis of VUR is by micturating cystography. Reflux can be graded from

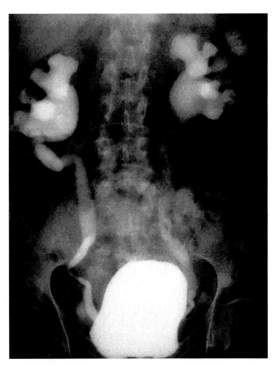

Fig 64 Micturating cystogram showing severe reflux nephropathy (grade III).

grade I (involving reflux into the ureter only) to grade V (gross dilatation and tortuosity of ureter, renal pelvis and calyces) (Fig 65).

Renal biopsy is not of diagnostic value.

Treatment
Renal scarring results from infection in young children. To try to prevent this, children with reflux are given antibiotic prophylaxis. Surgery for VUR is not proven to protect against scarring and its role is therefore controversial. Operations that have been performed include endoscopic injection of collagen behind the intravesical ureter, lengthening of the submucosal ureteric tunnel and ureteric reimplantation, but none have been shown to improve renal prognosis.

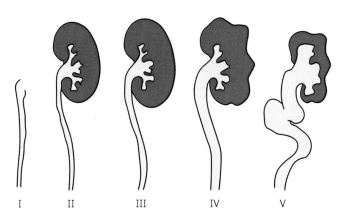

I   II   III   IV   V

Fig 65 Classification of vesicoureteral reflux (VUR): grade I, ureter only; grade II, up to pelvis and calyces, but with no dilatation; grade III, mild-to-moderate dilatation, but with only minimal blunting of fornices; grade IV, moderate dilatation, with obliteration of sharp angles of fornices; grade V, gross dilatation, tortuosity of the ureter and pelvicalyceal system, and calyces severely clubbed.

As with all forms of chronic and potentially progressive renal disorders, control of hypertension is of vital importance in retarding progression (see Section 2.1.2).

Prevention

> Of children with a UTI, 15–60% will have VUR and about 10% will have evidence of reflux nephropathy.

> All children with a UTI should be investigated for VUR.

> If VUR is present treatment with prophylactic antibiotics is recommended and screening of siblings should be considered, especially in those with high-grade reflux.

2.5 Diseases of renal vessels

2.5.1 Renovascular disease

Aetiology

Renovascular disease refers to disorders primarily affecting the renal arteries, and which lead to hypertension and renal dysfunction. Atherosclerosis accounts for 90% of cases of renovascular disease (atheromatous renovascular disease (ARVD)) and may produce discrete narrowing of the renal arteries at their origin (renal artery stenosi) or diffuse atherosclerotic disease of the renal arteries and smaller vessels.

Fibromuscular dysplasia is a much less common cause of renal artery stenosis and hypertension. It is seen mainly in young woman and is of unknown aetiology. Rarer causes of renovascular disease include dissection, vasculitis and extrinsic compression, such as by a tumour.

Epidemiology

ARVD is associated with generalised vascular disease, and has the same risk factors as atherosclerosis. It is present in up to 30% of patients undergoing coronary angiography, up to 60% with peripheral vascular disease, and about 30% with congestive heart failure who are aged >70 years. As older patients are now readily admitted to dialysis programmes, ARVD is an increasing cause of end-stage renal failure (ESRF) (about 20%) in this population.

Clinical presentation

Presentation is with hypertension (ARVD accounts for 80% of all secondary hypertension instances, ie 4% of all cases of hypertension), chronic kidney disease (CKD) or ESRF. Less commonly there may be angiotensin-converting enzyme (ACE) inhibitor-related acute kidney injury, and rarely but dramatically there can be 'flash' pulmonary oedema.

Predominant symptoms usually relate to coexisting extrarenal vascular disease (eg angina, intermittent claudication). Clinical examination may demonstrate vascular disease elsewhere (reduced or absent peripheral pulses, arterial leg ulcers or carotid and femoral bruits); renal artery bruits are occasionally present.

Investigations

General investigations include serum creatinine to estimate GFR, serum potassium (hypokalaemia or low-normal potassium suggests activation of renin–angiotensin–aldosterone system) and urinalysis (in the absence of coexistent diabetic nephropathy or hypertensive nephrosclerosis, ARVD is usually non-proteinuric).

Investigations are aimed at identifying atheromatous disease in the renal arteries – particularly if a discrete stenosis can be found. A renal ultrasound followed by either magnetic resonance angiography (MRA) or CT angiography is a reasonable approach for investigation.

> Ultrasonography – a discrepancy in renal length >2 cm is predictive of renovascular disease, and imaging will also give an indication of how much chronic damage there is and exclude obstruction. However, Doppler ultrasonography is time consuming, highly observer dependent and not usually suitable as a screening tool.

> Gadolinium-enhanced MRA of the renal arteries is the screening test of choice. It avoids the use of nephrotoxic contrast media and exposure to ionising radiation, but tends to overestimate the severity of stenoses. It should, however, be avoided in those with severe renal impairment (eGFR < 30 mL/min) due to the risk of gadolinium-induced nephrogenic systemic fibrosis.

> CT angiography – disadvantages are risks of allergy, contrast nephropathy and radiation exposure, although it may be appropriate if MRA is not available or contraindicated. Discussion with a radiologist is advised.

> Captopril renography – this is of limited value if there is significant renal dysfunction. It cannot delineate the anatomy of stenoses, but is useful to determine the relative contribution to function of each kidney prior to intervention. It is now uncommonly used because of its complexity and availability of other tests.

> Renal angiography – this remains the definitive investigation for renovascular disease (Fig 66). Often angiography and treatment (angioplasty ± stenting) will be performed as part of the same procedure. Risks include volume overload and/or acute renal dysfunction related to contrast, cholesterol emboli, bleeding – both at the site of catheter introduction and retroperitoneal – and dissection of the artery.

Treatment

All patients with ARVD should receive aspirin and cholesterol-lowering therapy for their general atherosclerotic risk. Other risk factors for vascular and renal disease, such as smoking and glycaemic control, should also be managed.

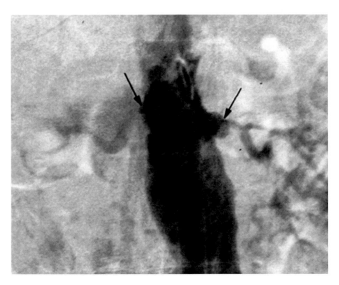

Fig 66 Aortic aneurysm in association with atheromatous renovascular disease (ARVD). An infrarenal aneurysm with bilateral renal artery stenoses (arrowed) are shown on this intravenous digital subtraction angiogram.

Most patients with ARVD have hypertension, and renin–angiotensin blockade with ACE inhibitor or angiotensin-receptor blocker (ARB) work well in many as it directly targets the mechanism of hypertension in these patients. However, some patients do not tolerate it, as maintenance of intraglomerular pressure and thus GFR may be dependent on angiotensin-II-mediated vasoconstriction of the efferent arteriole. It is thus important to check renal function 7–10 days after initiating therapy and discontinuing if there is a significant fall in eGFR (>25% reduction).

Patients with significant stenoses, especially ostial lesions, may be considered for treatment with angioplasty with or without a stent. However, three large randomised control trials (STAR, ASTRAL and CORAL) do not support the routine use of such radiological intervention, which was shown to have: 1 no benefit over medical therapy in reducing primary and composite endpoints of death, myocardial infarction (MI), stroke, heart failure, progression of CKD or need for RRT, and 2 was associated with increased adverse events. As a result of these trials nephrologists are now less inclined to pursue imaging of the renal arteries of patients, excepting

in the following circumstances when intervention might be appropriate:

> episodes of recurrent flash pulmonary oedema not explained by left ventricular dysfunction

> bilateral stenoses with acute deterioration in renal function, especially in the context of ACE inhibitor

> when there is a small kidney on one side and tight stenosis affecting the opposite functioning kidney

> renal artery stenosis with refractory hypertension on multiple drugs.

In a small and select group of patients, surgical reconstruction of the renal arteries may be considered – usually restricted to those patients who are also undergoing aortic surgery for an abdominal aortic aneurysm or severe aortoiliac atherosclerotic disease.

In contrast to ARVD, in fibromuscular dysplasia, along with lifestyle modifications and antihypertensive therapy, renal angioplasty is considered first-line treatment. It is often curative, with an initial success rate and 10-year patency of 90%. Stenting is usually not required, except where there have been procedural complications such as dissection.

Prognosis

The prognosis of ARVD is poor as a result of comorbid vascular events; the 5-year survival rate on dialysis is <20%.

2.5.2 Cholesterol atheroembolisation

Aetiology/pathophysiology

Cholesterol atheroembolisation syndrome occurs following embolisation of the contents of an atherosclerotic plaque (predominantly cholesterol crystals) from a large vessel to distal small to medium vessels, where it results in end-organ damage by occluding the vessel, thus causing ischaemia, and by provoking an inflammatory response.

It typically occurs in patients with widespread atheromatous disease, often following trauma to the vessels such as:

> vascular surgery – especially to the abdominal aorta

> angiography or stenting procedures – usually coronary.

Ruptured or unstable plaques release showers of cholesterol crystals that embolise to the vessels of the kidneys and other distal vessels (eg the gut, feet and skin of the lower extremities, and skeletal muscle), resulting in a variety of clinical presentations. Systemic anticoagulation may cause or exacerbate the condition by preventing the formation of stable thrombus on atheromatous plaques.

Clinical presentation

> There may be a recent history of vascular intervention and patients often have evidence of generalised vascular disease.

> Patients may present with acute, subacute or chronic kidney failure. In the former two settings, an eliciting event is often clear. Chronic kidney disease (CKD) may be due to

non-resolution of an acute insult, or due to spontaneous low-grade embolisation over a long period.

> Skin changes are variable and include livedo reticularis, cyanosis (in the feet it can cause 'blue toe syndrome' or 'trash feet'), gangrene, ulceration and purpura. The appearances can mimic features of a vasculitis.

> Gut ischaemia may result in intestinal blood loss.

> Low-grade fever, myalgia and anorexia may occur as manifestations of a systemic inflammatory response.

Hazard
Cholesterol atheroembolisation can mimic vasculitis.

Investigations

> Cholesterol crystals ('cholesterol clefts') within vessels on renal biopsy (Fig 67).

> Skin biopsy is less invasive and may demonstrate a similar appearance.

> Non-diagnostic findings include: elevated erythrocyte sedimentation rate (ESR), hypocomplementaemia and eosinophilia.

Treatment

Treatment is supportive. Anticoagulation should be withdrawn if implicated. Statin therapy may be beneficial (purported to stabilise atheromatous plaques). Avoid further angiography.

Prognosis

> Prognosis is poor because of underlying vascular disease.

> Chronic renal failure (CRF) may stabilise if precipitating factors can be removed.

> Some patients never recover renal function.

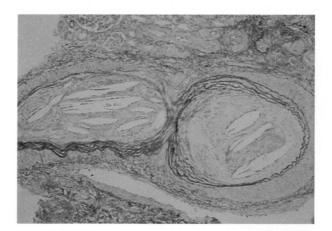

Fig 67 Intrarenal cholesterol emboli. Large cholesterol crystals are seen within renal arterioles – producing the appearance of 'cholesterol clefts' (H&E; magnification ×120).

2.6 Post-renal problems

2.6.1 Obstructive uropathy

Aetiology/pathophysiology/ pathology

Obstruction can arise at any point along the urinary tract (Fig 68). If pressure rises proximal to the obstruction, then the glomerular filtration rate (GFR) will fall and renal damage may occur.

Key point
Obstruction can arise from:

> within the lumen of the urinary tract (eg stones)

> within the wall of the system (eg urothelial tumours)

> outside the system (eg pressure from a pelvic tumour).

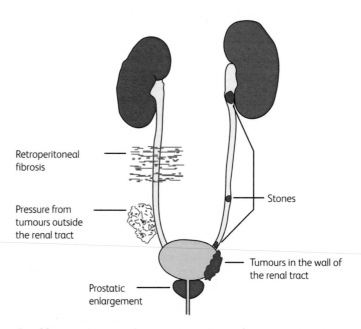

Retroperitoneal fibrosis

Pressure from tumours outside the renal tract

Prostatic enlargement

Stones

Tumours in the wall of the renal tract

Fig 68 Urinary tract obstruction can arise from outside the wall of the urinary tract, within the wall or within the lumen of the urinary system. The major sites at which obstruction to the urinary tract can occur are shown.

Epidemiology

Lower tract obstruction is common in older people, particularly in older men with prostatic disease.

Clinical presentation

Acute obstruction, especially with stones, can cause severe pain in the areas to which the urinary tract refers pain – from the loin down to the external genitalia (see Section 1.5.6).

Chronic obstruction is often asymptomatic until there is substantial renal impairment. A poor urinary stream suggests significant obstruction in a patient with prostatic disease; hesitancy, terminal dribbling and urinary frequency also occur.

Key point

Always consider prostatic obstruction in an older man with renal impairment or UTI.

Physical signs

> prostate enlargement

> large palpable residual bladder volume

> note that urinary obstruction does not cause the kidneys to become palpable.

Investigation

> Imaging of the renal tract, usually by ultrasonography – this may show a distended bladder, hydroureter or hydronephrosis.

> Further imaging may be necessary to define the site and nature of the obstruction, eg CT kidneys, ureters and bladder (KUB).

> Blood tests to check for evidence of renal impairment and hyperkalaemia.

> Specific tests may be relevant, such as prostate-specific antigen.

Differential diagnosis

The differential diagnosis is from other causes of renal impairment.

Treatment

> Lower urinary tract obstruction may often be relieved by insertion of a bladder catheter.

> For upper urinary tract obstruction, surgical or radiological relief of obstruction with nephrostomies or ureteric stents may be necessary.

> Following relief of urinary obstruction, particularly if it has been chronic, patients often have a significant diuresis and may require large volumes of intravenous or oral fluid to maintain hydration before this settles.

> In the long term, patients with prostatic disease may benefit from treatment with 5-alpha-reductase inhibitors or alpha-blockers.

Complications

> end-stage renal disease

> infection

> stone formation in static urine.

Prognosis

The renal prognosis depends on the amount of renal damage caused by the obstruction before it is relieved.

Disease associations

> tumours

> retroperitoneal fibrosis

> stones.

Pelviureteric junction obstruction: quite commonly a ring of fibrous tissue where the renal pelvis joins the ureter can obstruct the renal pelvis and calyces. This can correct spontaneously, but if there is pain or evidence of declining renal function then surgery is needed.

2.6.2 Stones

Aetiology/pathophysiology/pathology

Stones form when the concentration of stone-forming substances in the urine exceeds their solubility. Conditions that raise urinary concentrations of stone-forming substances or lower urinary levels of stone-inhibiting compounds therefore predispose an individual to stones. In particular, if the urine volume is reduced then the concentration of stone-forming substances rises and stone formation increases. Compounds such as citrate reduce stone formation by chelating stone substances.

Hypercalciuria occurs in 65% of patients with stones and is usually idiopathic. It is associated with obesity and hypertension. Major causes of stone formation are shown in Table 25.

Key point

Major sites of stone obstruction in the ureters are at:

> the pelviureteric junction

> the point where the ureters cross over the rim of the pelvic bones

> the entry site of the ureters into the bladder.

Epidemiology

Stones are common, with a prevalence of up to 10% in men and 5% in women. They are much more common in hot climates. There is a strong familial predisposition, with first degree relatives having a relative risk of 2.5 compared to controls. After one stone, there is a >50% chance of having a second stone in the next 10 years.

Clinical presentation

The clinical presentation varies:

> asymptomatic haematuria and uncomplicated passage of small stones or gravel

Table 25 Major causes of stone formation

Stone type	Causes
Calcium stones (oxalate, phosphate or both; 80% of cases)	Hypercalciuria: causes of hypercalcaemia, especially primary hyperparathyroidism; idiopathic Hyperoxaluria: primary hyperoxaluria, excess intake, ileal disease and ileal bypass Hypocitraturia: inflammatory bowel disease, chronic metabolic acidosis, distal tubular disease
Uric acid stones (10% of cases)	Acid urine (pH <5) causes uric acid precipitation High purine intake High cell turnover: tumours and tumour lysis
Cystine stones (2% of cases)	Cystinuria: autosomal recessive defect in dibasic amino acid transporter
Magnesium ammonium phosphate (struvite) stones (5% of cases)	Chronic infection with urea-splitting organisms causing an alkaline urine (eg *Proteus*, *Pseudomonas*, *Escherichia coli*, *Klebsiella*)
Other stones (3% of cases)	Include xanthine stones in xanthinuria Rare renal chloride channel mutations can cause stone formation

> acute renal colic with loin pain, nausea, vomiting and sometimes visible haematuria (see Section 1.5.6)

> incidentally demonstrated on imaging.

Physical signs
Obstruction may cause renal tenderness.

Investigations
Acute setting

> Urine: look for non-visible or visible blood.

> Imaging by plain radiography, ultrasonography, radiographic contrast studies (intravenous urogram (IVU), CT, antegrade or retrograde ureterography): calcium and infection stones are radio-opaque; cystine stones are weakly radio-opaque; and urate stones are radiolucent, but may be seen on ultrasound.

> Culture urine to exclude infection.

Outpatient setting
To identify a predisposing metabolic disorder:

> Analyse any stone passed to determine its constituents.

> Perform a spot urinalysis – check pH, specific gravity, microscopy for crystals, culture and qualitative test

for cystine (if there is a radiolucent stone). A pH above 7 with phosphate crystals is suggestive of magnesium ammonium phosphate / calcium phosphate 'infection stones'; hexagonal cystine crystals are diagnostic of cystine stones.

> Check serum sodium, potassium, creatinine, urea, calcium, phosphate, albumin, urate and bicarbonate.

> Collect a 24-hour urine sample with acid preservative – check volume, creatinine, calcium, magnesium, sodium, potassium, phosphate, oxalate and citrate.

> Collect a 24-hour urine sample in a plain container (no preservative) – check volume, creatinine, pH, protein, urate and cystine (qualitative test).

Consider an anatomical as well as a biochemical predisposition to stone formation – stone formation can occur because of urinary stasis, infection or around catheters. Ultrasonography is a good screening test for an anatomical abnormality.

Key point
Hypercalciuria, usually idiopathic, is found in 65% of patients with urinary stones.

Differential diagnosis

> clot retention

> papillary necrosis

> tumours.

Treatment
Asymptomatic stones not associated with obstruction or infection require conservative treatment only (see Prevention). Symptomatic, obstructing or large stones may be removed by percutaneous or surgical intervention, or by extracorporeal shock-wave lithotripsy.

Complications

> infection

> urinary obstruction

> permanent renal damage.

Prognosis
Fifty per cent of those who pass a urinary stone will do so again. Untreated or repeated obstruction can cause chronic renal failure (CRF), most commonly in those with infection stones.

Prevention

Key point
The most important preventive measure is to increase fluid intake.

Prevention of stone recurrence is by:

> All types of stones:

>> maintain a high fluid intake to keep the urinary concentration of stone-forming substances low – patients who form urinary stones should be told to drink enough liquids to ensure a urine output (UO) of at least 2–3 L/day

>> eradicate (if possible) any chronic infection

>> potassium citrate – helpful in most stone-forming situations because, as well as causing alkalinisation, the citrate chelates calcium.

> Calcium stones:

>> correct hyperparathyroidism if present

>> restrict dietary sodium, animal protein (meat, fish and poultry), and oxalate-containing foods (rhubarb and spinach) – do not advise a low dietary calcium intake, as this causes an increase in intestinal absorption of oxalate and can thereby increase the risk of stone formation

>> thiazide (not loop) diuretics inhibit urinary calcium excretion.

> Urate stones:

>> alkalinisation of the urine to a pH >6.5 with potassium citrate; the use of sodium citrate or bicarbonate is less preferable, as these predispose to hypercalciuria

>> if hyperuricosuria is present, then reduction of purine intake and reduction of urate production with allopurinol will also help.

> Struvite stones:

>> eradication of infection with antibiotics

>> as the stones themselves often harbour bacteria, they need to be removed as well.

> Cystine stones

>> alkalinisation of the urine with potassium citrate.

>> D-penicillamine and alpha-mercaptopropionylglycine contain sulphydryl groups that can bind to cysteine, reduce the formation of cystine and make it more soluble. Captopril has also been used in some studies.

2.6.3 Retroperitoneal fibrosis
Aetiology/pathophysiology/pathology
Refers to development of fibrosis in the retroperitoneal space leading to entrapment and obstruction of structures located there, most notably the ureters. This obstruction leads to progressive renal impairment.

The pathogenesis of primary/idiopathic retroperitoneal fibrosis (RPF) is unclear, but it may develop as an inflammatory response to contents of atherosclerotic plaques – it often begins around an atherosclerotic aortic aneurysm and may regress following repair. Leakage of plaque contents into the periaortic tissue may trigger an autoimmune response, hence the alternative name of periaortitis.

More recently, idiopathic RPF has been described as part of the spectrum of IgG4-related diseases as patients often have eosinophilia, raised levels of circulating IgG4 and the inflammatory infiltrate contains large numbers of IgG4-rich plasma cells. Whether this is the same condition as 'periaortitis' is unclear.

There is also an association of RPF with other connective tissue diseases and with HLA-B27, suggesting a genetic component.

Secondary causes of RPF are less common, but include drugs (ergot alkaloids and dopamine agonists), biological agents such as infliximab and etanercept, retroperitoneal metastases, radiotherapy and histiocytoses.

Epidemiology
> Incidence is between 0.1 and 1.4 per 100,000 people per year.

> Peak age of incidence is 50–60 years.

> Male to female ratio is 3:1.

Clinical presentation and associations
> dull and constant flank, abdominal or back pain is common; colic-like pain may develop when ureters become involved

> constitutional symptoms – low-grade fever, myalgia, weight loss

> incidental finding when investigating impaired renal function or vascular disease

> less commonly, lower limb oedema or DVT due to chronic compression of lymphatic vessels or veins.

Idiopathic RPF is strongly associated with other autoimmune/inflammatory disease (eg autoimmune thyroid disease, psoriasis). Patients with IgG4-related RPF often have a history of atopy.

Physical signs
There may be hypertension and signs of vascular disease.

Investigations
> Inflammatory markers – raised ESR, CRP with a normochromic/normocytic anaemia.

> Autoimmune markers – ANA and anti-smooth muscle antibody most commonly positive; also ANCA, rheumatoid factor (RF).

> Raised IgG4 levels.

> Ultrasound – may demonstrate hydroureter or hydronephrosis, but this may be minimal even in the presence of significant obstruction. May also show an abdominal aortic aneurysm (AAA).

- Contrast-enhanced CT or MRI is the imaging modality of choice to diagnose RPF, and can often help distinguish between primary and secondary forms. It is also useful to exclude secondary causes such as malignancy, which may worsen with immunosuppressive therapy.
- Tissue biopsy – if imaging studies do not show the findings typical of idiopathic RPF, in patients refractory to conventional steroid therapy or when another surgical intervention (eg ureteral decompression) is about to take place.

Differential diagnosis

- other causes of urinary tract obstruction
- malignancy with obstruction.

Treatment

The aim of therapy is to reduce inflammation, relieve obstruction to ureters and prevent recurrence.

- High-dose steroid therapy is first-line treatment to reduce inflammation. For refractory or relapsing cases, other immunosuppressive agents (eg azathioprine) may be considered. Steroid dose is tapered and then maintained at low dose for 1–3 years.
- Steroids should be combined with relief of renal tract obstruction by placement of bilateral ureteric stents (either retrograde or anterograde following nephrostomies). Occasionally open or laparoscopic ureterolysis is used to release the ureters from the surrounding fibrous tissue – this also allows biopsy of the mass.

Prognosis

With treatment the prognosis for renal function is good.

2.6.4 Urinary tract infection

Aetiology/pathophysiology/pathology

Urinary tract infections (UTIs) result from invasion of the urothelium by pathogenic organisms resulting in an inflammatory response. They may be symptomatic or asymptomatic. The laboratory definition requires 10^5 colony-forming units of bacteria per mL of urine. UTIs may be regarded as:

- uncomplicated – infection in a healthy woman, with a structurally and functionally normal urinary tract
- complicated – infection in anyone else, eg men, in pregnancy, immunosuppressed individuals or those with abnormal urinary tracts.

The most commonly isolated organism in acute UTIs is *Escherichia coli*. In hospital-acquired infections, *Klebsiella* and *Pseudomonas* species may be seen. *Proteus* infections are often associated with calculi in the urinary tract.

Infection usually enters the urinary tract through the urethra, and can cause urethritis or cystitis. A competent non-refluxing vesicoureteric junction prevents the spread of bladder infections to the upper urinary tracts, but blood-borne infections can sometimes deposit in the kidney.

There is a higher incidence of UTI in women; this is attributed to easier access for pathogens through the shorter female urethra. Also, in sexually active females, intercourse can facilitate ascent of infection to the bladder, and in postmenopausal women, the reduction in oestrogens (which are known to reduce urethral pH and improve mucosal protection) may increase the risk of infection. During pregnancy the ureters are relatively dilated and have a lower tone, which increases the risk of infection ascending to the kidneys.

UTI in older men is most often related to urinary stasis / incomplete bladder emptying secondary to prostatomegaly or neurogenic bladder.

Key point
- The usual organisms are Gram-negative *E coli*, *Klebsiella* and *Proteus* species.

- Lower UTI is restricted to the bladder and urethra, usually involves only the superficial mucosa and has no long-term effects.
- Upper UTI affects the kidney or ureters, involves the deep renal medullary tissue and can permanently damage the kidney.

Infection of the urinary tract by *Mycobacterium tuberculosis* is uncommon in the UK but is a cause of sterile pyuria (white cells in the urine, but no organism grown in standard culture conditions). Early morning urine samples should be cultured specifically for mycobacteria when this diagnosis is considered.

Diagnosis

The diagnosis of UTI on clinical presentation is not always straightforward. Some patients will meet the laboratory criteria for UTI but have no clinical symptoms – asymptomatic bacteriuria. Older patients with UTI may present with delirium, falls or reduced mobility rather than urinary tract symptoms.

The gold standard for diagnosis of UTI is culture of a midstream specimen of urine (MSU). This not only identifies the organism but also guides antimicrobial therapy. However, recent antibiotics may reduce the sensitivity of urine culture and some fastidious organisms may not grow under standard techniques. Patients with urinary catheters often have 'positive' cultures due to bacterial colonisation rather than infection.

Dipstick testing of urine for the presence of nitrites or leukocytes is often used as a quick alternative to urine culture for diagnosis. However, while sensitive, this has poor positive predictive value; in the general population the positive predictive value of standard urine dipstick testing is 45% and this drops to 30% in older people.

Prevention and treatment

General measures include increased fluid intake, double micturition (particularly if bladder outflow problems), post-coital voiding, and wiping from front to back in women.

Treatment – the first choice antibiotics for community-acquired UTI in the UK are trimethoprim and nitrofurantoin. In patients with recurrent UTIs initial antibiotic treatment should be based on previous resistance patterns. In cases where an MSU has been performed and produced a growth, the antibiotic regimen may be adjusted according to sensitivities. Note that trimethoprim often results in a rise in serum creatinine independent of an effect on GFR due to interference with creatinine secretion in a reversible manner – the creatinine returns to baseline when the trimethoprim is stopped.

Prevention – some patients may benefit from UTI prophylaxis. For recurrent UTI associated with intercourse, post-coital antibiotics taken within 2 hours may be beneficial. For recurrent UTI not related to intercourse, and which do not remit with general measures, regular low-dose antibiotics may be appropriate, although the rate of relapse on stopping is high. There is no convincing evidence

that rotating antibiotics has benefit. Cranberry extract and methenamine hippurate are effective in some patients and have the advantage of not increasing the risk of antibiotic resistance. Patients with suspected structural abnormalities of their urinary tract should be considered for urological evaluation.

2.7 The kidney in systemic disease

2.7.1 Myeloma
Pathology

The commonest cause of renal dysfunction in patients with myeloma is cast nephropathy or 'myeloma kidney', which is characterised by the renal biopsy finding of intratubular cast deposition (Fig 69). Other renal biopsy findings in patients with myeloma include glomerular lesions, amyloidosis or chronic interstitial nephritis.

Pathophysiology

In cast nephropathy kappa (κ) or lambda (λ) light chains form casts, and these casts obstruct the distal tubules

and collecting ducts. The proteinaceous casts may be directly toxic to the tubules and are usually associated with an interstitial infiltrate, often with multinucleate giant cells (Fig 69). Acute tubular necrosis (ATN) and tubular atrophy also occur.

Epidemiology

Renal involvement occurs in around 50% of patients with myeloma, usually subacute or chronic kidney disease (CKD), but acute kidney injury (AKI) is not infrequent.

Clinical presentation

AKI is frequently associated with cast nephropathy, but hypercalcaemia, hyperuricaemia, sepsis, drugs (eg NSAIDs) and radiocontrast agents may also contribute. Renal amyloid light-chain (AL) (primary) amyloidosis associated with myeloma usually presents with proteinuria (which may be massive) and/or renal impairment.

Diagnosis

See Section 1.5.7 for general investigations. All patients require investigations to confirm diagnosis, stage disease and risk stratify for

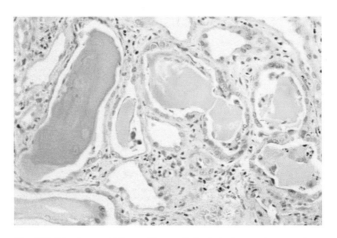

Fig 69 Myeloma kidney. Dense intratubular casts are shown with accompanying tubular cell atrophy (H&E; magnification ×200).

treatment. Diagnosis of myeloma requires:

> bone marrow biopsy and aspirate showing >10% plasma cells *or* plasmacytoma *and*

> end-organ damage (CRAB – raised Calcium, Renal impairment, Anaemia, Bone lesions) *or* presence of biomarkers associated with high risk of end-organ damage (eg plasma cells >60%, MRI with multiple bone lesions).

A renal biopsy is not necessary if bone marrow biopsy has confirmed the diagnosis of myeloma and patients have clinical features and laboratory investigations consistent with cast nephropathy. If there is a poor response to treatment, biopsy can help rule out alternative causes of renal impairment and assess renal prognosis.

Treatment

> General – correct volume depletion, treat hypercalcaemia, hyperuricaemia and sepsis, stop any drugs that may contribute to AKI.

> Dialysis – is given for the usual indications.

> Chemotherapy – a bortezomib-based regimen should be initiated as soon as possible to decrease light-chain production.

> Plasmapheresis – may provide some additional benefit and increase the likelihood of renal recovery by removing free light chains, but the evidence is limited. Haemodialysis removes small quantities of light chains, but at much lower levels, and there is no evidence to recommend it instead of plasmapheresis for this reason.

Prognosis

With the advent of bortezomib-based chemotherapy regimens, the prognosis of renal disease in myeloma has improved dramatically in the past few years. If there is a response to chemotherapy, 50–80% of patients gain improvement in renal function, which may allow dialysis independence.

The prognosis of myeloma still remains poor, even with haematopoietic cell transplantation, but for patients who tolerate and respond to treatment, persistent CKD or ESRF do not appear to significantly worsen the prognosis. Unfortunately, due to many factors, including the complications of renal impairment, many patients are not eligible for or do not tolerate treatment.

2.7.2 Amyloidosis

Aetiology

Amyloid deposits consist of proteins that have adopted an abnormal fibrillar conformation in conjunction with non-fibrillar constituents, including serum amyloid P (SAP) component and the glycosaminoglycans, heparan and dermatan sulphate. There are many types of amyloidosis, classified according to the protein from which the amyloid fibrils are derived. The types of amyloid that typically affect the kidneys are shown in the Table 26. Tissue biopsy is required for definitive diagnosis of amyloidosis.

Clinical presentation

Renal amyloid presents with proteinuria, nephrotic syndrome or chronic kidney disease (CKD).

Investigation

> Renal ultrasonography demonstrates normal-sized or enlarged, echogenic kidneys.

> Renal biopsy demonstrates extracellular amorphous material that may be within the mesangium, interstitium and/or vessel walls, and which shows red–green birefringence when stained with Congo red and viewed under cross-polarised light (Fig 70). If renal biopsy is not possible, alternatives include abdominal fat, salivary gland or rectal mucosa biopsy, again showing birefringence.

> A SAP scintigraphy scan is useful to demonstrate whole body amyloid load, delineate organ involvement and monitor response to treatment, but is not diagnostic alone.

Table 26	Types of amyloid that affect the kidneys	
Type of amyloid	**Amyloid protein involved**	**Underlying cause**
Systemic AL (primary) amyloidosis	Monoclonal immunoglobulin Light chains	Plasma cell dyscrasia
Systemic AA amyloidosis	SAA protein	Chronic inflammatory illness, eg rheumatoid arthritis
Hereditary amyloidosis	Fibrinogen A alpha-chain Apolipoprotein A1 Lysozyme	Mutations in the genes encoding the relevant proteins Autosomal dominant inheritance

AA, amyloid A; AL, amyloid light-chain; SAA, serum amyloid A.

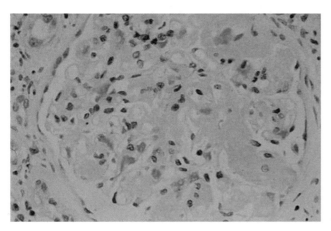

Fig 70 Renal amyloidosis. Renal biopsy specimen showing diffuse material staining with Congo red within the glomeruli; the patient had rheumatoid arthritis for 25 years (H&E; magnification ×250).

Treatment

Treatment of amyloidosis aims to suppress production of the fibril precursor protein and is therefore type-specific:

> AL (primary) amyloidosis is treated with cytotoxic chemotherapy to suppress the production of monoclonal light chains or haematopoietic cell transplantation.

> AA amyloidosis is treated by control of the underlying inflammatory or infective process, thereby suppressing SAA production.

> Liver transplantation may remove production of all (fibrinogen) or a proportion (apolipoprotein A1) of the mutant proteins that are amyloidogenic.

With the above treatments amyloid deposits can sometimes slowly regress and proteinuria can improve. Some patients progress to end-stage renal failure (ESRF). Patients with ESRF due to amyloidosis should be considered for renal transplantation, but not all are suitable.

Prognosis

The prognosis is dependent on the amyloid type. AL (primary) amyloidosis has a relatively poor prognosis (median survival of <5 years); amyloid A (AA)

and hereditary amyloidosis usually have a markedly better prognosis.

2.7.3 Thrombotic microangiopathy (haemolytic–uraemic syndrome)

Introduction/epidemiology

The thrombotic microangiopathies (TMAs) are a group of disorders presenting with a common clinical presentation: microangiopathic haemolytic anaemia (MAHA) and thrombocytopenia. MAHA and thrombocytopenia describe the blood picture, whereas TMA is a histological term used to describe the finding of arteriolar and capillary thrombosis due to endothelial injury.

Classification/definition

Primary TMA syndromes

> Thrombotic thrombocytopenic purpura (TTP) – classically described as a pentad of MAHA, thrombocytopenia, neurological abnormalities (coma, stroke, seizures), renal impairment and fever. There is a severe (inherited or acquired) deficiency of the matrix metalloproteinase a disintegrin and metalloproteinase with a thrombospondin type 1 motif, member 13 (ADAMTS13) (<10% of normal activity), which cleaves

von Willebrand factor (vWF) multimers. When this process is disrupted, the vWF multimers attract activated platelets and form the basis for the platelet thrombi.

> Diarrhoea-associated / typical haemolytic–uraemic syndrome (dHUS) – MAHA with thrombocytopenia and AKI. Seen in association with bloody diarrhoea secondary to infection with a Shiga toxin-producing bacterium, usually *Escherichia coli* O157:H7 or *Shigella*. This form is commonest in children and can be sporadic or in outbreaks from contaminated food. Approximately two to three cases per 100,000 per year. Approximately 6–9% of patients with the infections develop HUS.

> Atypical HUS (aHUS) – similar presentation to dHUS but without prodromal bloody diarrhoea (although there may be some diarrhoea – possibly a triggering infection). aHUS is caused by inherited or acquired (autoantibody-mediated) defects in the proteins that regulate complement deposition/activation on cell surfaces, particularly endothelium. It is rare – two cases per million population per year.

> Drug-induced TMA – causative drugs include quinine, immunosuppressants (calcineurin inhibitors (CNIs) – ciclosporin and tacrolimus), chemotherapeutic agents (mitomycin C).

Secondary TMA syndromes

The following may also present consistent with TMA:

> pregnancy – pre-eclampsia and haemolysis, elevated liver enzymes and low platelet count (HELLP) syndrome

> accelerated-phase hypertension

> infections (subacute bacterial endocarditis (SBE), HIV)

> malignancy (often disseminated)

> rheumatological disorders – SLE, scleroderma.

Pathology

In HUS, abnormal activation of complement, either through the activity of bacterial toxins (dHUS) or lack of normal regulatory proteins (aHUS), leads to endothelial damage and hence platelet activation and thrombus formation. Although biopsy is not required for diagnosis, affected organs show platelet-based thrombi lodged in the microcirculation, leading to the clinical manifestations. It is not clear why the central nervous system (CNS) and kidneys are more prone to development of TMA (Fig 71).

Clinical presentation

> AKI and MAHA with thrombocytopenia

> hypertension – usually present and often severe

> neurological symptoms – may be present in those with TTP

> other – fatigue, dyspnoea, bleeding, petechiae, haematuria.

Investigations

Bloods

> FBC and clotting – with an urgent blood film if TMA is suspected to look for characteristic abnormalities: fragments and schistocytes (fragmented red cells, also termed 'helmet cells')

> haemolysis screen – bilirubin (high), lactate dehydrogenase (LDH) (high), haptoglobins (low), direct antiglobulin test (DAT) (Coombs) test (typically negative)

> renal function and urinalysis

> liver function

> ADAMTS13 activity – check if clinical suspicion of TTP.

Other

> CT or MRI head – in patients presenting with abnormal neurology

> renal biopsy – may confirm the diagnosis but is not required and is high risk for bleeding.

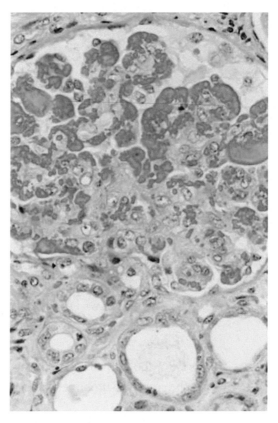

Fig 71 Haemolytic–uraemic syndrome (HUS). Typical renal histological appearance with intraglomerular thrombi (H&E; magnification ×300).

In all cases, urgent discussion with a local or national centre may be appropriate.

Treatment

Specific treatment depends on the presentation – current recommendations are:

Primary TMAs

> TTP – plasma exchange and steroids

> dHUS – best supportive care

> aHUS – plasma exchange has been the mainstay of treatment, but is now being superseded by eculizumab.

Secondary TMAs

> Treat the underlying cause.

Special note must be made of eculizumab (a C5 inhibitor, see Fig 72). This monoclonal antibody has recently been licensed for the treatment of paroxysmal nocturnal haemoglobinuria and aHUS. It binds to C5 and blocks its conversion to C5b, which is the final common pathway in complement activation. By thus preventing formation of the membrane attack complex (MAC), much of the endothelial damage is prevented, and hence platelet activation and aggregation prevented. It has been shown to significantly improve outcomes in aHUS.

Prognosis

The overall mortality rate is 10%, although this may fall with the advent of eculizumab. The prognosis is worse in adults. aHUS previously had a poor prognosis, with over 40% progressing to end-stage renal failure (ESRF) with a high recurrence rate post transplantation, but with eculizumab both risk of dialysis and risk of recurrence have been reduced. Trials are ongoing, as treatment is expensive and at present continued indefinitely, but it may prove possible to stop it safely in some individuals.

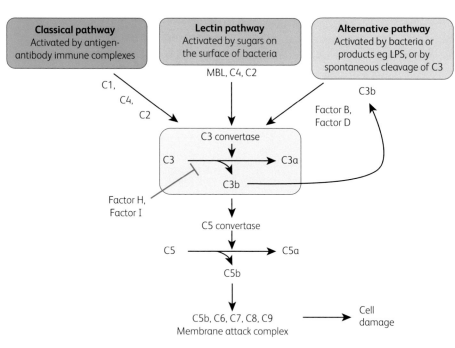

Fig 72 Simplified complement cascade, with the final common pathway shown in orange. Defective function of factor H, factor I, factor B, C3 and thrombomodulin (not shown) have been discovered in patients with atypical haemolytic–uraemic syndrome (HUS). From the efficacy of eculizumab (C5 blockade) it appears the final common pathway is a key step in the damage associated with TTP–HUS. LPS, lipopolysaccharide; MBL, mannose-binding lectin.

2.7.4 Sickle cell disease
Pathophysiology
Homozygous sickle cell disease can cause:

> glomerular disease (thought to result from hyperfiltration injury in childhood)

> ischaemic injury to the renal medulla (from papillary necrosis as a result of sickle-related occlusion of the vasa rectae).

Clinical presentation

> Enuresis occurs in about 40% of cases (poor concentrating ability).

> Haematuria, resulting from papillary necrosis, occurs in both homozygotes and sickle cell trait.

> Chronic kidney disease (CKD) in adult homozygotes, especially those aged over 40 years.

> Nephrotic syndrome can occur but is less common.

Investigations
Renal ultrasound can exclude other abnormalities and an intravenous urogram (IVU) may show 'cup and spill' calyceal deformities of papillary necrosis (Fig 62). If there is haematuria, a CT should be done to look for medullary carcinoma. Renal biopsy is usually not required for diagnosis, but can help exclude differentials in nephrotic range proteinuria or rapidly declining renal function. Findings in those with CKD typically demonstrate widespread nephron loss and glomerulosclerosis.

2.7.5 Autoimmune rheumatic disorders
Most autoimmune rheumatic disorders can cause renal disease, but most commonly renal problems are seen in:

> rheumatoid arthritis

> systemic lupus erythematosus (SLE)

> systemic sclerosis

> Sjögren's syndrome.

Rheumatoid arthritis
Pathology
Renal disease may be caused by amyloid A (AA) amyloidosis, a proliferative glomerulonephritis or as a complication of drug therapy. Gold and penicillamine can cause membranous glomerulonephritis and NSAIDs may cause interstitial nephritis. A rheumatoid-related mesangioproliferative glomerulonephritis (with IgM deposition) can occur.

Clinical presentation
Presentation is with proteinuria, nephrotic syndrome (especially amyloid) or renal impairment. Patients with mesangioproliferative glomerulonephritis will have non-visible haematuria and an 'active' urine sediment with red cell casts.

Treatment
Withdraw offending drugs. Attempt to avoid NSAIDs in all cases of renal impairment (although this is not always possible). In cases of AA amyloidosis, take vigorous measures to suppress the inflammation associated with rheumatoid arthritis. Standard management of CKD and ESRF is applicable.

Prognosis
Patients with amyloidosis and chronic interstitial nephritis may progress to ESRF. Drug-related glomerulonephritis usually resolves within 6 months of withdrawing the offending agent.

Systemic lupus erythematosus
Pathology
Several patterns of renal disease may be seen on histological examination of the kidneys in patients with SLE (Table 27; Fig 74):

> 'wire-loop' lesions (thickened capillary walls – electron microscopy shows electron-dense deposits) are characteristic of SLE (Fig 74)

Table 27 Abbreviated International Society of Nephrology / Renal Pathology Society classification of lupus nephritis (2003)

Class	Biopsy findings	Frequency (%)
I	Minimal mesangial lupus nephritis	5–10
II	Mesangial proliferative lupus nephritis	10
III	Focal lupus nephritis (<50% of glomeruli)	10
IV	Diffuse (>50% glomeruli) segmental (IV-S) or global (IV-G) lupus nephritis	50
V	Membranous lupus nephritis	20
VI	Advanced sclerosing lupus nephritis (>90% global glomerulosclerosis)	0–5

Class V lupus nephritis may occur in combination with class III or IV, in which case both are diagnosed.

> immunofluorescence is often positive for most immunoglobulins (IgG, IgM and IgA) and complement components (C3, C4 and C1q).

Key point

In SLE nephritis there is usually a 'full house' of immunoglobulins and complement components on the renal biopsy (viewed under immunofluorescence).

Epidemiology
Up to 50% of patients with SLE have evidence of renal involvement at presentation; lupus nephritis is more common in black patients and in women (the male:female ratio is 1:9). Most patients present between 16 and 55 years of age.

Clinical presentation
Renal disease in patients with SLE can present in a variety of ways, which reflect the different pathologies, eg asymptomatic proteinuria, nephrotic syndrome and rapidly progressive renal failure (Fig 73).

Treatment
Treatment depends on the class of lupus nephritis, disease activity and the degree of chronic damage. Rapidly progressive glomerulonephritis is usually due to class III or IV lupus nephritis and is treated with immunosuppressive agents such as cyclophosphamide, mycophenolate mofetil, azathioprine and steroids. Randomised trials support the use of oral or pulsed intravenous steroids with intermittent intravenous cyclophosphamide. Membranous lupus nephritis is usually responsive to steroids and azathioprine. General management is as for chronic kidney disease (CKD) (see Section 2.1.2) and end-stage renal disease (see Section 2.1.3). Several biologic treatments have been trialled; rituximab and belimumab are promising.

Prognosis
The pattern of renal histological damage is of prognostic value:

> membranous (class V) lesions have a favourable renal outcome

> class III and IV (proliferative) lupus nephritis predicts the worst renal prognosis.

Systemic sclerosis
Pathology
Prominent pathological changes occur in interlobular arteries (severe intimal proliferation with deposition of

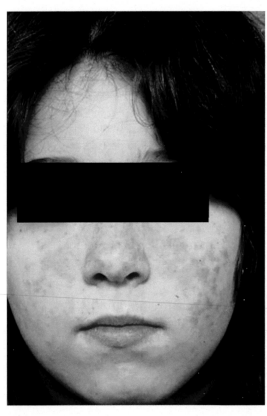

Fig 73 Typical rash of systemic lupus erythematosus (SLE).

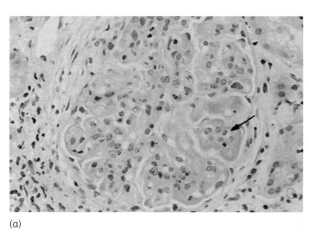 (a)

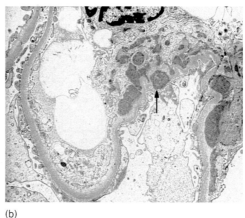 (b)

Fig 74 Renal histological changes in systemic lupus erythematosus (SLE). **(a)** Proliferative glomerulonephritis: a typical wire-loop capillary (arrowed) is shown (H&E; magnification ×200). **(b)** Electron microscopy reveals subendothelial deposits (arrowed) (magnification ×20,000).

mucopolysaccharides, forming an 'onion skin'); fibrinoid necrosis of afferent arterioles and secondary glomerular ischaemia are common (Fig 75).

Clinical presentation
Renal disease is almost invariably accompanied by hypertension. In classic 'scleroderma renal crisis' there is accelerated-phase hypertension, microangiopathic haemolytic anaemia (MAHA) and acute kidney injury (AKI).

Treatment
Treatment is with ACE inhibitor for control of hypertension and may include prostaglandin analogues. Management is as for CKD (see Section 2.1.2)

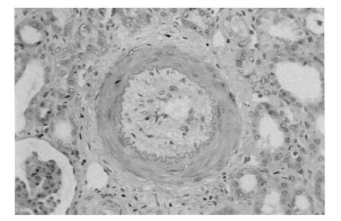

Fig 75 Vascular changes in scleroderma. Renal biopsy specimen showing obliterative arteriolar lesions with 'onion skin' appearance and intimal hyperplasia (H&E; magnification ×250).

and end-stage renal disease (see Section 2.1.3).

Prognosis
In many patients AKI is irreversible. Renal impairment may improve after months of dialysis but the prognosis is still poor due to the frequency of extrarenal disease involvement (especially restrictive cardiomyopathy, pulmonary fibrosis and bowel involvement).

Sjögren's syndrome
Pathology
The most common renal abnormality is interstitial nephritis.

Clinical presentation
Presentation is with proteinuria, CKD or renal tubular dysfunction such as renal tubular acidosis (RTA), which may be proximal and/or distal.

Treatment
The condition responds to steroids and cyclophosphamide, but these are rarely required for renal manifestations alone. Oral bicarbonate can help to correct RTA.

2.7.6 Systemic vasculitis
The term vasculitis refers to a group of diseases that are characterised by the presence of inflammation in the blood vessels, resulting in tissue ischaemia. The spectrum of disease is wide and is classified according to the size of the blood vessels affected. The kidney is commonly involved in small vessel vasculitides, which are usually associated with the presence of anti-neutrophil cytoplasmic antibodies (ANCA). ANCA-negative small vessel vasculitides include cryoglobulinaemia, various autoimmune rheumatic disorders and Henoch–Schönlein purpura.

Pathology
The ANCA-associated vasculitides include microscopic polyangiitis (MPA), granulomatosis with polyangiitis (GPA, previously Wegener's granulomatosis),

polyarteritis nodosa (PAN) and eosinophilic granulomatosis with polyangiitis (eGPA, previously known as Churg–Strauss syndrome). Renal histology typically shows necrotising glomerulonephritis, associated with focal proliferative and/or crescentic glomerulonephritis (Fig 76). Necrotising granulomas are characteristic in GPA. Vasculitis is typically 'pauci-immune', meaning that there is little or no detectable immunoglobulin deposition by immunohistochemistry. Findings in PAN, which is a medium-sized arterial vasculitis, may show renal infarction rather than glomerulonephritis.

Clinical presentation

Patients with renal vasculitis classically present with acute nephritic syndrome, but they may also present with extrarenal manifestations of vasculitis and be discovered incidentally to have renal involvement. A purpuric vasculitic skin rash is common. Pulmonary involvement is most frequent in GPA, where there may be characteristic necrotising granulomas in the upper respiratory tract with sinusitis and nasal discharge. Pulmonary haemorrhage may be life-threatening. In PAN patients may present with acute kidney injury (AKI) which is usually associated with severe hypertension. Pulmonary infiltrates and haemorrhage, gastrointestinal (GI) ischaemia, mononeuritis multiplex, cutaneous vasculitis (Fig 77) and systemic features (myalgia and pyrexia of unknown origin) may occur.

Investigations

> MPA is typically associated with ANCA directed against myeloperoxidase (MPO).

> GPA is strongly associated with ANCA directed against proteinase 3 (PR3).

> PAN can show ANCA positivity by immunofluorescence, but this is often non-specific. If enzyme-linked immunosorbent assay (ELISA)

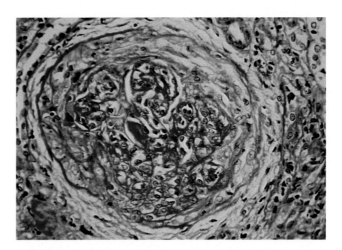

Fig 76 Crescentic glomerulonephritis. The crescent derives from the epithelial cells of Bowman's capsule (periodic acid–Schiff; magnification ×300). This appearance is recognised in many forms of aggressive glomerulonephritis, including anti-GBM antibody disease, ANCA-positive vasculitis and idiopathic rapidly progressive glomerulonephritis.

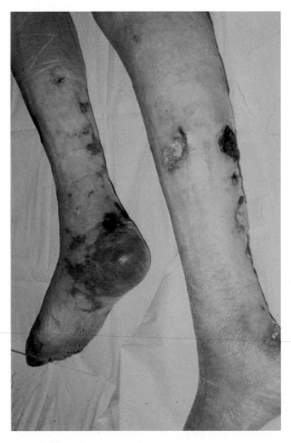

Fig 77 Vasculitic skin ulcers in polyarteritis nodosa (PAN). The ulcers are deep, 'punched-out' and caused by necrosis.

confirms PR3 or MPO antibodies this suggests that either GPA or MPA may be the diagnosis. In PAN there may be an eosinophilia. About 30% of cases are positive for hepatitis-B surface antigen (HBsAg). Mesenteric angiography characteristically shows microaneurysms (Fig 78).

> Renal or other tissue biopsy is usually necessary in cases of suspected vasculitis to confirm the diagnosis.

Treatment
Initial treatment

> Immunosuppressive therapy – standard therapy would be corticosteroids and cyclophosphamide for 3 months, followed by azathioprine and low-dose steroid maintenance. Rituximab with steroids has been shown to be non-inferior to cyclophosphamide for induction, and effective as maintenance therapy in ANCA vasculitis, with a better safety profile than cyclophosphamide. It is currently used in patients for whom cyclophosphamide is contraindicated or as a second-line therapy.

> Plasma exchange – evidence supports use in patients with ANCA-associated vasculitis who present with a serum creatinine >500 µmol/L, and in those with pulmonary haemorrhage.

Maintenance treatment
Vasculitis can relapse at any time and patients need careful lifelong monitoring after the initial diagnosis. PR3-associated vasculitis (generally GPA) is more likely to relapse than MPO-associated vasculitis (generally MPA).

2.7.7 Diabetic nephropathy
Pathology
Initially there is hyperfiltration and enlargement of the glomeruli. In established diabetic nephropathy Kimmelstiel–Wilson nodules (focal glomerular sclerosis) are characteristic, but mesangial matrix expansion and diffuse glomerular sclerosis with vascular changes are more common (Fig 79).

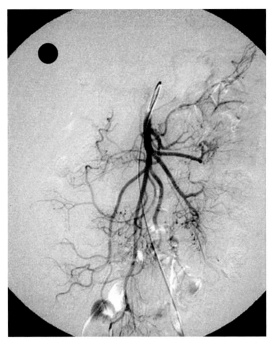

Fig 78 Mesenteric angiogram showing microaneurysms in polyarteritis nodosa (PAN).

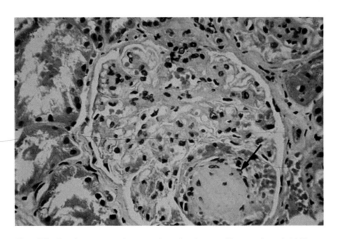

Fig 79 Diabetic nephropathy. A classic Kimmelstiel–Wilson nodule (arrowed) is present with a background of diffuse mesangial sclerosis (H&E; magnification ×250).

Epidemiology
Diabetic nephropathy is the most common cause of ESRF in the Western world. Approximately 20–30% of patients with type 1 diabetes mellitus will have albuminuria by 15 years after diagnosis, but only half will progress to overt nephropathy. This has reduced significantly over the past 2 decades with improvements in treatment. Current data suggest approximately 25% of patients with type 2 diabetes mellitus develop nephropathy. The incidence of type 2 diabetes is much higher, so most patients with diabetic nephropathy have type 2 diabetes.

Clinical presentation

> The earliest finding is microalbuminuria (albumin excretion of 20–200 µg/min or 30–300 mg/day), but this is not reliably detected by standard dipstick.

> The majority (>50%) of patients with microalbuminuria develop overt

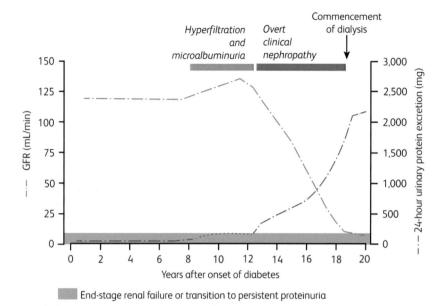

Fig 80 The clinical course of diabetic nephropathy. This schema demonstrates the typical temporal relationship between the development of microalbuminuria, proteinuria and progressive decline in glomerular filtration rate (GFR).

diabetic nephropathy with proteinuria >0.5 g/day (Fig 80), and subsequently develop hypertension and chronic kidney disease (CKD). About 30% of patients with diabetic nephropathy become frankly nephrotic.

> Diabetic nephropathy is usually associated with retinopathy (common basement membrane pathology) – if there is no retinopathy then question the diagnosis.

> Macrovascular disease (ie renal artery stenosis) should be considered in all diabetics with renal impairment (particularly if minimal/no proteinuria).

Treatment

> Blood pressure control – ACE inhibitors and angiotensin-II receptor blockers (ARBs) can prevent progression from microalbuminuria to overt nephropathy. They exert their renoprotective effect both by limiting proteinuria and through BP control. Combination therapy with ACE inhibitor and ARB is not recommended, due to the high incidence of adverse events.

> Glycaemic control – should be as tight as possible.

> Risk factors for cardiovascular disease – should be corrected wherever possible.

> Pancreatic transplantation (either at the time of renal transplantation or as a separate procedure) – to be considered in selected patients with type 1 diabetes mellitus, and occasionally in patients with type 2 diabetes and ESRF who are insulin dependent.

Prognosis

Once there is renal impairment in diabetic nephropathy, decline to ESRF is usually inexorable. Mortality is high – patients with type 1 diabetes have a 20-fold greater mortality than the general population; and relative risk is increased further in those with proteinuria, largely due to cardiovascular disease.

Survival with all modalities of renal replacement therapy (RRT) among diabetic patients is reduced compared to other causes of ESRF (recent data suggest the median survival from

initiation of dialysis is around 4 years for type 1 diabetes and 2.5 years for type 2 diabetes). Diabetic patients obtain substantial survival benefit from renal transplantation.

2.7.8 Hypertension

Hypertension is a very common association of chronic kidney disease (CKD). The evidence is not strong that essential hypertension causes CKD, but there is no doubt that it increases the rate at which renal function declines in patients with CKD.

CKD is an important cause of secondary hypertension in which some of the following mechanisms may play a role:

> renin release and activation of the renin–angiotensin–aldosterone axis

> reduced natriuretic capacity

> disorganisation of intrarenal vascular structures.

Pathology

> Characteristic findings on renal biopsy specimens in hypertensive subjects include vascular wall thickening and luminal obliteration, with interstitial fibrosis and glomerulosclerosis (hypertensive nephrosclerosis).

> Accelerated-phase hypertension is characterised by arterial fibrinoid necrosis with tubular and glomerular ischaemia (Fig 81).

> A wide range of renal pathologies can be complicated by hypertension.

Epidemiology

Hypertension affects up to 15% of the population, and is of unknown aetiology (essential hypertension) in the vast majority. It is more common in certain ethnic groups than others (eg those of African ancestry). Renal disease is the most common cause of secondary hypertension. Among patients approaching ESRF, 80% are hypertensive.

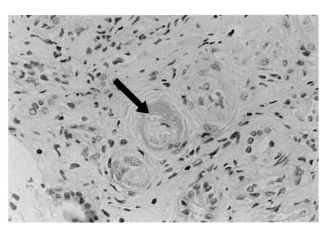

Fig 81 Accelerated-phase hypertension: renal biopsy showing severe arteriolar lesions with intimal hyperplasia and fibrinoid necrosis of the media (arrowed) (H&E; magnification ×200).

Clinical presentation

> Patients diagnosed as having 'essential hypertension' may be found to have proteinuria or CKD. The term 'hypertensive nephrosclerosis' is often applied, but it is often impossible to determine whether the renal disease is secondary to the hypertension, or vice versa.

> Accelerated-phase hypertension is a cause of AKI.

Physical signs

> Essential hypertension – can cause end-organ damage: heart (left ventricular hypertrophy and cardiac failure); eyes (grade I and II retinopathy); brain (stroke).

> Accelerated-phase hypertension – the characteristic finding is grade III (haemorrhages and exudates) or IV (with papilloedema) retinopathy (Fig 82); end-organ damage is as for essential hypertension but occurs with higher frequency. There may be thrombotic microangiopathy (TMA).

Investigations

Current UK guidelines suggest that all patients with a clinic BP of >140/90 mmHg should have ambulatory BP measurement (ABPM) or home BP measurement (HBPM) to confirm the diagnosis; although in severe hypertension, treatment can be initiated while waiting for results of ABPM or HBPM.

All hypertensive patients should have investigations for end-organ damage, including a serum creatinine and dipstick urinalysis check. Consider secondary causes, particularly in patients presenting at a young age, in the absence of family history, or with accelerated-phase hypertension and low serum potassium. Take a comprehensive drug history and ask about recreational drugs. Consider renovascular disease, particularly fibromuscular dysplasia in younger patients, and consider undiagnosed obstructive sleep apnoea in overweight patients. Screen for renal disease and endocrine disorders with baseline bloods (renal function, electrolytes, thyroid function, bone profile).

Treatment

Treatment of hypertension involves general measures such as regular exercise, weight loss if appropriate, and reduction in salt intake, as well as modification of cardiovascular risk factors. Pharmacological treatment is offered to those with low-grade hypertension (<160/100 mmHg in clinic or 150/95 mmHg ABPM/HBPM) only if they are <80 years with target organ damage, established cardiovascular or renal disease, diabetes, or have a 10-year cardiovascular risk equivalent of ≥20%. All patients with moderate or severe hypertension should be offered treatment. Those <40 years should be investigated for secondary causes.

Antihypertensive choice is based on age and race, and follows a stepwise progression.

> Treatment step 1 if <55 years – ACE inhibitor or ARB.

> Treatment step 1 if >55 years or of African-Caribbean origin – calcium

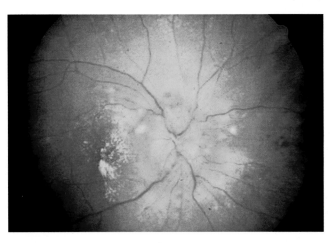

Fig 82 The retina in accelerated-phase hypertension. There is papilloedema, cotton-wool spots and hard retinal exudates, as well as haemorrhage (grade IV hypertensive retinopathy).

channel blockers (CCB). If these are
not tolerated or appropriate (oedema,
risk of congestive cardiac failure
(CCF)), thiazide diuretics should be
used as an alternative.

> Treatment step 2 – the combination
  of ACE inhibitor / ARB with a CCB
  (or thiazide).

> Treatment step 3 – the combination
  of ACE inhibitor / ARB with CCB and
  a thiazide.

> Treatment step 4 – review of
  medication, check of concordance,
  and then consider adding
  spironolactone, increasing the
  thiazide, or adding an alpha- or
  beta-blocker (the National Institute
  for Health and Care Excellence (NICE)
  recommends beta-blockers are no
  longer considered as first-line options
  except in those who are younger and
  intolerant of ACE inhibitor / ARB
  treatment, women of childbearing
  age, or those with increased
  sympathetic drive).

2.7.9 Sarcoidosis

Epidemiology

Hypercalciuria occurs in 65% of patients
with sarcoidosis and hypercalcaemia in
about 20%. Clinically significant renal
impairment is uncommon.

Clinical presentation

This is usually with renal impairment
in the context of other features of
sarcoidosis. Tubular proteinuria,
Fanconi syndrome and distal or proximal
renal tubular acidosis (RTA) are all
recognised. Nephrocalcinosis sometimes
occurs, but renal calculi are not
common.

Investigation

Among patients with CKD, renal biopsy
usually shows a granulomatous interstitial
nephritis (Fig 83). Sarcoid-related
glomerulopathy (usually membranous
glomerulonephritis) is rare.

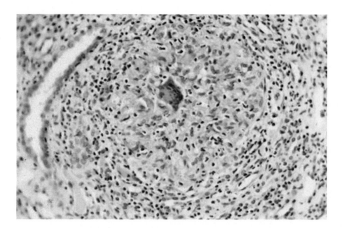

Fig 83 Sarcoidosis. Typical renal histological appearance with chronic interstitial
nephritis and giant-cell granulomatous change (H&E; magnification ×160).

Treatment

Both hypercalcaemia and interstitial
nephritis generally respond to
corticosteroids in moderate dosage.
Steroid-sparing agents such as
methotrexate, azathioprine or
(occasionally) TNF blockers have been
used in patients who do not tolerate or
respond to steroids.

2.7.10 Hepatorenal syndrome

Pathophysiology

Severe liver disease is associated with
marked intrarenal hypoperfusion
secondary to excessive renal
vasoconstriction. Renal parenchymal
damage generally does not occur
and, if normal hepatic function
is restored by liver transplantation,
renal function usually recovers.

Epidemiology

Hepatorenal syndrome occurs in
about 10% of patients hospitalised
with cirrhosis and ascites. It is also
common in jaundiced patients requiring
major surgery for biliary or pancreatic
disease.

Clinical presentation

Usually with AKI in the context
of severe liver disease and
hyperbilirubinaemia. Precipitants
include hypovolaemia (eg variceal

bleed) and sepsis (eg spontaneous
bacterial peritonitis).

Investigations

Other causes of renal impairment in the
context of liver disease, of which there
are several, always need to be excluded
to make the diagnosis of hepatorenal
syndrome. Urine dipstick is typically
bland, with no or minimal proteinuria.
Urinary biochemistry in hepatorenal
syndrome characteristically shows
a very low sodium concentration
(<10 mmol/L).

Treatment

The goal of treatment is to support the
patient while waiting for the liver to
recover, or until liver transplantation.
Treatment with terlipressin and albumin
(or midodrine, octreotide and albumin)
has been shown to improve renal
function. Transjugular intrahepatic
portosystemic shunts (TIPS) create a
low-pressure shunt bypassing the liver,
and may lead to an improvement in
hepatorenal syndrome. Dialysis
is appropriate only in patients
with potentially remediable liver
disease, or in candidates for liver
transplantation.

Prognosis

The mortality of hepatorenal syndrome is
high. Median survival of patients who

present with rapidly deteriorating renal function is 2 weeks and virtually all are dead within 10 weeks of the onset of renal impairment. Median survival among patients with gradual reduction of their glomerular filtration rate (GFR) due to hepatorenal syndrome is 4–6 months.

2.7.11 Pregnancy and the kidney

Circulatory and other physiological changes during pregnancy affect the kidneys:

> Glomerular filtration rate (GFR) increases by up to 50% in the first trimester of normal pregnancy.

> The ureters and renal pelvis become dilated (Fig 84) and the risk of lower UTI is increased.

Pre-eclampsia constitutes new-onset hypertension and proteinuria, and manifests after the 20th week of pregnancy. It is the most common medical complication of pregnancy affecting 4–7% of expecting mothers, and is associated with increased fetal morbidity and mortality. Placental abruption, thrombotic microangiopathy (TMA) and severe pre-eclampsia are all causes of acute kidney injury (AKI) in the latter stages of pregnancy: irreversible cortical necrosis can occur, although reversible acute tubular necrosis (ATN) is more common (Fig 85).

Chronic kidney disease (CKD) of any sort before pregnancy has big implications for both the fetus and the mother (Table 28). If pregnant women with CKD have hypertension, the risks of permanent deterioration in renal

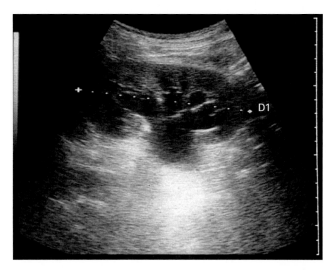

Fig 84 Hydronephrosis of pregnancy: typical ultrasonographic appearance.

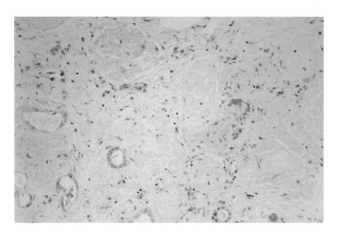

Fig 85 Renal biopsy showing cortical necrosis. There is complete necrosis of the majority of visible structures (including glomeruli) (H&E; magnification ×160).

function, intrauterine growth retardation and preterm delivery all increase considerably, and this is true whether the patient is pre-dialysis, on dialysis or has a functioning renal transplant. Additionally, the likelihood of successful conception is lower with increasing CKD.

Epidemiology

> Asymptomatic bacteriuria occurs in up to 5% of pregnancies, and symptomatic infection develops in about 25% of these cases if they are not treated.

Table 28 Pregnancy-related problems in women with pre-existing renal disease		
Impairment of renal function pre-pregnancy or in the first trimester[1]	**Maternal complications**	**Fetal loss**
Mild (creatinine <125 µmol/L)	Common (≈25%)	Rare (5–10%)
Moderate (creatinine 125–250 µmol/L)	Very common (≈50%)	Uncommon (<10%)
Severe (creatinine >250 µmol/L)	Nearly all (≈90%)	Very common (≈50%)

1 Normal range for serum creatinine 60–110 µmol/L.

- Pre-eclampsia occurs in 4–7% of pregnancies and is more common in first pregnancies and multiple pregnancies.
- AKI complicates one in 6,000 pregnancies.

Clinical presentation

Varies from mild urinary infection, to pre-eclampsia or AKI. In proteinuric disease, it is important to distinguish between pre-existing renal disease and pre-eclampsia by determining the timing of the onset of proteinuria, hence women are screened at booking. Idiopathic postpartum AKI may be associated with severe hypertension and disseminated intravascular coagulation.

Investigations

Proteinuria most commonly occurs in the context of pre-eclampsia, and should be screened for, along with BP, throughout pregnancy. This typically resolves within 3 months of delivery and requires further investigation if it does not.

In the context of pre-eclampsia, women should be monitored closely with weekly FBC (platelets), liver function and creatinine, but if stable do not require inpatient care.

Peripartum AKI is usually haemodynamically mediated and recovery is anticipated. If recovery does not occur postpartum, renal perfusion can be assessed by radionuclide scintigraphy and renal biopsy should be considered.

Treatment

- Bacteriuria – patients with significant bacteriuria should receive antibiotics regardless of symptoms.
- Hypertension – suitable agents include methyldopa or labetalol as first-line therapy, nifedipine as second line.
- Pre-eclampsia – treatment is to deliver the fetus (and placenta), hence delivery is normally induced at around 37 weeks if the mother is stable, but earlier if there are features of instability (worsening renal function, HELLP syndrome, central nervous system (CNS) symptoms/signs).

Patients with CKD who become pregnant should have close monitoring every 2–4 weeks and regular screening for bacteriuria, pre-eclampsia and intrauterine growth restriction (IUGR).

Prognosis

Pre-eclampsia is the second leading cause of maternal mortality, accounting for 12–18% of pregnancy-related maternal deaths. It is also associated with increased fetal morbidity and mortality, usually as a result of iatrogenic prematurity.

In patients with AKI during pregnancy, renal recovery is anticipated in those with ATN, but not in those with cortical necrosis. AKI in the mother is associated with a high perinatal fetal mortality rate. In patients with CKD, the chance of a successful conception and live birth declines as the GFR falls, and is unusual with a GFR of <20 mL/min.

Pregnancy and kidney transplantation

Women who wish to become pregnant after renal transplantation should be reassured that this is generally safe with good outcomes. The following should be considered:

- Timing – waiting until a year after transplantation is considered sensible. Remember contraceptive advice in women who have been transplanted: fertility (lost in ESRF) may return rapidly with good graft function.
- Graft (renal) function – creatinine should be <150 μmol/L.
- Immunosuppression – steroids, azathioprine and CNIs (ciclosporin and tacrolimus) are all safe. Mycophenolate mofetil and sirolimus are teratogenic: patients taking these should be switched to safe alternatives.
- Other medications – avoid ACE inhibitors and ARBs.
- Actively monitor for and treat UTIs.
- There is an increased risk of hypertension, pre-eclampsia, preterm birth, IUGR and graft dysfunction/loss.

- Think about inherited conditions pre-conception – autosomal dominant polycystic kidney disease (ADPKD), reflux nephropathy.
- Patients should be managed in a joint obstetric/renal clinic.

2.8 Genetic renal conditions

2.8.1 Autosomal dominant polycystic kidney disease

Aetiology/pathophysiology

There is progressive development of renal cysts (Fig 86). Two genetic loci have been described:

- Polycystic kidney disease 1 (*PKD1*) on chromosome 16 (85% of cases) – encodes polycystin 1, a large transmembrane molecule likely to be involved in cell/matrix interactions.
- *PKD2* on chromosome 4 (10% of cases) – encodes polycystin 2, tends to produce a milder disease than *PKD1*.

Polycystin 1 and 2 proteins probably form a physical complex and are important in the function of the primary cilium, a hair-like appendage that is thought to sense the flow of urine along the tubule.

Note that autosomal recessive polycystic kidney disease is distinct from autosomal dominant polycystic kidney disease (ADPKD): it is a rare disease (one in 10,000 to one in 40,000) that typically presents in infancy and is frequently associated with congenital hepatic fibrosis, which is characterised by cysts, fibrosis and portal hypertension.

Epidemiology

- The most common inherited renal disease.
- Accounts for 5–10% of end-stage renal disease.
- Prevalence: one per 400 to one per 1,000.

Fig 86 Macroscopic appearance of a polycystic kidney. (Courtesy of Dr D Peat.)

Clinical presentation

Common features

> Discovered through screening of an affected family (an increasingly likely way for these patients to present).

> Acute abdominal pain (usually due to bleeding into a cyst or cyst infection) in 30% of cases. Chronic abdominal/back pain may occur.

> Hypertension in 20% of cases.

> Gross haematuria in 20% of cases.

> Urinary tract infection (UTI) in 5–40% of cases; and this is more common in women.

> Incidental discovery of an abdominal mass.

Uncommon feature

> ESRF.

Rare feature

> intracranial haemorrhage.

Physical signs

> palpable kidneys and/or liver

> hypertension

> murmurs associated with mitral regurgitation or mitral valve prolapse (mitral valve prolapse occurs in 20% of polycystic kidney disease patients).

Investigations

Diagnosis is by demonstration of multiple bilateral renal cysts and a positive family history.

> Ultrasonography: in *PKD1* families, diagnostic criteria are age-related (two cysts in those <30 years old, at least two cysts in each kidney in those aged 30–59, and four cysts in each kidney for those aged >60). Normal ultrasonography after the age of 30 (but not before) excludes the diagnosis. Associated cysts in the liver and pancreas can be helpful in supporting the diagnosis.

> Genetic testing is available for both *PKD1* and *PKD2* mutations.

> Cranial magnetic resonance angiography (MRA): in patients with a family history of intracranial aneurysm. In other PKD families screening for cerebral aneurysms is controversial.

Other investigations are as for CKD (see Section 2.1.2).

Differential diagnosis

Simple renal cysts.

Treatment

> Antihypertensives – control of blood pressure reduces cardiovascular complications and progression of renal disease.

> Treat UTIs – it is often difficult to eradicate infection in a cyst. Prolonged antibiotic courses are often required, and sometimes cyst drainage is helpful.

> Analgesia – some patients suffer considerable renal pain. Occasionally drainage or deroofing of large cysts may give long-term relief.

> Tolvaptan, a vasopressin (antidiuretic hormone (ADH)) receptor antagonist, lowers renal epithelial cell intracellular cAMP levels and has been shown to reduce cyst growth in animal models, and to reduce rate of renal enlargement and rate of decline in eGFR in humans (TEMPO study). It has recently been approved for use by NICE in the UK, but at the time of writing is not yet used routinely in clinical practice.

Complications/prognosis

> Renal – ESRF will occur in at least 75% of cases: in *PKD1* typically at about 50–60 years of age; and in *PKD2* at about 65–75 years of age. UTIs and bleeds into cysts are also common.

> Cardiovascular disease – associated with hypertension and chronic renal failure (CRF). Cardiac valve diseases, most commonly mitral valve prolapse or aortic regurgitation, occur in 25% of patients.

> Cerebrovascular disease – ruptured intracranial aneurysm complicates 5–10% of patients with ADPKD and is more common in some families than others.

> Liver disease – the incidence of hepatic cysts increases with age (<10% if younger than 30 and >40% if aged over 60) and they are found more commonly in patients with significant renal disease. Apart from pain in some cases, these do not usually cause symptoms.

> Colonic diverticulae.

> Herniae – both abdominal wall and inguinal.

2.8.2 Alport syndrome

Aetiology/pathophysiology

Alport syndrome consists of:

> nephritis and progressive renal impairment

> sensorineural deafness (in two-thirds of cases)

> eye abnormalities (in one-third of cases).

The defect is in type IV collagen, a key component of the glomerular basement membrane (GBM). It can be:

> X-linked dominant (85–90% of cases). Mutations in the *COL4A5* gene encoding alpha 5 chain of type IV collagen – this alteration prevents integration of the alpha 3 chain into the GBM. The alpha 3 chain contains the Goodpasture antigen. Affected males develop progressive renal failure.

> Autosomal recessive (10% of cases). Similar to X-linked disease but equally severe in females. Due to mutations in *COL4A3* or *COL4A4*.

> Autosomal dominant. This is uncommon, due to dominant-negative mutations in *COL4A3* or *COL4A4*.

Benign familial haematuria is also due to mutations in *COL4A3* and *COL4A4*.

Epidemiology

> Gene frequency is one per 5,000 to one per 10,000.

> Of European dialysis patients, 0.6% have Alport syndrome.

Clinical presentation

This can typically include:

> non-visible or haematuria

> renal impairment

> hearing loss

> visual problems.

Physical signs

> high-tone sensorineural hearing loss

> bilateral anterior lenticonus (protrusion of the lens into the anterior chamber).

Investigations

The following may be considered:

> Audiometry.

> Slit-lamp examination of the eye.

> Renal biopsy will demonstrate structural abnormalities of the GBM under electron microscopy (but is not required in all cases).

> Skin biopsy – in suspected X-linked Alport, a defect in *COL4A5* can be established on skin biopsy in affected males or as a mosaic in carrier females.

> Genetic testing is available.

Treatment

There is no specific treatment.

Complications/prognosis

> End-stage renal failure (ESRF) – all affected males with X-linked disease progress to ESRF, usually by age 30. Most carrier females never reach ESRF, but do have persistent haematuria and/or proteinuria. Some develop ESRF at 45–60 years of age.

> Progressive hearing loss.

> Visual impairment through lens rupture and cataract formation.

> Following transplantation patient's may develop antibodies to type IV collagen and anti-GBM disease.

2.8.3 X-linked hypophosphataemic vitamin-D resistant rickets

Aetiology/pathophysiology

This is the most common hereditary form of isolated renal phosphate wasting. Hypophosphataemia, together with a functional defect in osteoblasts, leads to abnormal mineralisation of growing bone. The defect is in the phosphate-regulating neutral endopeptidase, X-linked (*PHEX*) gene, which codes for a zinc metallopeptidase. The pathogenesis is unclear.

Clinical presentation

> Growth delay is usually noted by 6 months.

> Rickets, which develop after the child starts walking.

> Bone pain.

Physical signs

> small stature

> rickets.

Investigations

> low serum phosphate with inappropriate phosphaturia

> normal serum calcium, potassium, glucose, bicarbonate and parathyroid hormone – these (and the absence of glycosuria and proteinuria on urinalysis) rule out syndromes with other renal tubular defects or nutritional rickets

> bone radiographs: rickets.

Treatment

> High-dose oral 1,25-dihydroxy-vitamin D (calcitriol).

> Oral phosphate supplements: these are often poorly tolerated as a result of associated diarrhoea.

> Recombinant growth hormone may reduce growth delay.

Complications

Treatment-associated hypercalcaemia can cause nephrocalcinosis and renal damage.

Prognosis

> A sufferer's growth rate can be improved, although their final stature is usually abnormal.

> Females are less severely affected.

Nephrology: Section 3

3 Investigations and practical procedures

3.1 Examination of the urine

3.1.1 Urinalysis

Indications

Urinalysis should be performed in all patients with renal disease/dysfunction. In addition, it is appropriate as a screening test in almost any clinical setting because:

> The consequences of renal failure are serious.

> Substantial loss of renal function occurs in a wide range of clinical settings with no specific clinical symptoms.

> Serious renal disease is virtually excluded if urinalysis is negative and the glomerular filtration rate (GFR) is normal.

Practical details

Urinalysis for blood and protein provides a sensitive, cheap and non-invasive screening test.

Estimation of protein content
Dipstick (routine)

Standard dipsticks are more sensitive to albumin than other proteins. Their threshold for albumin is 150–300 mg/L.

Interpretation of dipstick tests for urinary protein:

> Measures concentration, not rate of protein loss; for the same rate of protein loss, concentrations will be lower when urine is dilute (eg after loop diuretic).

> Contamination with skin cleanser / antiseptics (eg chlorhexidine) can give false-positive results.

> Trace results, especially in concentrated urine, are usually not clinically significant.

> Positive results should usually be followed by quantitative urine protein determination.

> A negative does not exclude immunoglobulin light chain excretion.

Dipstick for microalbuminuria

In people with diabetes, development of microalbuminuria (30–300 mg/24 hour) identifies a group at high risk of progressive renal failure. This degree of albuminuria is not reliably detected by standard urine dipsticks, but is with antibody (rather than chemical) detection (eg Micral-Test II).

Laboratory measurement

Used to quantify protein excretion, eg after positive dipstick urinalysis; 24-hour urinary collections to measure protein excretion have now been superseded by estimation of urinary protein:creatinine ratio (PCR) or urinary albumin:creatinine ratio (ACR) in a spot urinary sample.

Urinary ACR:

> normal value: <2.5 mg/mmol (men); <3.5 mg/mmol (women)

> proteinuria: >30 mg/mmol

> nephrotic: usually >200 mg/mmol.

Urinary PCR:

> normal value: <15 mg/mmol

> proteinuria >50 mg/mmol

> nephrotic: usually >300 mg/mmol.

Key point

Measures of urinary ACR and PCR are now the standard methods of quantitating proteinuria: 24-hour urinary collections are no longer required for this purpose.

Testing for haem
The urine dipstick threshold is 150 µg haemoglobin/L – equivalent to 5,000 red cells/mL – and:

> Will give a positive test with red cells, haemoglobin or myoglobin.

> A negative test effectively excludes the presence of abnormal numbers of red cells in the urine.

> If urine discoloration is present but testing for haemoglobin is negative, consider rare causes of discolouration such as porphyria, beetroot ingestion or drugs (such as rifampicin).

All people excrete some red cells in their urine, hence positive tests are common: 2.5–4% of healthy adult men in population-based studies. It is prudent to avoid testing for several days after severe exercise ('joggers nephritis' or menstruation). Urethral catheterisation or bladder trauma can also increase the number of erythrocytes in the urine. However, the possibility that a positive urinary test for blood could be caused by serious renal or urological disease (eg transitional cell carcinoma) should always be considered, especially in those over the age of 40, smokers, and those with a history of pelvic irradiation or previous cyclophosphamide use (see Section 1.1).

Key point

Intact red cells will sediment on centrifugation, whereas haemoglobin or myoglobin will not. In haemoglobinuria or myoglobinuria the supernatant will remain pink/red and positive on dipstick testing, whereas in haematuria it will not (Fig 87).

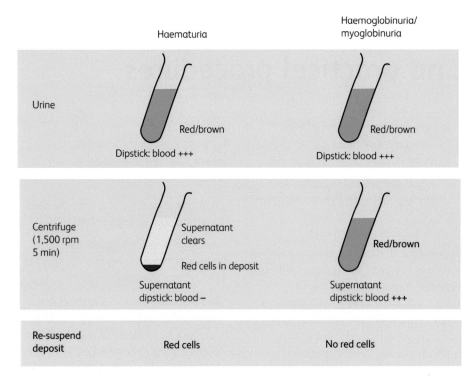

Haematuria

Haemoglobinuria/
myoglobinuria

Urine

Red/brown

Dipstick: blood +++

Red/brown

Dipstick: blood +++

Centrifuge
(1,500 rpm
5 min)

Supernatant
clears

Red cells in deposit

Supernatant
dipstick: blood –

Red/brown

Supernatant
dipstick: blood +++

Re-suspend
deposit

Red cells

No red cells

Fig 87 Distinguishing haematuria (red cells in urine) from haemoglobinuria/
myoglobinuria.

Other selected urine tests

> Urinalysis for nitrites: screening test
for urine infection (urinary nitrate
converted to nitrite by the presence
of Enterobacteriaceae).

> Urinalysis for leukocytes: screening for
infection (pyuria); is also positive
when white cells present in sterile
urine (eg interstitial nephritis).

> If nitrites, leukocytes and blood
(urinalysis) are positive this has
reasonable positive predictive value for
a urinary tract infection (UTI) – but
there is still a substantial false-positive
rate (particularly in older people, where
asymptomatic bacteriuria is common).

> Urinalysis for glucose: glucose will be
present if there is a lowered renal
threshold for glucose or elevated
blood glucose concentration.

> Urine sodium content: 24-hour
excretion is useful in assessing sodium
intake; a low sodium concentration in
a spot sample can be useful in
establishing that renal failure is
pre-renal or associated with
hepatorenal syndrome.

> Urine osmolality: used in diagnosis of
diabetes insipidus and syndrome of
inappropriate secretion of antidiuretic
hormone.

> Urine pH: for diagnosis of renal
tubular acidosis (RTA); monitor in
situations where a particular urine pH
is desirable (eg preventing urate
deposition in tumour lysis or in the
alkalinisation of urine in the
treatment of rhabdomyolysis).

> Urine electrophoresis: for light chains
(Bence Jones protein).

> Urine calcium, oxalate and citrate
determination in those with stones.

3.1.2 Urine microscopy
Principle

> Centrifuge a 10 mL urine sample at
1,500 revolutions/min (rpm) for
5 minutes: this will sediment the
cellular elements, casts and crystals.

> Re-suspend sediment in 1 mL of the
sample (with a staining agent if
desired).

> View under microscope.

> Red cell casts are particularly
important in establishing that
there is glomerular inflammation
(Fig 88). They are pathognomonic
of glomerulonephritis – but only
present in about 30% of cases.

> Micro-organisms can also be detected.

Indications

> reduced glomerular filtration rate (GFR)

> abnormality on dipstick urinalysis.

3.2 Estimations of glomerular filtration rate

Principle

An ideal marker for glomerular filtration
rate (GFR) would have the following
characteristics:

> steady-state level in plasma

> freely filtered at the glomerulus

> no tubular absorption or secretion

> no extrarenal clearance.

In this situation:

GFR = (concentration in urine × urine
production rate) / concentration
in plasma

Accurate determinations for research
and certain clinical purposes are
based on the administration of
various filtered markers including
inulin, iohexol, or radiolabelled
ethylenediaminetetra-acetic acid or
diethylenetriaminepenta-acetic acid.

In routine clinical practice these markers
are not practical to use because of
complexities related to administration
and measurement, or due to radiation
exposure. Instead the marker used to
estimate GFR is creatinine, a waste
product of muscle metabolism that is
the closest endogenous approximation
to an ideal marker for GFR that is
relatively easily measured. It is not a

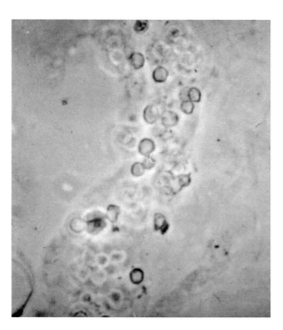

Fig 88 Red cell cast from the urine of a patient with glomerulonephritis, viewed with phase contrast.

perfect marker of GFR because there is some tubular secretion of creatinine in addition to glomerular filtration, plus extrarenal clearance of about 2 mL/min.

Cystatin C, a cysteine protease filtered by the kidney, can be used to estimate GFR when creatinine measurements may be unreliable or where more accuracy is required, but this does not yet form part of routine clinical practice.

Practical details

Estimated GFR

There are many formulae that can be used to estimate a patient's GFR based on their serum creatinine, age, sex and (sometimes) weight and/or race. The most widely used is the abbreviated 'modification of diet in renal disease' (MDRD) equation, which – in the form typically used by clinical chemistry laboratories – reports estimated GFR (eGFR) based on the patient's serum creatinine, age and sex. More recent guidance suggests that instead of MDRD, the 'Chronic Kidney Disease Epidemiology Collaboration' (CKD-EPI) formula should be used instead to estimate GFR, as it is less biased. Most laboratories now routinely report eGFR

in conjunction with any measurement of serum creatinine (see Section 2.1.2).

When considering eGFR as derived by these formulae it is important to recognise:

> It is an estimate, not a precise value – eg it will be inaccurate in people with extreme body types, underestimating true GFR in those with increased muscle bulk and overestimating true GFR in those with little muscle.

> It needs to be adjusted for ethnicity – if the patient is of African-Caribbean or African origin, then the reported eGFR must be multiplied by 1.21 or 1.159 for the MDRD or CKD-EPI formulae, respectively.

> The creatinine level must be stable – eGFR calculations are not valid if serum creatinine is changing, as in acute kidney injury (AKI).

> It is not valid in pregnant women or children (aged <18 years).

Creatinine clearance

GFR can be predicted from measurement of creatinine clearance. Before routine calculation of eGFR this was often used in clinical practice to give a more precise estimate of GFR

than measurement of serum creatinine alone, but a substantial problem with the technique is its dependence on timing and completeness of urine collection, which are often unreliable.

Key point
Incomplete urine collections will underestimate the creatinine clearance.

Key point
Plasma creatinine will be normal (for a short time) even if there is no glomerular filtration! In cases of AKI, creatinine will be accumulating rapidly in the plasma, but this cannot be discerned from a single value. GFR can be predicted only if the plasma creatinine is stable.

3.3 Imaging the renal tract

By far the most commonly used method is ultrasonography, which is cheap, reliable and non-invasive. Other tests are used in specific clinical settings.

3.3.1 Ultrasonography

This should be performed in all those with reduced GFR or abnormal urinary findings. Important findings on ultrasonography include the following:

> renal size (Fig 89)

> obstruction (Fig 90)

> scars (reflux nephropathy)

> cysts (autosomal dominant polycystic kidney disease)

> renal tumours

> renal stones

> thickness of renal cortex.

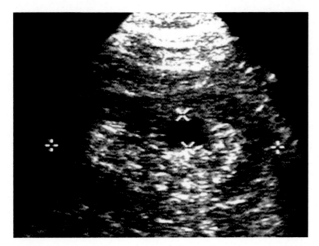

Fig 89 Ultrasonogram of the kidney in chronic kidney disease (CKD). The length is reduced (8.15 cm), the cortex thinned and there is a simple cyst (1.1 cm).

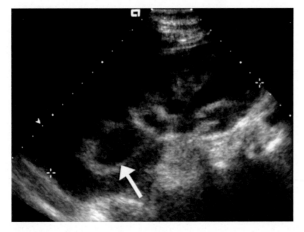

Fig 90 Ultrasound image of an obstructed kidney. Its length is enlarged at 14 cm, calyces are dilated (arrow) and cortical thickness is preserved.

Key point

Occasionally obstruction is not evident on ultrasonography – usually when it has occurred rapidly, recently and the patient is volume depleted. Negative ultrasound findings can also occur when obstruction is caused by malignant encasement of the kidneys. If there is a high index of suspicion, repeat the ultrasonography after correcting the volume depletion, or obtain a (non-contrast) CT.

3.3.2 Plain abdominal radiograph

This can be useful in detecting calculi and nephrocalcinosis (Fig 91), but in practice these are now diagnosed on CT urogram (non-contrast) and so plain films are mostly used only for monitoring known renal calculi.

3.3.3 Computed tomography

CT urography has superseded other contrast studies, eg intravenous urography (IVU), in imaging the kidney. Non-contrast imaging is used as first choice in renal colic, as it misses <2% of

stones with no risk of AKI from contrast. Contrast CT can be used for:

> evaluation of space-occupying lesions in the kidney or to meet requirement for detailed anatomical knowledge (Fig 92 and Fig 93)

> investigation of extrinsic problems impinging on the renal tract (eg ureteric compression in retroperitoneal fibrosis)

> spiral CT can be used to examine the renal arteries.

3.3.4 Intravenous urography

Radiographic contrast medium is filtered by the glomerulus and concentrated in the tubule. The contrast medium is radio-opaque and visible on radiographs as it passes through the kidney, ureter and bladder. With the widespread availability of cross-sectional imaging and improved resolution of ultrasound, IVU is now rarely performed.

3.3.5 Percutaneous or retrograde ureteric imaging

These techniques are used for assessment of pelvi-calyceal and ureteric anatomy. Percutaneous nephrostomy (anterograde pyelogram, where contrast is injected through a needle or catheter placed into the renal pelvis through the back/flank) also allows decompression of obstructed kidneys with or without anterograde placement of stents. Alternatively, imaging can be performed as a retrograde study during cystoscopy, where radiographic contrast medium is injected into the ureter from below (Fig 94). Carrying out imaging during cystoscopy allows immediate intervention, such as retrograde placement of stents or removal of transitional cell cancers (TCCs).

3.3.6 Isotopic imaging

The following compounds are often used:

> ^{99m}Tc-dimercaptosuccinic acid (DMSA): filtered by the glomerulus and then taken up by the tubules

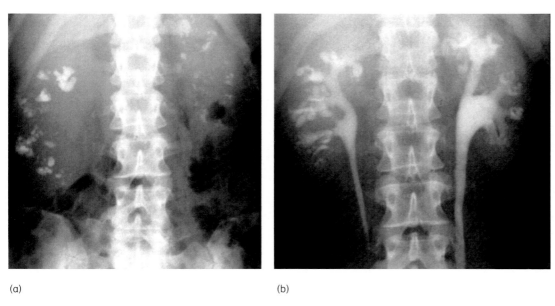

(a)   (b)

Fig 91 **(a)** Plain abdominal radiograph and **(b)** intravenous urogram (IVU) of a patient with medullary sponge kidney with marked nephrocalcinosis.

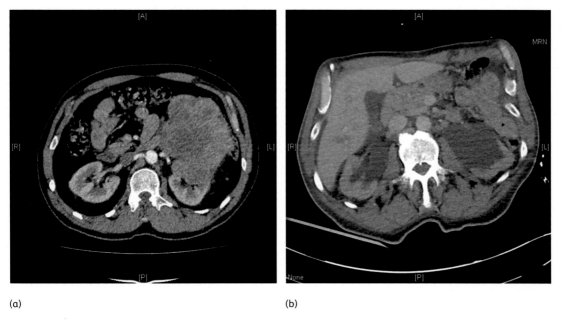

(a)   (b)

Fig 92 **(a)** CT with large (17 cm) mass arising from left kidney – renal cell carcinoma. The right kidney is normal. **(b)** CT with bilateral hydronephrosis (worse on the left, where there is also thinning of the renal cortex – suggesting longstanding obstruction).

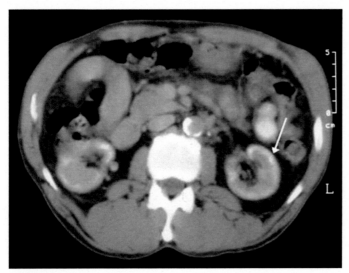

Fig 93 CT scan of the abdomen without contrast showing calcification of the renal cortex of both kidneys (arrowed on the left). This patient had acute cortical necrosis as a complication of severe acute pancreatitis.

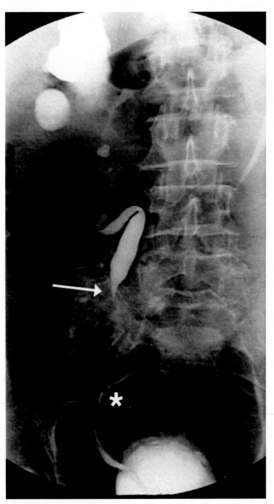

Fig 94 Retrograde ureterogram. A catheter is inserted in the lower ureter from the bladder (*). Contrast outlines a tapered stricture (arrow) and the obstructed calyceal system.

> 99mTc-mercaptoacetyltriglycine (MAG3): secreted by the tubules
> 99mTc-diethylenetriamine penta acetic acid (DTPA): filtered by the glomerulus.

Indications

> DMSA – gold standard for detection of renal scars, eg for screening children with suspected reflux nephropathy or UTI (Fig 95).
> DTPA – ideal for assessing GFR, and can help assess split (left/right) function, eg before nephrectomy.
> MAG3 – allows assessment of split (left/right function) as well as uptake time – decreased, delayed uptake by one kidney can indicate renal artery stenosis, sensitivity for which will be enhanced by the administration of captopril 1 hour previously (but is not useful if GFR is substantially reduced).

3.3.7 Renal angiography

Is now predominantly used for therapeutic intervention, as the radiation dose and contrast load are high, therefore major uses include:

> the diagnosis of renal artery stenosis and fibromuscular hyperplasia (Fig 96a), with stenting or balloon angioplasty if appropriate
> establishing (and potentially embolising) a site of bleeding in the kidney, eg after renal biopsy or percutaneous nephrostomy (Fig 96b).

3.3.8 Magnetic resonance imaging

Is widely used in renal arterial imaging because of the lack of radiation. magnetic resonance angiography (MRA) is used in the assessment of living donors in renal transplantation, to identify arterial anatomy, but can also assess for renal artery stenosis. MRA is also used following angiographic intervention to assess response to treatment, eg following embolisation of arteriovenous (AV)

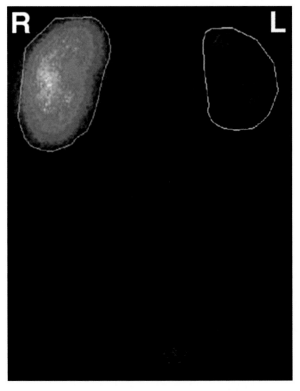

malformations. MRA is relatively contraindicated in those with a low GFR (<30 mL/min) or on dialysis because of the risk of nephrogenic systemic fibrosis with gadolinium-based contrast agents.

3.4 Renal biopsy

Principle

Renal biopsy remains the gold standard for diagnosis of most forms of intrinsic renal disease, and also for investigating transplant kidney dysfunction.

Needle biopsies of the kidney are taken and processed as follows (Fig 97):

> paraffin: for haematoxylin and eosin staining, and also special stains (eg silver stain and Congo red)

> frozen sections: immunofluorescence for immunoglobulins and complement components

> resin embedding: for electron microscopy.

Fig 95 DMSA scintigraphy of the kidneys. The left kidney is not seen because it is non-functioning: it was subsequently removed.

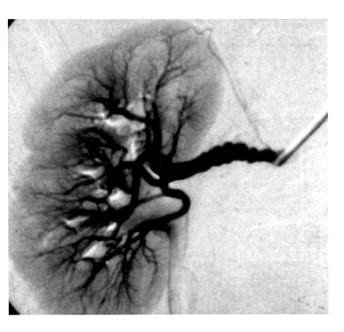

(a)

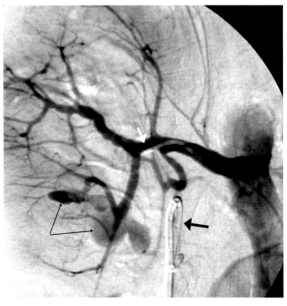

(b)

Fig 96 (a) Renal angiogram showing fibromuscular hyperplasia. **(b)** Renal angiogram showing a fistula from the renal circulation into the pelvicalyceal system after percutaneous nephrostomy. A catheter is seen in the renal artery (white arrow). Also seen is the upper end of a ureteric stent (heavy black arrow). Contrast is seen to enter the dilated pelvicalyceal system (fine black arrows). The fistula was successfully embolised along with resolution of the haematuria.

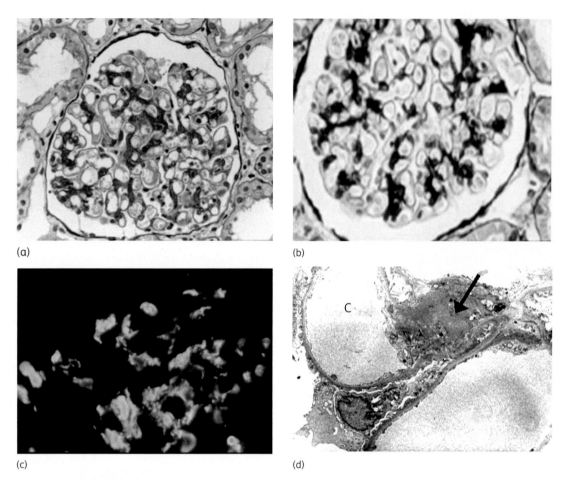

(a)

(b)

(c)

(d)

Fig 97 (a) Light microscopy of a glomerulus. The section has been stained by the periodic acid–Schiff method, and shows expansion of the mesangium. **(b)** Silver-stained section of a glomerulus showing mesangial expansion characteristic of IgA nephropathy. **(c)** Immunofluorescence of part of a glomerulus for IgA: there is mesangial deposition of IgA. **(d)** Electron micrograph showing dense deposits in the mesangium, between capillary loops (C). (Courtesy of Dr D Davies, Oxford Radcliffe Hospitals.)

Indications

> Used to investigate unexplained acute kidney injury (AKI) and some cases of chronic renal disease.

> Should be performed only if the result could alter management.

> Renal histopathological expertise must be available.

Renal biopsy can be performed on inpatients, or as a day-case outpatient procedure.

Contraindications

These are relative, rather than absolute, and the decision as to whether or not to biopsy a particular patient will always depend on the clinical setting and the balance of benefits and risks. The contraindications include:

> single kidney: possibility of losing the kidney

> reduced renal size: biopsy is less likely to be diagnostic, and more likely to cause a significant bleed

> uncontrolled hypertension: increased risk of haemorrhage; blood pressure should be corrected before biopsy

> reduced platelet count, reduced haematocrit and abnormal coagulation tests: these increase the risk of haemorrhage and should be corrected before biopsy – anticoagulants must be stopped

> patient compliance: must be able to lie still and breath hold while the biopsy is taken.

Practical details

Before the investigation

> ultrasonography or other formal imaging to determine the size, location and number of kidneys

> FBC, urea and electrolytes (UE), coagulation screen, blood group and save

> appropriate premedication

> in severe renal impairment, consider desmopressin acetate (DDAVP) infusion (it raises levels of

von Willebrand factor and factor VIII, and ameliorates the bleeding tendency related to uraemia).

The investigation

> The patient lies prone.

> The kidney to be biopsied is localised using ultrasonography.

> The kidney moves down with inspiration, and the operator directs the patient's respiration.

> A spinal needle is used to anaesthetise the track.

> Once the biopsy track is anaesthetised, the biopsy needle is then passed into the lower pole of the kidney under ultrasound guidance (and with the patient holding their breath in inspiration).

> Usually two cores of tissue are taken.

Special handling of biopsy material is sometimes needed:

> oxalate nephropathy: alcohol-containing fixative

> culture for *Mycobacterium tuberculosis:* no fixative.

After the investigation

> bed rest (usually 6 hours)

> monitor pulse, BP and urine colour.

Complications

The major complication is haemorrhage. Perirenal haematoma is very common (>30% of cases) if looked for by ultrasonography. There is haematuria in about 8% of cases. Up to 2% of patients require blood transfusion, and <1% need embolisation/ nephrectomy.

4 Self-assessment

4.1 Self-assessment questions

MRCP(UK) Part 1 examination questions

Question 1

Clinical scenario

A 24-year-old Caucasian male presented to the emergency department of his local hospital with dyspnoea and haemoptysis. Blood tests demonstrated acute kidney injury (AKI) with a creatinine of 528 µmol/L (normal range 60–110). A chest X-ray showed bilateral diffuse alveolar opacities.

Question

Which investigation is most likely to be diagnostic of the cause of his chest X-ray abnormality?

Answer

A bronchoscopy
B echocardiography
C high-resolution computerised tomography (CT) scan
D spirometry
E transfer coefficient (K_{CO})

Question 2

Clinical scenario

A 25-year-old woman presented with haemoptysis. On examination, she was found to have bilateral coarse crepitations. Investigations:
Urine dipstick: 3+ protein, 3+ blood
Serum urea: 14 mmol/L (normal range 2.5–7.0)
Serum creatinine: 265 µmol/L (normal range 60–110)
Renal biopsy revealed necrotising glomerulonephritis with cellular crescents and linear deposition of immunoglobulin G (IgG) and complement along the glomerular basement membrane (GBM).

Question

Which is the most appropriate test to confirm the diagnosis?

Answer

A anti-centromere antibody
B anti-glomerular basement membrane (GBM) antibody
C anti-neutrophil cytoplasmic antibody (ANCA)
D anti-nuclear antibody (ANA)
E anti-smooth muscle antibody

Question 3

Clinical scenario

A 50-year-old man with end-stage renal failure (ESRF) had been on maintenance haemodialysis for several years. On a routine biochemical screen he was found to be hypocalcaemic. An X-ray of his hands revealed loss of cortical outline and fine fraying of the tips of his distal phalanges.

Question

What is the most likely underlying diagnosis?

Answer

A amyloid deposition
B gout
C hyperparathyroidism
D osteoarthritis
E osteoporosis

Question 4

Clinical scenario

A 22-year-old man presented with a purpuric rash over his lower limbs, knee pain and frank haematuria coincident with an upper respiratory tract infection. Investigations:
Urinalysis: 3+ protein, 3+ blood
Serum creatinine: 145 µmol/L (normal range 60–110)
Ultrasound of kidneys: normal
He proceeded to undergo a renal biopsy.

Question

What is the most likely finding on light microscopy?

Answer

A focal and segmental sclerosis
B fusion of foot processes
C mesangial deposition of immunoglobulin A (IgA)
D pauci-immune glomerulonephritis
E thickened basement membranes

Question 5

Clinical scenario

A 78-year-old man with end-stage renal failure (ESRF) due to type 2 diabetes mellitus underwent maintenance haemodialysis via a tunnelled right internal jugular haemodialysis catheter. At the start of a dialysis session he complained of feeling unwell and had rigors. Examination revealed a temperature of 38°C, pulse 100 beats per minute, blood pressure (BP) 90/60 mmHg and oxygen saturation 98% on room air. His chest was clear.

Question

What is the most likely pathogen?

Answer

A *Escherichia coli*
B *Klebsiella pneumoniae*
C *Pseudomonas aeruginosa*
D *Staphylococcus epidermidis*
E *Streptococcus pneumoniae*

Question 6

Clinical scenario

A 60-year-old man presented with a 5-day history of haemoptysis. Closer questioning revealed a 1-year history of lethargy and general malaise. He also complained of deafness in his left ear and had recurrent sinusitis.

On examination, he was pale with coarse crackles in both lung bases.

Investigations:

Erythrocyte sedimentation rate (ESR): 75 mm/1st h (normal threshold <20)

Serum creatinine: 200 µmol/L (60–110)

Haemoglobin: 85 g/L
(normal range 130–180)

Anti-neutrophil cytoplasmic antibody (ANCA)

immunofluorescence staining: positive for cytoplasmic ANCA

Proteinase 3 titre: 75 U/mL
(normal range 0–10)

Rheumatoid factor: 40 kIU/L (normal threshold <30)

Question
What is the most likely diagnosis?

Answer
A granulomatosis with polyangiitis (GPA)
B microscopic polyangiitis
C mixed cryoglobulinaemia
D systemic lupus erythematosus (SLE)
E systemic rheumatoid disease

Question 7

Clinical scenario
A 77-year-old man who had undergone resection and radiotherapy for colon cancer 10 years previously presented with back pain, weight loss, nausea and reduced urine output. On closer questioning, he also described frequency, urgency and poor stream.

Investigations:

ESR: 85 mm/1st h
(normal threshold <20)

Haemoglobin: 92 g/L
(normal range 130–180)

Serum creatinine: 265 µmol/L
(normal range 60–110)

Renal tract ultrasound: bilateral hydronephrosis and a retroperitoneal mass

Question
What is the most likely diagnosis?

Answer
A amyloidosis
B benign prostatic hypertrophy

C recurrence of colonic carcinoma
D retroperitoneal fibrosis
E urinary tract infection

Question 8

Clinical scenario
An 18-year-old student presented with progressive sensorineural deafness. He wore glasses and his mother reported that the optician mentioned that he had an abnormality of the lens of his eye. Physical examination was otherwise unremarkable. Dipstick urinalysis revealed non-visible haematuria.

Question
What is the most likely diagnosis?

Answer
A Alport syndrome
B Bartter syndrome
C Berger's syndrome
D IgA nephropathy
E minimal change disease

Question 9

Clinical scenario
A 81-year-old man with recent fatigue was found to have serum creatinine 800 µmol/L (normal range 60–110) and potassium 6.2 mmol/L (normal range 3.5–4.9), and he was referred to the medical take by his general practitioner (GP). Key findings on examination were BP 147/82 mmHg, jugular venous pressure (JVP) not elevated and a clear chest on auscultation. A renal ultrasound showed a post-micturition (residual) volume of 800 mL in his bladder, and bilateral pelvicalyceal dilatation.

Question
Which is the most appropriate initial treatment?

Answer
A antegrade nephrostomies
B haemodialysis
C intravenous saline
D optical urethrotomy
E urethral catheterisation

Question 10

Clinical scenario
A 68-year-old woman presented with red itchy rash over her trunk and limbs that has been present for 5 days. Her renal function had deteriorated, with serum creatinine 327 µmol/L (baseline 98 µmol/L 1 month previously; normal range 60–110). She was taking a considerable number of medications.

Question
Which medication is the most likely cause of her acute kidney injury (AKI)?

Answer
A amoxicillin
B aspirin
C digoxin
D lisinopril
E rosuvastatin

Question 11

Clinical scenario
A 65-year-man with a history of hypertension, type 2 diabetes mellitus, ischaemic heart disease and peripheral vascular disease attended clinic for routine review. On a combination of amlodipine 10 mg daily and bendroflumethiazide 2.5 mg daily his BP was 156/90 mmHg. Ramipril 2.5 mg daily was commenced, and his blood tests were repeated 2 weeks later.

Investigations – baseline:

Serum sodium: 145 mmol/L
(normal range 137–144)

Serum potassium: 4.5 mmol/L
(normal range 3.5–4.9)

Serum urea: 6.0 mmol/L
(normal range 2.5–7.0)

Serum creatinine: 97 µmol/L
(normal range 60–110)

Investigations – 2 weeks later:

Serum sodium: 143 mmol/L

Serum potassium: 6.5 mmol/L

Serum urea: 16.7 mmol/L

Serum creatinine: 170 µmol/L

Question
What is the most likely diagnosis?

Answer

A hypertensive nephropathy
B hypovolaemia
C interstitial nephritis
D renal artery stenosis
E retroperitoneal fibrosis

Question 12

Clinical scenario

A 31-year-old woman presented with seizures. On examination she had a facial rash. Dipstick urinalysis revealed blood 1+ and protein 3+. A biochemical screen was normal, excepting creatinine 175 µmol/L (normal range 60–110). Immunological testing demonstrated a positive anti-nuclear antibodies (ANA) and antibodies to double-stranded DNA.

Question

Which renal condition is most likely?

Answer

A acute interstitial nephritis
B amyloidosis
C IgA nephropathy
D membranous nephropathy
E nephrocalcinosis

Question 13

Clinical scenario

A 42-year-old man with end-stage renal disease due to IgA nephropathy received a cadaveric renal transplant. The procedure was uncomplicated, and he had good graft function, with baseline serum creatinine 105 µmol/L (normal range 60–110). Ten months later he complained of anorexia and night sweats, and he had lost 5 kg in weight in the preceding month. Physical examination revealed no unexpected abnormalities.

Question

Which investigation is most likely to provide the diagnosis?

Answer

A bronchoalveolar lavage
B CT chest/abdomen/pelvis
C renal transplant biopsy
D serum cytomegalovirus polymerase chain reaction (CMV PCR)
E urine for decoy cells

Question 14

Clinical scenario

A 37-year-old man with end-stage renal failure (ESRF) secondary to diabetic nephropathy had been on peritoneal dialysis for 1 year. He presented with abdominal pain and cloudy dialysate in his drainage bag. A diagnosis of peritoneal dialysis-associated peritonitis was made.

Question

What is the most likely causative organism?

Answer

A *Campylobacter jejuni*
B *Candida albicans*
C *Escherichia coli*
D *Mycobacterium tuberculosis*
E *Staphylococcus epidermidis*

Question 15

Clinical scenario

A 51-year-old woman with polycystic kidney disease and a slowly rising serum creatinine, which had been 320 µmol/L (normal range 60–110) at her last clinic visit 1 month ago, was brought to the emergency department after being found collapsed at home by her partner. She was fully conscious (Glasgow Coma Scale (GCS) score 15/15) but complained of a headache.

Question

What is the most likely diagnosis?

Answer

A aortic dissection
B renal cyst infection
C subarachnoid haemorrhage
D transient ischaemic attack
E uraemic encephalopathy

Question 16

Clinical scenario

A 64-year-old woman with stable chronic kidney disease (CKD) stage IV (creatinine 270 µmol/L (normal range 60–110), estimated glomerular filtration rate (eGFR) 16 mL/min/1.73 m² (normal threshold >60)) presented with an uncomplicated lower urinary tract infection, for which she was prescribed an antibiotic by her GP. She attended a routine renal outpatient appointment later that week, when she said she felt perfectly well, but routine blood testing revealed creatinine 350 µmol/L.

Question

What is the most likely cause for her deterioration in renal function?

Answer

A acute pyelonephritis
B acute tubular necrosis
C amoxicillin
D trimethoprim
E urinary tract obstruction

Question 17

Clinical scenario

A 57-year-old man was referred by his GP to the medical team on take to exclude a deep venous thrombosis. All tests were normal/negative, excepting that he had 2+ non-visible haematuria on urinalysis (with nil else of note). This remained positive on subsequent samples, and there was no growth on urine culture. His serum creatinine was normal.

Question

What action should you take next?

Answer

A check a serum autoimmune screen
B refer him to local renal services
C refer him to local urology services
D request a urinary tract CT
E request a urinary tract ultrasound

Question 18

Clinical scenario

A 37-year-old woman with a history of recurrent *Klebsiella* urinary tract infections presented to the emergency department with severe right-sided flank pain. A non-contrast CT kidneys, ureters and bladder (KUB) demonstrated a stone in the right ureter.

Question

What is the most likely chemical composition of the stone?

Answer

A calcium acetate

B cysteine

C magnesium ammonium phosphate

D potassium citrate

E uric acid

Question 19

Clinical scenario

A 25-year-old man, generally fit and well apart from moderate hearing impairment, presented to his local emergency department with a 3-week history of lethargy, nausea and vomiting. Dipstick urinalysis showed 2+ blood and 2+ protein. Laboratory test results included urea 59 mmol/L (normal range 2.5–7.0), creatinine 1,600 µmol/L (normal range 60–110) and haemoglobin 79 g/L (normal range 130–180). Renal ultrasound demonstrated two 7 cm kidneys.

Question

Which gene is most likely to be abnormal?

Answer

A *ADPKD1*

B *COL4A5*

C *NPHS2*

D *PHEX*

E *TRPC6*

Question 20

Clinical scenario

A 28-year-old woman with biopsy-proven IgA nephropathy and stable chronic kidney disease (CKD) stage III (eGFR 45 mL/min/1.73 m^2 (normal threshold >60); creatinine 130 µmol/L (normal range 60–110)) contacted you for advice about her medications because she thought that she might be pregnant, had performed a pregnancy test, and found this to be positive.

Question

Which medication is it most important to stop and replace with a safer alternative?

Answer

A aspirin

B fish-oil supplements

C folic acid

D ramipril

E simvastatin

Question 21

Clinical scenario

A pregnant woman with pre-eclampsia had severe hypertension.

Question

What is the definitive treatment for the condition?

Answer

A delivery of the baby

B dexamethasone

C labetalol

D magnesium

E nitrates

Question 22

Clinical scenario

A 39-year-old woman with a history of hypertension was found referred to have impaired renal function, with creatinine 160 µmol/L (normal range 60–110) (eGFR 33 mL/min/1.73 m^2 (normal threshold >60)). Dipstick urinalysis revealed 1+ proteinuria, and ultrasound examination of the kidneys showed both to have reduced size with upper and lower pole scarring.

Question

What is the most likely underlying diagnosis?

Answer

A amyloidosis

B hypertensive nephropathy

C IgA nephropathy

D membranous glomerulonephritis

E reflux nephropathy

Question 23

Clinical scenario

A 47-year-old man with known nephrotic syndrome due to focal segmental glomerulosclerosis attended hospital with acute flank pain, proteinuria 3+ and haematuria 3+ on dipstick urinalysis, and a rise in serum creatinine from 115 to 167 µmol/L (normal range 60–110). He was taking prednisolone, tacrolimus, ramipril and furosemide as regular medications.

Question

What is the most likely cause of his presentation?

Answer

A acute interstitial nephritis

B calcineurin inhibitor (tacrolimus) nephrotoxicity

C renal artery stenosis

D renal vein thrombosis

E spontaneous bacterial peritonitis

Question 24

Clinical scenario

A 27-year-old woman with type 1 diabetes since childhood presented with peripheral oedema, which she said had 'come and gone' a few times in the last couple of months. Her diabetes had always been very well controlled, with a urine albumin: creatinine ratio (ACR) 1.5 mg/mmol (normal) and normal retinal photography at her recent annual review. Urinalysis demonstrated 3+ proteinuria as the only abnormality. Her serum creatinine was normal. A renal biopsy was arranged.

Question

What is the renal biopsy most likely to demonstrate?

Answer

A amyloidosis

B diabetic nephropathy

C immunoglobulin A (IgA) nephropathy

D minimal change disease

E tubulointerstitial nephritis

Question 25

Clinical scenario

A 38-year-old man with a family history of autosomal dominant polycystic kidney disease was referred with renal impairment and hypertension. An ultrasound scan of the abdomen confirmed bilateral enlarged polycystic kidneys. He had a question regarding the risk to his children.

Question

What do you think is the chance that both of my two children will have polycystic kidney disease?

Answer

A 0%

B 25%

C 33.3%

D 50%

E 75%

MRCP(UK) Part 2 examination questions

Question 26

Clinical scenario

A 65-year-old man had received a renal transplant for polycystic kidney disease 5 years previously. He had good graft function with a baseline creatinine of 120 µmol/L (normal range 60–110), and was immunosuppressed with tacrolimus, mycophenolate mofetil and prednisolone. He had been unwell with a respiratory tract infection for which his GP had prescribed a course of clarithromycin (he was allergic to penicillin). He attended his routine follow-up clinic a week later. He was feeling much better, but his blood tests demonstrated a significant decline in renal function with a creatinine of 340 µmol/L.

Question

What is the most likely cause for his deterioration in renal function?

Answer

A acute allergic interstitial nephritis

B acute cellular rejection

C calcineurin inhibitor (tacrolimus) nephrotoxicity

D cyst infection

E obstructive uropathy

Question 27

Clinical scenario

A 74-year-old man was referred to the emergency department by his GP with lethargy and exertional dyspnoea. Examination revealed BP 165/82 mmHg and mild ankle oedema, but nil else of note. Blood test results included urea 38 mmol/L (normal range 2.5–7.0) and creatinine 568 µmol/L (normal range 60–110). No old biochemical values were available.

Question

Which investigation result would provide the best indication that this is chronic – rather than acute – kidney disease?

Answer

A anaemia (haemoglobin 82 g/L; normal range 130–180)

B bilateral small (8 cm) kidneys on ultrasonography

C elevated C-reactive protein (CRP) (87 mg/L; normal threshold <10)

D hyperphosphataemia (serum phosphate 2.7 mmol/L; normal range 0.8–1.4)

E proteinuria (3+ protein on dipstick urinalysis)

Question 28

Clinical scenario

A 72-year-old woman with a history of total abdominal hysterectomy and salpingo-oophorectomy for cervical carcinoma 6 months previously, presented to the medical take. She had been unwell with nausea and vomiting for 1 week, and reported that she had not passed any urine for 3 days. She did not appear to be very unwell, and on examination seemed to be euvolaemic. Urgent blood tests were arranged, and these revealed serum creatinine 700 µmol/L (normal range 60–110). She remained anuric when catheterised and after being given 1 L of 0.9% saline intravenously. An urgent renal ultrasound is reported as 'normal, with no hydronephrosis'.

Question

What is the most likely diagnosis?

Answer

A acute interstitial nephritis

B acute tubular necrosis

C obstructive uropathy

D paraneoplastic vasculitis

E renal vein thrombosis

Question 29

Clinical scenario

A 75-year-old man had been on haemodialysis for the last 15 years. He was anuric. He was getting increasingly frail and had developed arterial insufficiency of his right foot. The vascular surgeons were considering an amputation. He felt that his quality of life was poor and he wanted to stop dialysing. He asked: 'How long will I survive after stopping dialysis, doctor?'

Question

What will you tell him is most likely?

Answer

A 1–2 weeks

B 1–7 days

C 2–4 weeks

D 3 days

E 3 months

Question 30

Clinical scenario

A 62-year-old man complained of generalised swelling for the last 2 months and presented himself to the emergency department, where you were asked to see him as the core medical trainee on call. On examination he had peripheral oedema and hypertension. His urinalysis demonstrated 1+ blood and 3+ proteinuria. Blood tests revealed normal serum urea and creatinine, although his serum albumin was low (28 g/L; normal range 37–49).

Question
Which management strategy is most appropriate?

Answer
A commencement of an angiotensin-converting enzyme (ACE) inhibitor

B initiation of steroid therapy

C referral to local renal services as an outpatient

D referral to radiology for a CT-guided renal biopsy

E urgent admission for further investigation

Question 31

Clinical scenario
A 52-year-old man with a renal transplant 18 months previously presented to hospital with a 3-day history of malaise. On examination he looked unwell, with a pyrexia of 38.4°C, low BP and tenderness over his transplant kidney. Urgent blood tests demonstrated deteriorating renal function.

Question
Which combination represents optimal management?

Answer
A blood cultures, intravenous fluids, broad-spectrum antibiotics

B blood cultures, intravenous fluids, renal transplant ultrasound

C intravenous fluids, broad-spectrum antibiotics, pulsed intravenous steroids

D intravenous fluids, renal transplant ultrasound, renal biopsy

E intravenous fluids, urgent cytomegalovirus polymerase chain reaction (CMV PCR), renal transplant ultrasound

Question 32

Clinical scenario
A 67-year-old man was referred to the on-take medical team on account of blood tests revealing acute deterioration in renal function. He had complained of feeling unwell for 2 weeks, with fevers, anorexia and a purple rash on his legs. Blood tests performed by his GP revealed a rise in serum creatinine from 127 to 254 µmol/L (normal range 60–110), together with an ESR of 72 mm/1st h (normal threshold <20). He had a past medical history of ischaemic heart disease, type 2 diabetes and hypertension, and had undergone diagnostic coronary angiography 1 month previously.

Question
What is the most likely diagnosis?

Answer
A anti-neutrophil cytoplasmic antibody (ANCA)-associated vasculitis

B cholesterol emboli

C contrast nephrotoxicity

D Henoch–Schönlein purpura

E multiple myeloma

Question 33

Clinical scenario
A 19-year-old woman, normally fit and well and without any significant past medical history, attended the emergency department complaining of a burning sensation on passing urine. She said that the urine looked cloudy and had an unpleasant smell. She said that she had never had a urinary tract infection before. Dipstick urinalysis was positive for nitrite.

Question
What is the most appropriate management?

Answer
A check midstream specimen of urine (MSU)

B prescribe amoxicillin

C referral to renal services

D request CT kidneys, ureters and bladder (KUB)

E request urinary tract ultrasound

Question 34

Clinical scenario
A 82-year-old man, on maintenance haemodialysis for 4 years, developed painful shingles and was started on aciclovir by his GP. Over the next week he became increasingly confused. He missed a regular dialysis session, and his wife brought him to the emergency department. His observations are unremarkable and, apart from delirium, there was nothing focal on examination.

Question
What is the most likely cause of his delirium?

Answer
A aciclovir toxicity

B hyperkalaemia

C pulmonary oedema

D uraemic encephalopathy

E zoster-associated encephalitis

Question 35

Clinical scenario
A 51-year-old man of African-Caribbean ethnicity was referred to the renal service after a routine blood test revealed serum creatinine 160 µmol/L (normal range 60–110) (eGFR 51 mL/min/1.73 m^2 (normal threshold >60)). Physical examination was unremarkable, apart from BP 180/104 mmHg. Dipstick urinalysis showed no abnormality. A 24-hour ambulatory BP record was obtained, which revealed mean BP 157/92 mmHg.

Question
What should be the first choice of antihypertensive agent?

Answer
A angiotensin-converting enzyme (ACE) inhibitor

B angiotensin-receptor blocker (ARB)

C beta-blocker

D calcium channel blocker (CCB)

E thiazide diuretic

Question 36

Clinical scenario

A 21-year-old woman was referred to the emergency department by her GP because of severe hypokalaemia (serum potassium 2.4 mmol/L; normal range 3.5–4.9).

Arterial blood gas analysis revealed:
pH 7.23 (normal range 7.35–7.45)
PO_2 13.2 kPa (normal range 11.3–12.6)
PCO_2 4.0 kPa (normal range 4.7–6.0)
HCO_3 10 mmol/L (normal range 21–29)
Cl^- 120 mmol/L (normal range 95–107)
Repeat serum biochemistry testing showed:
Sodium 137 mmol/L
(normal range 137–144)
Potassium 2.3 mmol/L
(normal range 3.5–4.9)
Creatinine 58 µmol/L
(normal range 60–110)

Question

Which is the most likely diagnosis?

Answer

A Balkan nephropathy

B ethylene glycol intoxication

C Gitelman syndrome

D type I renal tubular acidosis

E type IV renal tubular acidosis

Question 37

Clinical scenario

A 67-year-old man was referred by his GP to the renal outpatient clinic after a routine blood test showed serum creatinine 187 µmol/L (normal range 60–110) (eGFR 33 mL/min/1.73 m^2 (normal threshold >60)). There were no abnormal findings on examination. Dipstick urinalysis revealed 2+ proteinuria and 1+ haematuria. Renal ultrasound examination demonstrated two 10.5 cm kidneys. Blood test results included corrected serum calcium 2.75 mmol/L (mild hypercalcaemia; normal range 2.20–2.60), prostate-specific antigen (not elevated), immunoglobulin electrophoresis (normal), serum

parathyroid hormone 2 pmol/L (low-normal; normal range 0.9–5.4). There was no Bence Jones proteinuria.

Question

Which investigation is most likely to establish the diagnosis?

Answer

A ACE level

B plasma vitamin D level

C renal biopsy

D serum free light chain assay

E sestamibi parathyroid scan

Question 38

Clinical scenario

A 68-year-old man who had felt non-specifically unwell for 6 weeks developed back pain and went to see his GP, who performed blood tests, including a screen for myeloma. When the blood test results were reported by the laboratory, these confirmed the diagnosis of myeloma and also demonstrated AKI (creatinine 491 µmol/L; normal range 60–110) and hypercalcaemia (corrected calcium 3.1 mmol/L; normal range 2.20–2.60). The patient was admitted by the on-take medical team the same day. Physical examination revealed no abnormalities.

Question

What would be the most appropriate immediate management?

Answer

A chemotherapy with a cyclophosphamide-based regime

B chemotherapy with bortezomib and dexamethasone

C intravenous bisphosphonate

D intravenous saline

E plasma exchange

Question 39

Clinical scenario

A 76-year-old man was admitted with pleuritic chest pain. His comorbidities

included CKD stage IIIb, ischaemic heart disease and hypertension. His regular medications were aspirin, atenolol, clopidogrel, nifedipine, ramipril and simvastatin. A CT pulmonary angiogram (CTPA) was planned to exclude a pulmonary embolism.

Question

What would be the most appropriate way of reducing the risk of contrast nephrotoxicity?

Answer

A arrange haemodialysis immediately after CTPA

B pre-hydrate with isotonic sodium bicarbonate

C stop ramipril and arrange haemodialysis after CTPA

D stop ramipril and prehydrate with normal saline

E stop ramipril and prescribe N-acetylcysteine infusion

Question 40

Clinical scenario

A 77-year-old man with end-stage renal failure (ESRF) of unknown cause for which he received haemodialysis three times per week was admitted to hospital with pneumonia. You are the core medical trainee (CMT) covering the renal ward in the evening, and the nurses contact you at 9.30 pm because the biochemistry laboratory technician has just phoned to say that his serum potassium is 2.9 mmol/L (normal range 3.5–4.9).

Question

What action should you take?

Answer

A arrange transfer to a bed with a cardiac monitor

B check when he last had dialysis

C contact the on-call renal specialist registrar (SpR) immediately for advice

D prescribe intravenous potassium replacement

E prescribe oral potassium replacement

Question 41

Clinical scenario

A 24-year-old woman presented to with joint pain, lethargy and a facial rash. On examination she had marked peripheral oedema and her BP was 168/92 mmHg.

Investigations:

Urine protein:creatinine ratio: 240 mg/mmol (normal threshold <30)

Serum creatinine: 167 µmol/L (normal range 60–110)

Serum albumin: 30 g/L (normal range 37–49)

Renal biopsy: Focal glomerulonephritis with subendothelial and mesangial immune deposits.

Question

What is the most likely diagnosis?

Answer

A lupus nephritis class II

B lupus nephritis class III

C lupus nephritis class V

D membranous glomerulonephritis

E Sjögren's syndrome

Question 42

Clinical scenario

A 65-year-old man presented with numbness and tingling in his fingers, consistent with carpal tunnel syndrome, and with diarrhoea. Examination was notable for multiple bruises, hepatomegaly and peripheral oedema.

Investigations:

Serum creatinine: 225 µmol/L (normal range 60–110)

Serum albumin: 27 g/L (normal range 37–49)

He underwent a renal biopsy.

Question

Which would be the most useful stain to use on the biopsy tissue to confirm the diagnosis?

Answer

A Congo red

B Gram

C haematoxylin and eosin

D periodic acid–Schiff

E silver

Question 43

Clinical scenario

A 68-year-old man who had been complaining of back pain for 2 months was found collapsed by a friend and brought to hospital. On examination, vital signs included temperature 36.8°C, pulse 90 beats per minute and BP 90/60 mmHg. His jugular venous pressure (JVP) was not visible. He was confused, but here was no focal neurological deficit.

Investigations:

Haemoglobin: 87 g/L (normal range 130–180)

White cell count: 9.1×10^9/L (4.0–11.0)

Platelets: 110×10^9/L (150–400)

ESR: 99 mm/1st h (normal threshold <20)

Serum sodium: 136 mmol/L (normal range 137–144)

Serum potassium: 6.5 mmol/L (normal range 3.5–4.9)

Serum corrected calcium: 3.2 mmol/L (2.20–2.60)

Serum urea: 20 mmol/L (2.5–7.0)

Serum creatinine: 275 µmol/L (60–110)

Serum alkaline phosphatase: 100 U/L (45–105)

Question

What is the diagnosis?

Answer

A Addison's disease

B multiple myeloma

C Paget's disease

D primary hyperparathyroidism

E prostate carcinoma with metastases

Question 44

Clinical scenario

A 72-year-old woman who was a heavy smoker had previously undergone a lobectomy for non-small-cell carcinoma of the lung. She presented with a 6-week history of leg swelling and lethargy. Examination revealed a well-healed thoracotomy scar and bilateral pitting oedema. Urinalysis showed 4+ protein.

Investigations:

Urine protein:creatinine ratio: 635 mg/mmol (normal threshold <30)

Serum creatinine: 180 µmol/L (normal range 60–110)

Serum albumin: 22 g/L (normal range 37–49)

Question

What is the most likely diagnosis?

Answer

A crescentic glomerulonephritis

B focal segmental glomerulonephritis

C hypertensive nephropathy

D membranous nephropathy

E minimal change disease

Question 45

Clinical scenario

A 65-year-old man with a history of type 2 diabetes mellitus presented with leg swelling. On examination his BP was 165/90 mmHg and he was found to have proliferative retinopathy.

Investigations:

Urine protein:creatinine ratio: 400 mg/mmol (normal threshold <45)

Serum creatinine: 177 µmol/L (normal range 60–110)

Serum albumin: 29 g/L (normal range 37–49)

Haemoglobin A_{1C}: 75 mmol/mol (normal range 20–42)

Question

What is the most likely diagnosis?

Answer

A amyloidosis

B diabetic nephropathy

C hypertensive nephropathy

D membranous nephropathy

E renal artery stenosis

Question 46

Clinical scenario

A 77-year-old man with a history of well-controlled type 2 diabetes mellitus and hypertension presented with fatigue and leg swelling. He had been taking ibuprofen for several weeks for pain due to osteoarthritis. Previous blood tests of renal function had been normal.

Investigations:
Urine dipstick: 2+ protein
Urine protein:creatinine ratio: 138 mg/mmol (normal threshold <45)
Serum urea: 11.5 mmol/L (normal range 2.5–7.0)
Serum creatinine: 177 µmol/L (normal range 60–110)

Question
What is the most likely diagnosis?

Answer
A diabetic nephropathy
B hypertensive nephropathy
C membranous nephropathy
D minimal change disease
E tubulointerstitial nephritis

Question 47

Clinical scenario
A 65-year-old man of no fixed abode was found unconscious and admitted to the emergency department. On examination he smelt strongly of alcohol, and vital signs included temperature 34.5°C and BP 110/65 mmHg. Dipstick urinalysis showed 3+ blood, but urine microscopy showed no cells or organisms.

Further investigations:
Serum creatinine: 280 µmol/L (normal range 60–110)
Gamma-glutamyl transferase (GGT): 40 U/L (normal threshold <50)
Aspartate transaminase (AST): 575 U/L (normal range 1–31)
Lactate dehydrogenase (LDH): 1,750 U/L (normal range 10–250)

Question
What is the most likely underlying diagnosis?

Answer
A hepatorenal syndrome
B hypothermia

C hypovolaemia
D paracetamol poisoning
E rhabdomyolysis

Question 48

Clinical scenario
A 62-year-old man was found to have poorly controlled BP when reviewed in clinic. He had received a deceased cardiac donor renal transplant 8 months previously. Delayed graft function meant that he had required three sessions of haemodialysis post transplant for hyperkalaemia, but he had reached a baseline serum creatinine of 180 µmol/L 3 weeks post transplant, which remained steady for the first 4 months. Since then the serum creatinine had started to creep up, and for the past month has been sitting at 280 µmol/L. His other blood tests had been stable, and he was passing good volumes of urine, which showed only a small amount of protein on dipstick. His BP was 180/80 mmHg on amlodipine 10 mg od, doxazosin 8 mg bd and bisoprolol 2.5 mg od, which had been restarted early post transplant and increased recently.

On examination there are no unexpected abnormalities: his transplant was in the left iliac fossa and was firm but non-tender to palpation, although he was obese, which made assessment difficult. Ultrasound examination showed a 12 cm transplant kidney, with normal corticomedullary differentiation and no pelvicalyceal dilatation. The technician thought the Doppler was normal, although the position of the kidney made the whole study technically challenging.

Question
What is the most likely cause of his raised creatinine?

Answer
A acute antibody-mediated rejection
B acute cellular rejection
C chronic transplant glomerulopathy
D transplant renal artery stenosis
E urinary tract infection

Question 49

Clinical scenario
A 34-year-old woman with end-stage renal failure (ESRF) of unknown cause had received a renal transplant 2 years previously. This had been complicated by an early rejection episode at 3 months, successfully treated with steroids.

On routine review in clinic she was well. Her medications were tacrolimus 2 mg bd, mycophenolate mofetil 500 mg bd, cefalexin 250 mg on, amlodipine 5 mg od and aspirin 75 mg od. Her BP was 110/70 mmHg, urine dipstick showed no protein and no blood, and serum creatinine was 110 µmol/L. All other blood tests were within normal range.

She said that she wished to become pregnant, and asked for advice about her medications.

Question
What would be your recommendation?

Answer
A stop amlodipine and start labetalol
B stop aspirin and start warfarin
C stop cefalexin and start trimethoprim
D stop mycophenolate mofetil and start azathioprine
E stop tacrolimus and start ciclosporin

Question 50

Clinical scenario
A 35-year-old woman received a renal transplant for end-stage renal failure (ESRF) due to adult polycystic kidney disease. She did well postoperatively, with serum creatinine rapidly falling to around 100 µmol/L, and was discharged home on tacrolimus (a calcineurin inhibitor), azathioprine and prednisolone as her immunosuppressive medications.
She was reviewed twice weekly in clinic for the next 5 weeks, and then weekly, as determined by standard protocol.

Progress was uncomplicated until week 9, when routine blood tests revealed that over the previous 7 days her serum creatinine had risen from 108 μmol/L to 180 μmol/L.

Question

What would you do first?

Answer

A arrange biopsy of transplant kidney

B arrange ultrasound of transplant kidney

C give intravenous steroids

D increase dose of oral prednisolone

E increase dose of tacrolimus

4.2 Self-assessment answers

Answer to Question 1

E: transfer coefficient (K$_{CO}$)

The picture is suggestive of a pulmonary–renal syndrome, probably antiglomerular basement membrane (GBM) disease (Goodpasture's). Pulmonary haemorrhage will cause an elevated transfer coefficient (K$_{CO}$).

Answer to Question 2

B: anti-glomerular basement membrane (GBM) antibody

The patient has symptoms suggestive of Goodpasture's syndrome, namely pulmonary haemorrhage in association with nephritis. The renal biopsy appearances indicate Goodpasture's disease, in which serologic assays for anti-GBM antibodies are useful for confirming the diagnosis and monitoring the response to therapy.

Answer to Question 3

C: hyperparathyroidism

Secondary hyperparathyroidism leads to renal osteodystrophy, which develops as a result of hyperphosphataemia, hypocalcaemia and impaired synthesis of renal vitamin D. This can result in

changes such as terminal tuft erosions (as described above), fractures and pruritus.

Answer to Question 4

C: mesangial deposition of immunoglobulin A (IgA)

Henoch–Schönlein purpura is a systemic small vessel vasculitis affecting the skin, joints, bowel and kidneys. Biopsy of the skin or kidneys will show IgA deposition. The association between upper respiratory tract infection and concomitant macroscopic haematuria is termed synpharyngitic haematuria.

Answer to Question 5

D: *Staphylococcus epidermidis*

Gram-positive organisms are responsible for most dialysis catheter-related infections. Risk factors include diabetes mellitus, long duration of catheter use, recent surgery and immunosuppression. Presentation is most often with fever and chills, although evidence of metastatic infection may often be the first clue.

Answer to Question 6

A: granulomatosis with polyangiitis (GPA)

GPA (previously known as Wegener's granulomatosis) is an autoimmune multisystem disorder of unknown aetiology. It is characterised by necrotising granulomatous inflammation and pauci-immune vasculitis affecting small- to medium-sized blood vessels.

Answer to Question 7

D: retroperitoneal fibrosis

Retroperitoneal fibrosis is characterised by inflammatory tissue around the aorta and iliac arteries, which can encase the ureters and lead to obstructive nephropathy. It can be idiopathic, or secondary to abdominal aortic aneurysms, renal tract injury, post radiation, malignancy or infection. A biopsy may be required for diagnosis.

Answer to Question 8

A: Alport syndrome

In patients with Alport syndrome, sensorineural deafness often starts in childhood and is progressive. Anterior lenticonus, an abnormal conical or spherical forward projection of the lens, is pathognomonic. Renal disease results from a defect of type IV collagen in the glomerular basement membrane (GBM), which leads to basement membrane thickening, impairment of selectivity and glomerulosclerosis.

Answer to Question 9

E: urethral catheterisation

This man appears to have obstruction at the level of bladder outflow, most likely due to benign prostatic hypertrophy. He should first be catheterised and then given intravenous fluids. He may well become polyuric when his obstruction is relieved.

Answer to Question 10

A: amoxicillin

She has a rash and recent-onset kidney impairment. The most likely cause is an acute (allergic) interstitial nephritis – common causes for which would be antibiotics (particularly penicillins, cephalosporins, sulphonamides and rifampicin), non-steroidal anti-inflammatory drugs (NSAIDs), proton-pump inhibitors and allopurinol.

Answer to Question 11

D: renal artery stenosis

The patient has a significant history of vascular disease on a background of risk factors such as diabetes and hypertension. In patients with renal artery stenosis there is reduced perfusion in the afferent arteriole and glomerular filtration is heavily dependent on the effect of angiotensin II on the efferent arteriole. Angiotensin-converting enzyme (ACE) inhibitors reduce the production of angiotensin II, reducing glomerular filtration.

Answer to Question 12

D: membranous nephropathy

Systemic lupus erythematosus (SLE) can affect the kidneys in a number of different ways. Typical patterns of renal involvement include focal or diffuse proliferative, membranous, mesangial and sclerosing glomerulonephritis.

Answer to Question 13

B: computerised tomography (CT) chest/abdomen/pelvis

While infectious complications of transplantation could cause this picture, the most likely diagnosis is post-transplant lymphoproliferative disorder (PTLD). This is most common in the first year after transplantation, and a whole-body CT is an appropriate initial investigative step.

Answer to Question 14

E: *Staphylococcus epidermidis*

While all the above organisms can cause peritoneal dialysis-associated peritonitis, the most common are coagulase-negative staphylococci (*S epidermidis*). Treatment is with intraperitoneal antibiotics.

Answer to Question 15

C: subarachnoid haemorrhage

There is an important association between intracranial (berry) aneurysms and autosomal dominant polycystic kidney disease. With this history, a subarachnoid haemorrhage is the most likely diagnosis.

Answer to Question 16

D: trimethoprim

Trimethoprim blocks tubular secretion of creatinine, although this effect is only generally evident (as a significant rise in serum creatinine) in patients with a low estimated glomerular filtration rate (eGFR), where this contributes to a greater proportion of creatinine clearance. Glomerular filtration of creatinine is unchanged. Trimethoprim also interferes with tubular secretion of potassium and may cause hyperkalaemia. The effect will be fully reversible on cessation of the drug – stop the trimethoprim and ask the general practitioner (GP) to repeat the blood tests a week later.

Answer to Question 17

C: refer him to local urology services

This patient has non-visible haematuria, without proteinuria. Given that he is over 40 years old, he needs referral to the local urology department for investigation to exclude a urinary tract malignancy (renal ultrasound, urine cytology and cystoscopy), as per national guidelines.

Answer to Question 18

C: magnesium ammonium phosphate

Struvite (magnesium ammonium phosphate) stones occur in patients with chronic infections with bacteria expressing urease (*Escherichia coli*, *Proteus*, *Klebsiella*, *Pseudomonas*). They account for about 5% of all stones.

Answer to Question 19

B: *COL4A5*

The *COL4A5* gene encodes the alpha-5 chain of type IV collagen – mutations in which prevent integration of the alpha-3 chain into the glomerular basement membrane (GBM) and cause X-linked dominant Alport syndrome (hence the patient's deafness).

Answer to Question 20

D: ramipril

Angiotensin-converting enzyme (ACE) inhibitors and angiotensin-receptor blockers (ARBs) are contraindicated in pregnancy, due to increased rates of fetal malformations, particularly with exposure in the second and third trimesters.

Answer to Question 21

A: delivery of the baby

While measures to control blood pressure (BP) (labetalol – not nitrates), prevent seizures (magnesium) and promote fetal lung maturation (oral steroids) are all sensible and may need to be employed, the only definitive treatment is to deliver the baby. The timing of this will depend on the balance of risk to the mother and baby of postponing delivery versus the risks of premature birth to the baby.

Answer to Question 22

E: reflux nephropathy

The patient is likely to have had undiagnosed congenital vesicoureteric reflux, which commonly presents many years later with hypertension, proteinuria and renal impairment. The finding of scars on renal ultrasound is characteristic.

Answer to Question 23

D: renal vein thrombosis

Nephrotic syndrome predisposes to renal vein thrombosis, which typically presents with flank pain, haematuria and a rise in serum creatinine.

Answer to Question 24

D: minimal change disease

Usually patients with diabetes and nephrotic-range proteinuria have diabetic nephropathy – but this is the exception that proves the rule! She has good diabetic control without pre-existing microalbuminuria or retinopathy, and the oedema has been intermittent – in this situation you should be suspicious that a lesion other than diabetic nephropathy is present, and minimal change disease is the most likely diagnosis.

Answer to Question 25

B: 25%

Assuming he has autosomal dominant polycystic kidney disease, each child has a 50% risk of being affected, so the risk of them both being affected is 25%.

Answer to Question 26

C: calcineurin inhibitor (tacrolimus) nephrotoxicity

Clarithromycin inhibits cytochrome P450 3A4 (CYP3A4), and if the dose of tacrolimus had not been significantly reduced, tacrolimus levels will have risen substantially, causing toxicity and acute graft dysfunction.

Answer to Question 27

B: bilateral small (8 cm) kidneys on ultrasonography

The finding of small kidneys (normal size 9–14 cm) on ultrasound is almost always indicative of chronic kidney disease (CKD) – all the other abnormalities could be caused by acute or chronic disease processes.

Answer to Question 28

C: obstructive uropathy

This woman had retroperitoneal metastatic disease from her malignancy, encasing her renal collecting systems, causing obstruction but preventing hydronephrosis. She required an urgent non-contrast CT of her abdomen/pelvis, and consideration of relief of obstruction by ureteric stenting / nephrostomies.

Answer to Question 29

A: 1–2 weeks

Anuric patients who stop dialysis usually survive for 1–2 weeks, in the absence of other significant intercurrent illness.

Answer to Question 30

C: referral to local renal services as an outpatient

This patient has nephrotic syndrome and requires outpatient assessment and a renal biopsy in due course to establish an underlying diagnosis. A loop diuretic (eg furosemide) will alleviate the oedema in the interim.

Answer to Question 31

A: blood cultures, intravenous fluids, broad-spectrum antibiotics

This man is septic, potentially with graft (transplant) pyelonephritis. He needs standard treatment (ie resuscitation), as for any patient with sepsis, before you proceed to further investigations.

Answer to Question 32

B: cholesterol emboli

The history is typical of cholesterol embolisation following instrumentation in a man with widespread vascular disease. As in this case, it can occur after an interval of days to weeks. Hypocomplementaemia may occur, and the finding of cholesterol clefts within vessels on renal or skin biopsy is diagnostic.

Answer to Question 33

B: prescribe amoxicillin

This clinical presentation is common and typical of lower urinary tract infection. Common organisms include *Escherichia coli*, and *Proteus* and *Klebsiella* species. In a young woman the presence of stones (CT-KUB) or an anatomical abnormality (ultrasound) would be unusual, and not sought at first presentation. It would not be unreasonable to check a midstream specimen of urine (MSU), but the most appropriate option would be to prescribe an appropriate antibiotic.

Answer to Question 34

A: aciclovir toxicity

The dose of aciclovir needs significant reduction in patients with end-stage renal failure (ESRF), otherwise it can cause neurological toxicity (particularly in those at increased risk – eg frail older people). A single missed haemodialysis session is unlikely to result in the other presentations listed above, and zoster-associated encephalitis is rare, and mostly seen in immunosuppressed individuals (especially HIV). If in doubt about medication doses in dialysis patients, seek help.

Answer to Question 35

D: calcium channel blocker (CCB)

Current guidelines suggest that CCBs should be the first-line choice of antihypertensive in patients of African-Caribbean origin. There is nothing else here to alter this (ie no proteinuria or oedema).

Answer to Question 36

D: type I renal tubular acidosis

This patient has a hypokalaemic, hyperchloraemic metabolic acidosis with a normal serum anion gap. Type I (distal) renal tubular acidosis is the cause – type IV renal tubular acidosis causes hyperkalaemia, ethylene glycol intoxication causes a metabolic acidosis with an elevated anion gap (and you would expect hyperkalaemia), Gitelman syndrome produces hypokalaemia with metabolic alkalosis, and Balkan nephropathy results in chronic renal impairment.

Answer to Question 37

C: renal biopsy

This man may have sarcoidosis – most other likely causes of hypercalcaemia have been excluded, although a comprehensive drug history would be sensible. A renal biopsy is the most appropriate and diagnostic of the listed investigations.

Answer to Question 38

D: intravenous saline

Before anything else is considered, this patient should receive aggressive rehydration with intravenous fluids both to try and preserve renal function and to treat hypercalcaemia. You should be aiming to provoke a diuresis – he will need close monitoring of their volume status and fluid balance.

Answer to Question 39

D: stop ramipril and prehydrate with normal saline

The best answer is to stop any potentially nephrotoxic agents (ramipril) and prehydrate with normal saline before the CT pulmonary angiogram (CTPA). There is no good evidence for the use of intravenous (although there is some evidence for the use of oral) N-acetylcysteine, and prophylactic haemodialysis is not indicated. Isotonic sodium bicarbonate is an alternative to normal saline, but there is no evidence that it is better in this context, and the ramipril should be stopped.

Answer to Question 40

B: check when he last had dialysis

In order to remove potassium, haemodialysis utilises a dialysate with a low potassium concentration. This is highly likely to be a blood sample taken at the end of dialysis, when patients' serum potassium will usually be around the 3 mmol/L mark – and this low value will rapidly return into the normal range. No other action is required than checking that this is correct.

Answer to Question 41

B: lupus nephritis class III

The patient presents with features suggestive of system lupus erythematosus (SLE). Lupus nephritis can present with nephrotic syndrome, hypertension and renal impairment. In class I nephritis, there is minimal change with some mesangial immune deposits and mild proteinuria. In class II, there is mesangial hypercellularity and immune deposits, usually presenting as mild renal disease. Biopsy findings in class III are as described above.

Answer to Question 42

A: Congo red

The symptoms described above are consistent with a diagnosis of primary amyloidosis. The kidney is one of the most frequent sites for amyloid deposition and this leads to progressive organ dysfunction. Congo-red stained amyloid has an orange-red appearance under light microscopy and produces apple-green birefringence under polarised light.

Answer to Question 43

B: multiple myeloma

Multiple myeloma is characterised by a neoplastic clonal proliferation of plasma cells, often leading to extensive skeletal destruction. Lytic lesions result in bone pain and hypercalcaemia. Renal impairment occurs via light chain deposition, dehydration, amyloidosis and drugs.

Answer to Question 44

D: membranous nephropathy

Membranous nephropathy is one of the most common causes of nephrotic syndrome in adults. It is often a primary disorder (associated with autoantibodies directed against the phospholipase A2 receptor), but can be caused by malignancy, especially in older patients.

Answer to Question 45

B: diabetic nephropathy

The patient has nephrotic syndrome on a background of poor diabetic control and evidence of diabetic retinopathy. Diabetic nephropathy is caused by thickening of the glomerular basement membrane (GBM) and mesangial expansion, with subsequent glomerulosclerosis and Kimmelstiel–Wilson nodule formation.

Answer to Question 46

E: tubulointerstitial nephritis

The recent onset of symptoms after non-steroidal anti-inflammatory drug (NSAID) use on a background of well-controlled diabetes suggests an acute interstitial nephritis. There would be evidence of acute interstitial inflammation on renal biopsy. Treatment is by cessation of the offending drug, but steroids may also be considered.

Answer to Question 47

E: rhabdomyolysis

The patient was found unconscious and had likely sustained muscle injury, which would explain the elevated aspartate transaminase (AST) and lactate dehydrogenase (LDH) (less likely from liver release due to the normal gamma-glutamyl transferase (GGT)). Myoglobin in the urine leads to a positive urine dipstick for blood but negative urine microscopy for red blood cells.

Answer to Question 48

D: transplant renal artery stenosis

This man is likely to have transplant renal artery stenosis, which is most commonly diagnosed about 6 months post transplant. The bland urine dipstick makes infection unlikely, and the slow creep in his creatinine makes rejection less likely. A renal angiogram would be the best choice for next investigation. Although this carries a risk of contrast-induced nephropathy, it also allows immediate intervention if a lesion is seen.

Answer to Question 49

D: stop mycophenolate mofetil and start azathioprine

There are excellent outcomes of pregnancy following renal transplantation. In general, it is recommended that women wait at least a year after the operation and at least 6 months after a bout of rejection. Mycophenolate mofetil is teratogenic: this should be switched to azathioprine and she should be advised not to conceive until she has been on this for 3 months.

Answer to Question 50

B: arrange ultrasound of transplant kidney

The first priority is to establish the diagnosis, with the first step being to ensure there is no blockage to the flow of urine by ultrasound examination. If ultrasound does not suggest this and there is no other obvious cause of acute kidney injury (AKI), then biopsy would be recommended, primarily to look for acute rejection.

Index

Note: page numbers in *italics* refer to figures, those in **bold** refer to tables.

D

deep venous thrombosis *79, 79–80, 80*

dermatan sulphate 114

desmopressin acetate (DDAVP) infusion 136–7

DETAIL trial 70

dexamethasone 24

dextran, polymerised 84

dextrose 39, 40

diabetes with CKD 16–18

   antihypertensives 70

diabetic nephropathy 16–18, 150

   clinical presentation 121–2, *122*

   epidemiology 121

   histological changes of 70

   management 18

   pathology 121, *121*

   prognosis 18, 122

   treatment 122

dialysis 25–7, 63, 82–4, 114

diarrhoea-associated/typical haemolytic–uraemic syndrome (dHUS) 115

diclofenac 57

diethylenetriaminepenta-acetic acid 130, 134

99mTc-diethylenetriamine penta acetic acid (DTPA) 134

diffuse proliferative glomerulonephritis 95–6

digoxin 39

99mTc-dimercaptosuccinic acid (DMSA) scintigraphy 105, 132, 134, *135*

dipstick haematuria 3–5

dipstick testing

   microalbuminuria 129

   protein 129

   see also urinalysis

distal RTA 103, 104

diuretics, rheumatoid arthritis with swollen legs 12

Doppler ultrasonography

   renovascular disease 106

   rheumatoid arthritis, with swollen legs 12

double-stranded DNA (dsDNA) 9

D-penicillamine 21, 111

Duke's B carcinoma 43

dyscrasias, plasma cell 12, 17

dysmorphic red cells 4

dyspnoea, in dialysis patients **29**

E

EBV (Epstein–Barr virus) 31, 34, 99

eculizumab 95, 116

electrocardiogram (ECG) 39–43

electrophoresis, urine 130

endocarditis 33, 37

end-stage renal failure (ESRF) 16, 23, 26, 37, 61, 67, 69, 70

   aetiology/pathophysiology/pathology 74

   causes 75, 106, 121

   clinical presentation 75

   complications 76

   epidemiology 74–5

   investigations 75

   physical signs 75

   prevention 76

   prognosis 76

   treatment 75

enzyme-linked immunosorbent assay (ELISA) 120

eosinophilic granulomatosis with polyangiitis (eGPA) 120

eosin staining 135

Epstein–Barr virus (EBV) 31, 34, 99

erythrocyte sedimentation rate (ESR) 9, 24

erythropoiesis-stimulating agents (ESAs) 16, 30

Escherichia coli 33, 99, 112, 115, 149

ESRF *see* end-stage renal failure (ESRF)

estimated glomerular filtration rate (eGFR) 5, 53, 131

etanercept 11, 111

ezetimibe 73

F

Fanconi syndrome 104

fever 34–7

fibromuscular dysplasia 106, 107, 123

fingertip, infarcts 51, *51*

flash pulmonary oedema 19

flucloxacillin 52

fluconazole 34

fluid management

   backache and renal impairment 60

   postoperative AKI with hypovolaemia 45

fluid overload, evidence 44

fluid status, backache and renal impairment 58

focal necrotising glomerulonephritis *see* crescentic glomerulonephritis

focal segmental glomerulosclerosis (FSGS) 9, 77, 90, 91, 99

furosemide 10, 60, 71, 78, 101

G

gadolinium-enhanced MRA, renovascular disease 106

genetic renal conditions 126–8

GFR *see* glomerular filtration rate (GFR)

gliclazide 16

glomerular diseases 87–99

   see also individual conditions

glomerular filtration rate (GFR) 5, 50

   estimations 130–1

   loss of 67, 69

   pregnancy and kidney 125

glomerulonephritis 23, 49, 51, 54, 117, 120

glucocorticoids, MCGN 95

glucose, urinalysis for 130

glycaemic control 18

glycosaminoglycans 114

Goodpasture's disease 53, 55, 96, 128

gout, CKD and 73

granulomatosis with polyangiitis (GPA) 53, 119, 120, 147

H

haematoxylin 135
haematuria
  dipstick *see* dipstick haematuria
  non-visible 17
  urine dipstick testing for 54–5, *55*
haemodialysis 81–3
  catheter 36
  complications 82, **85**
  postoperative AKI 46
haemofiltration, postoperative AKI 46
haemoglobin, testing for 129–30, *130*
haemolysis, elevated liver enzymes and
      low platelet count (HELLP)
      syndrome 115
haemolytic–uraemic syndrome (HUS)
      see thrombotic microangiopathies
      (TMAs)
haemoptysis 52–55
hantavirus 101
Henoch–Schönlein purpura 94, 119, 147
heparin, low-molecular-weight 10
hepatitis B 99
hepatitis C 99
hepatorenal syndrome 124–5
history taking 3–21
  atherosclerosis and renal failure
      18–20
  diabetes with CKD 16–18
  dipstick haematuria 3–5
  pregnancy with renal disease 5–8
  recurrent loin pain 20–1
  rheumatoid arthritis with swollen legs
      11–13
home BP measurement (HBPM) 123
human leukocyte antigen (HLA) 98
hydronephrosis, of pregnancy 125, *125*
hypercalcaemia 20, 58, 59, 60–1
hypercalciuria 109, 110
hypercholesterolaemia 9, 10
hypercoagulability 8
hyperfiltration 16
hyperkalaemia

abdominal system 41
assessment 39, *39*
CKD 71, **72**
ECG changes 39–40, 66, *66*
investigation 41
management 41–3, 62, 75
treatments 39–40
hyperlipidaemia 8, 79
hyperparathyroidism 147
  bone function tests 59
  hypercalcaemia, causes of **58**
  stones, causes of 21
  symptoms 20
  treatment 16
hypertension 122–4
  CKD 71
  epidemiology 122
  investigations 123
  pathology 122, *123*
  physical signs 123
  treatment 11, 123, 124
hyperuricosuria 111
hypoalbuminaemia, aetiology/
      pathophysiology/pathology 77
hypoglycaemia 40
hypophosphataemia 128
hypovolaemia, postoperative AKI and 45

I

ibuprofen 24
icodextrin 84
IgA *see* immunoglobulin A (IgA)
imaging
  computed tomography 132, *133*, *134*
  isotopic imaging 132, 134, *135*
  intravenous urography 132
  magnetic resonance imaging 134,
      135
  percutaneous/retrograde ureteric
      imaging 132, *134*
  plain abdominal radiograph 132, *133*
  renal angiography 134, *135*

ultrasonography 131–2, *132*
immunofluorescence test, for ANCA 52
immunoglobulins 93–4, 147
immunosuppressive therapy 7
  pulmonary haemorrhage 55
  renal transplantation 86
  systemic vasculitis 121
incidence, of UTI 112
indications
  isotopic imaging 134, *135*
  renal biopsy 136
  RRT 66
  for urgent dialysis **42**
  urinalysis 129
  urine microscopy 130
indinavir 20
infection(s) 9, 21, 41, 57, 80, 99, 111
infliximab 11, 111
insulin 39, 40
intermittent haemodialysis,
      postoperative AKI 46
international normalised ratio (INR) 10
intravenous urography (IVU) 5, 132
iohexol 130
iron 102
isotopic imaging, renal tract 132, 134, *135*
itching, CKD 13

J

joints, renal impairment and 46
jugular venous pressure (JVP) 30, 45

K

Kidney Disease: Improving Global
      Outcomes (KDIGO) guidelines 44,
      44, 65, **68**
kidney in systemic disease 113–26
kidney transplantation *see*
      transplantation, renal
Kimmelstiel–Wilson nodules 121, *121*
Klebsiella spp 112, 149

PD *see* peritoneal dialysis (PD)

PE (pulmonary embolism) **29**, **37**, 47

pelviureteric junction obstruction 109

penicillamine 11

penicillin 80, 90, 101

pentamidine 34

percutaneous antegrade nephrostomy 21

percutaneous/retrograde ureteric imaging 132, *134*

peritoneal dialysis (PD) 35, 37
  advantages and disadvantages 81, **81**
  complications 85, **89**, *89*
  conservative management 81
  failure of 84, 85
  practical details 84, 85, *87*, *88*
  principle 83, *85*, *86*

peritonitis, PD associated 37

pH, urine 130

phosphate stones 21

plain abdominal radiograph 132, *133*

plasma cell dyscrasias 17

plasma exchange 55, 121

plasmapheresis 55, 114

pleuritic chest pain 46

pneumococcal vaccine 80

Pneumocystis jirovecii 33, 34, 86

pneumonia 53, 80

podocin 77

polyarteritis nodosa (PAN) 120, 121, *121*

polycystic kidney disease 21–2
  ADPKD *see* autosomal dominant polycystic kidney disease (ADPKD)

polymerase chain reaction (PCR) test 33

postoperative acute kidney injury 43–6

post-renal problems 108–13

post-renal renal impairment
  causes of 43–4
  evidence 44

post-streptococcal glomerulonephritis *see* diffuse proliferative glomerulonephritis

post-transplant lymphoproliferative disorder (PTLD) 31, 33, 34, 148

potassium, removal 40

prednisolone 55, 61, 98, 101

pre-eclampsia, complication of pregnancy 5–6, 7, 125, 126

pregnancy and renal disease 5–8, 23–4, 73, 126

pre-renal failure 19

primary glomerular diseases 88–98

primary TMA syndromes 115, 116

prodromal bloody diarrhoea 115

proliferative disease 87–8

protein:creatinine ratio (PCR) 4, 9, 47, 77, 90

proteinuria
  aetiology/pathophysiology/pathology 77
  diabetic nephropathy 17
  haematuria and 4
  nephrotic-range 8
  quantitation of 9
  reduction of 79
  urine dipstick testing for 54–5, *55*

Proteus spp 112, 149

proximal RTA 103, 104

Pseudomonas spp 112

PTLD (post-transplant lymphoproliferative disorder) 31, 33, 34, 148

pulmonary embolism (PE) **29**, **37**, 47

pulmonary oedema 41–2, **42**

pulmonary renal syndrome
  cause 53
  defined 53

R

radiography
  chest, hyperkalaemia 41

ramipril 148, 150

rapamycin 23

rapidly progressive glomerulonephritis *see* crescentic glomerulonephritis

recurrent loin pain 20–1

red blood cell casts 4

reflux nephropathy (chronic pyelonephritis) 7, 105–6, 148

renal angiography 106, *107*, 134, *135*

renal artery stenosis
  imaging for 19, 147
  transplant 150

renal biopsy 60, 69, 90, 100, 101, 128, 114, 115
  complications 137
  contraindications 136
  indications 136
  practical details 136–7

renal colic 55–7

renal disease, pregnancy with 5–8, 23–4

Renal drug handbook 73

renal failure 13, 23
  atherosclerosis and *see* atherosclerosis and renal failure

renal hypoperfusion, evidence of 44

renal impairment
  backache and *see* backache and renal impairment
  causes of 44, 68–9
  coma and *see* coma
  fever and 49–52
  haemoptysis and *see* haemoptysis
  multisystem disease and 46–9
  symptoms 41

renal inflammatory condition 19

renal investigations, renal impairment and haemoptysis 54–5, *55*

renal microscopic polyangiitis *see* crescentic glomerulonephritis

renal pathologies, evidence to support specific 44

renal replacement therapy (RRT) 16, 21, 66, 73, 80–7
  conservative management 81
  haemodialysis 81–3
  nephrectomy and 79
  overview 80
  peritoneal dialysis 83–5, *87*, 88, *89*

triamterene 20
triglycerides 17
trimethoprim 34, 69, 113, 148
troponin, measurements 38
tubulointerstitial diseases 100–6
tubulointerstitial nephritis with uveitis
        (TINU) syndrome 101, 150

U

ultrasound 41, 45, 100, 105, 106, 111,
        114, 117, 127, 131–2, 150
uraemia 13
uraemic toxins 74
urate stones 21, 111
urethral catheterisation 147
uric acid stones 20
urinalysis 129–30
    acute interstitial nephritis 101
    atherosclerosis and renal failure 19
    dipstick 4–5
urinary ACR 129
urinary alkalinisation 63
urinary obstruction 19
urinary outflow obstruction, symptoms 41
urinary PCR 129
urinary stone(s)
    disease, diagnosis 57

pain from 20
risk factors for 20
urinary tract infections (UTIs) 112–13
    symptoms 14
    ultrasonography 41, *42*
urinary tract ultrasonography
    atherosclerosis and renal failure 19
    diabetes with CKD 17
urine
    cytology 5
    dipstick testing 3, 54–5, *55*, 113
    examination of 21
        microscopy 130
        urinalysis 129–30
    frothy 77, *79*
    output (UO) 50, 60, 62, 64

V

valganciclovir 34, 80
vancomycin 37, 52
vascular access, haemodialysis 82, *83, 84*
vasculitis
    ANCA-associated 55, 98
    defined 119
    diagnosis 51
    pneumonia to 53

pulmonary–renal syndromes 5, 54
signs of active 53, *54*
systemic *see* systemic vasculitis
vasopressin, ADPKD 127
vesicoureteral reflux (VUR) 7, 105, *105,*
        106
vitamin D 61
volume depletion and fluid replacement
        42, 42–3
vomiting, CKD 13
von Willebrand disease 4
von Willebrand factor (vWF) multimers 115

W

warfarin, anticoagulation with 10
Wegener's granulomatosis 53, 102, 119

X

X-linked hypophosphataemic vitamin-D
        resistant rickets 128

Z

zoledronate 61